MARTIN VAN BUREN

AND THE MAKING OF THE

DEMOCRATIC PARTY

MARTIN VAN BUREN

AND THE MAKING OF THE

DEMOCRATIC PARTY

By ROBERT V. REMINI

COLUMBIA UNIVERSITY PRESS, NEW YORK

1959

LIBRARY OF CONGRESS CATALOG CARD NUMBER: 58-13671

COPYRIGHT © 1951, 1959 COLUMBIA UNIVERSITY PRESS
FIRST PUBLISHED IN BOOK FORM 1959

PUBLISHED IN GREAT BRITAIN, CANADA, INDIA, AND PAKISTAN
BY THE OXFORD UNIVERSITY PRESS
LONDON, TORONTO, BOMBAY, AND KARACHI

MANUFACTURED IN THE UNITED STATES OF AMERICA

For Ruth, Beth, and Joan

PREFACE

SOME YEARS AGO I began work on a biography of Martin Van Buren. Although that work continues in progress, I have interrupted it to describe in greater detail Van Buren's unique contribution to the formation of the Democratic party.

In no way does this volume purport to be a complete study of the early history of the party. A thorough investigation would include biographical information on such men as Amos Kendall, John Eaton, James Buchanan, William B. Lewis, Francis P. Blair, and others, along with an account of the Jacksonian movement in the several states. Moreover, the narrative of this book stops with Andrew Jackson's election to the presidency in 1828, after a basic party structure began to emerge.

Historians have tended to disregard the organizational work involved in the making of the Democratic party to pursue the more important question of the meaning of Jacksonian Democracy. No study has been made of just how, when, and for what reasons men such as Van Buren, Buchanan, Ritchie, Livingston, and other national figures united behind the Hero of New Orleans. This work will attempt to answer these questions as far as they relate to Van Buren; it can not speak for the others. Scholars have recently called for more intensive research of Jacksonianism on the state and local levels. I would add to this the need for a number of critical biographies of the men who engineered Jackson's election in 1828.

If Van Buren can be regarded as representative of this group of aspiring politicians, then it would appear that Jacksonian Democracy began as a movement to initiate political changes—

changes in the organization and conduct of the national party. The notion that the Democratic party simply evolved as Jacksonians struggled to find a sense of direction is patently false. There was a certain amount of drift involved, particularly in the final link-up of the party organization with the large masses of people; nevertheless, conscious efforts were made to redirect party policies and restate a fundamental political philosophy. None of these efforts, it should be noted, were inspired by economic or social changes taking place in the nation. As examples, it need only be pointed out that the Tariff of Abominations and the Anti-Masonic movement in New York were regarded primarily as political problems. Whatever Jacksonian Democracy became later on in the 1830's it did not begin over clashing economic and social interests.

Although I have tried to maintain an objective approach in this study, I must admit to one prejudice: I believe that Van Buren—even in the field of partisan politics—deserves a better reputation than he has enjoyed from Americans generally and historians particularly.

I wish to thank Professors Henry Steele Commager and Richard B. Morris of Columbia University and Joseph R. Frese, S. J., of Fordham University for their generous encouragement and incisive comments and suggestions. I am also grateful to the Fordham University Research Fund for making possible the final research connected with the publication of this book. My deepest personal debt is to Professor Dumas Malone of Columbia University, who guided the study from its beginning as a doctoral dissertation, and who has given immeasurably of his time, patience, and wisdom.

The chapter dealing with the Tariff of Abominations first appeared in a slightly altered form in the *American Historical Review,* LXIII (July, 1958), and is used here with the kind permission of the publishers.

ROBERT V. REMINI

Fordham University
December, 1958

CONTENTS

MARTIN VAN BUREN
AND THE MAKING OF THE
DEMOCRATIC PARTY

I: THE LITTLE MAGICIAN

A PHRENOLOGIST one day was examining the bumps on the head of a man sitting before him. He did not know the man but he recognized the bumps.

"What a head!" he cried. "Who is he?"

"You wouldn't suppose him to be a clergyman, would you?" asked a woman who was watching the examination.

"A clergyman! Great Heavens. No! . . . If he had been an educated man, he could have set the world in arms! This is a Van Buren head. . . ." [1]

Indeed, Martin Van Buren had quite a head. He may not have set the "world in arms," but he did play a significant role —perhaps the most significant role—in the making of the Democratic party. Many of his contemporaries—those who lacked a proper "feel" for greatness—regarded him as something less than a political statesman and dubbed him the "Little Magician," the "Red Fox of Kinderhook," and the "Master Spirit." That charlatan Davie Crockett was once asked for his opinion of Van Buren, and his statement has since become the prototype of more subtle critiques.

What have I to say against Martin Van Buren? He is an artful, cunning, intriguing, selfish, speculating lawyer, who, by holding lucrative offices for more than half his life, has contrived to amass a princely fortune. . . . His fame is unknown to the history of our country, except as a most adroit political manager and successful officeholder. . . . Office and money have been the gods of his idolatry; and at their shrines has the ardent worship of his heart been devoted. . . . He can lay no claim to pre-eminent services as a statesman; nor has he ever given any evidences of superior talent, except as a political electioneerer and intriguer. [2]

Van Buren was only some of these things. An intriguer, yes
—but only occasionally, when a situation demanded it. A political manager, absolutely—and one of the foremost in the history of this nation. But he was neither selfish nor cunning; he
was an intelligent, clever, honest, and enterprising lawyer with
a sure knowledge of the fine art of making money. To say that
he was not a statesman is to dispute the facts of his life and
the value of the services he performed for his country.

Martin Van Buren was born in the little village of Kinderhook in Columbia County, New York, on December 5, 1782.
The son of a tavernkeeper, he received his earliest education
helping his father manage the tavern, where he watched the
patrons eat and drink and listened to their conversation—political and otherwise. Observers later commented on his great
knowledge and understanding of human nature; undoubtedly
much of it was acquired during these early years. He went to
the village academy for a formal education,[3] and then to the
law offices, successively, of Francis Silvester and William P. Van
Ness. In 1803 he began the practice of law and slowly built a
reputation for himself as a hard-working and resourceful lawyer.
Like his father, Van Buren joined, and assumed an active
role in, the Republican party. This organization and its rival,
the Federalist party, evolved from the disagreements between
Thomas Jefferson and Alexander Hamilton while they were
members of George Washington's first cabinet. In theory,
Hamilton and the Federalists favored a strong centralized government, directed by the propertied classes (especially the
manufacturing and commercial classes), and encouraging a di-
versified economic life. Jefferson and the Republicans, on the
other hand, opposed concentration of political power and
visualized a country ruled by vast numbers of educated American people, most of whom would be farmers.
Once he had become a party member, Van Buren's political
astuteness, his instinctive understanding of the nature of power
and patronage, and his ability to manage men were soon discovered. He rose rapidly through the ranks. He was appointed

a fence-viewer, then surrogate of Columbia County, and finally was elected to the Senate of the New York legislature.

Fundamentally Van Buren was no "magician" or "intriguer," but when he began his career he was thrown headlong into an arena of conniving and scheming politicians in Albany who knew and obeyed the law of the jungle. Politics in New York was dirty, and its muck could be found on many distinguished statesmen of the period, including De Witt Clinton, Rufus King, Silas Wright, Jr., William H. Seward, and William L. Marcy. To stay alive in the New York political world one had to be clever, shrewd, and sometimes unscrupulous. It did not take the intelligent young lawyer Van Buren very long to learn what he must do to survive.

Within ten years after his arrival in Albany as a senator, Van Buren gained control of the state's Republican organization. His success was due partly to his personality as a leader, partly to his ability to conceive and execute intricate plans to weaken his opponents, partly to his above-average talents as a speaker and writer, and partly to his genius for political organization.

Martin Van Buren was probably one of the most charming men of his age. Without that charm, that ingratiating, refined, and affable manner,[4] he could never have succeeded as well as he did. Men and women vied for his companionship, went out of their way to engage him in conversation, and maneuvered to get him to accept invitations to their dinners. He was courteous to all—which some misinterpreted—and possessed the "high art of blending dignity with ease and suavity."[5] His mild, open, and sociable disposition induced one observer to write that he was "as polished and captivating a person in the social circle as America has ever known. . . ."[6] Although endowed with no exceptional wit himself, he had a sense of humor and a keen appreciation of the humorous.[7]

But as friendly as he tried to be, he was constantly attacked by the newspapers. And, on rare occasions, he complained. "Why the deuce is it that they have such an itching for abusing me?" he asked. "I try to be harmless, and positively good natured, & a most decided friend of peace."[8] Because of the abuse he was subject to—and it came not only from newspaper editors—he trained himself to disregard or seem impervious "to attacks on his feelings or character even in his own presence." [9] His "good nature and complacency could scarcely be moved by any amount of sarcasm, wit, pasquinade, caricature, or ridicule. . . . He possessed a happy philosophy which enabled him to laugh . . . at all such attempts to injure him. . . . This self control, amiability, and imperturbable composure undoubtedly constituted his strength, and enabled him to navigate successfully the troubled waters of politics when others, possessing more talent but less tact, were wrecked or engulfed." [10]

His aloofness, in turn, led to the charge that he was "too cautious, too circumspect—too uniformly under the control of a cool, collected sagacity of judgment,—never either warmed or warped from the line of calculated policy, by any of the disturbing impulses of heart or imagination." [11] This was Van Buren's defense, or so he said, against "the catalogue of calumnies which the malice of my enemies have heaped upon me." [12] His insurance against the future lay in being ever cautious and wary. He "never was off his guard, never 'slopped over.' " [13]

Van Buren's physique brought him many nicknames. Although he was just below medium height for a man, he gave the appearance of being small. Slender, his body was nevertheless compact and solid. His hair—before he began losing it— was a light sandy color. The most prominent feature of his face was a fine high forehead.

With all these endowments at his command Van Buren propelled himself forward. His ambition was the dynamo of his strength,[14] but it is to his credit that he prevented it from distorting his perspective or becoming all-consuming. He knew when to step aside and let another pass. He knew when to back off and applaud the advance of another. Although he believed that he must "husband" all those things which would promote his success,[15] he recognized that ambition tempered with moderation would be to his advantage in the long run. This, together with a remarkable ability to predict political developments, a natural tact in his dealings with others, and an instinctive knowledge of the sources of power, brought him success in virtually all his undertakings.

During the War of 1812, a number of Federalist extremists tried to engineer New England's secession from the Union. They succeeded only in bringing disgrace to themselves and their party. They were mocked as traitors; and this ridicule became a weapon which the Republicans wielded with gusto until the Federalist party breathed no more.

On the national level the party of Hamilton ceased to exist by 1816, although in many states it lingered for the next six years. The principles of Federalism, however, never died—a fact which Van Buren knew and which he had to teach his contemporaries. The former members of this so-called traitorous party drifted into Republican ranks, and the "Era of Good Feelings" began. It was a period in which one party ruled the nation, but it was also a period of violent quarreling and factious bickering within that party.

In New York the happy phrase "Era of Good Feelings" had little meaning. The Republican party had always been divided one way or another, and outsiders invariably found it difficult to understand New York's political history. New Yorkers hardly understood it themselves. At one time there were three separate groups claiming the title Republican: the followers of Aaron Burr, of George Clinton, and of the Livingston family. Later there were the members of Tammany Hall, sometimes called Quids or Martling Men. Finally, there were the Bucktails and Clintonians.

By the time Van Buren had learned everything that New York politics had to teach him, he assumed command of the Bucktail faction, so named because the sachems of New York City wore a buck's tail in their hats whenever they attended a Tammany meeting. (Some, but not all, Bucktails were Tammany men, and most, but again not all, Tammany men were Bucktails.) By 1819 the term had a single meaning: it referred to all Republicans sworn to exterminate the political power of De Witt Clinton and the Clintonians, his personal following.

New York has had few men of Clinton's statue. The record of his governorship has rarely been equaled. He himself, however, is something of an enigma. At once brilliant and dull, popular and despised, displaying unique powers of foresight at one moment and the complete lack of them at the next, he ran hot and cold throughout his useful public career. He was a man of widespread interests which touched both the artistic and the scientific; his activities in some respects resembled those of a dilettante, yet in others he demonstrated scholarly acumen and penetrating insight.

In his relations with others Clinton was a complete failure. His reckless disregard for the feelings, whims, prejudices, and sympathies of others cost him the loyalty of countless politicians who could have strengthened his position. His egotistic mania for praise and flattery was disgusting to most.[16] He was continually charged with being niggardly and ungrateful toward his sympathizers as well as overly vindictive toward his enemies. The highest emotion he could command in others was admiration for his catholic interests.[17]

Politically speaking, Clinton personified the doctrine of expediency. One congressman who was not embroiled in New York politics said that Clinton had "his price & may be bought." [18] The price was the gratification of his ambitions, and his ambitions often drove him to excess. Although he rarely took into account the numerous details connected with the grandiloquent schemes he was perpetually proposing, there were exceptions.[19] The years he struggled to have the Erie Canal built, his pleading, coaxing, cajoling, arguing to persuade legislators into committing themselves to its construction, constitute just one example.

From the moment he entered politics Clinton was a Republican at least in name—and too often in name only. Repeatedly he was found on the Federalist side of the fence, speaking the purest brand of Hamiltonianism. When he ran against James Madison for the presidency in 1812 he received both Republican and Federalist support. Disregarding party discipline, he could never be made to abide by caucus decisions unless they happened to agree with his own way of thinking. Incapable of any real loyalty himself, he demanded a slavish kind of loyalty from others. Yet, despite his character, he had a large personal following who joined him in a pitched battle against Van Buren for control of New York.

In 1821 the Bucktails, in response to the demands of the people, forced the convoking of a convention to amend the state's anachronistic constitution. The Clintonians fought it, knowing that one of its objects was their ouster from office. This was not, obviously, the avowed aim of the Bucktails; they talked righteously of cleaning house from top to bottom, of widening the franchise, and of reforming outmoded practices within the legislative, executive, and judical departments of the government. The people, brushing Clinton and his party aside, instructed the Bucktails to do as they promised.

The constitutional revisions which were overwhelmingly approved in January, 1822, did reflect the democratic advances which had been made during the past forty years, and many of them resulted from the sincere desire for reform among the men who attended the convention. The suffrage was extended to include city worker and country farmer, more frequent elections were guaranteed, the governor was given the veto power, the greater part of the patronage was turned over to the legislature and to the governor for distribution, new courts were created, some old ones were abolished, and the independence of the state Supreme Court was lessened. In short, many of the great citadels of aristocratic power were demolished.

Because of his opposition to the convention, Governor Clinton prepared to retire at the end of his term in office. His faction was denounced as Federalist and then was swept from the legislature. Bucktails flocked into the Assembly and Senate. Van Buren, about to leave for Washington as the newly elected

United States Senator, finished work on his political machine, the Albany Regency, which was to run New York in his absence.

Van Buren organized the Regency to maintain his firm grip on the state. Moreover, he meant it as a springboard for the furtherance of his own ambitions and the ambitions of those who legitimately claimed membership in his party. A theory underlying the establishment of this machine was that all men who would attain political prominence must do so within the framework of the organization, recognizing the authority of those in control. With power thus derived, the state would be given an efficient, energetic, and forceful government run along Republican lines, according to the Jeffersonian creed.

The Regency was nothing more than a governing council located in Albany, composed of men of the highest political skills. Into the hands of these politicians the Little Magician transferred his control of the party. By adroit use of the patronage they were to discipline Republicans into a fighting, resourceful, and unbeatable body of men. They were also to formulate and direct party policies. However else it may have seemed to New Yorkers, this was never a one-man show. The most notable Regency members—almost all chosen by Van Buren—included William L. Marcy, Silas Wright, Jr., Edwin Croswell, Benjamin F. Butler, Azariah C. Flagg, John A. Dix, Roger Skinner, Benjamin Knower, Thomas Olcott, and Samuel A. Talcott.

To exercise effective control of the party and thereby of the state, Van Buren had to adopt a system by which he could extend Regency sway over the lowest ranks of Republicans. A governing council in Albany directing affairs was all well and good up to a point, but without auxiliary agencies in every county to carry out and enforce party edicts the organization was incomplete. As Van Buren conceived his machine, an order once given to the Bucktails should be obeyed right down to the last officeholder in the smallest hamlet of New York.

Events subsequently proved that establishing local headquarters in the several counties, or converting those already in existence, was comparatively simple, since the Little Magician had previously laid a solid foundation by personally meeting and winning the support of the leading anti-Clinton politicians from most of the principal communities. After 1822, those men who remained obdurate, refusing to accept Regency over-lordship, were denied patronage and removed from any appointive positions they held. The procedure was rigorously applied after the collapse of the Clintonian party, and thereafter Bucktailism was the only political faith acceptable when applying for office.[20]

The word "patronage" has varied meaning. To say that it was used to effect Regency control of New York is of course correct, but this does not tell the entire story. It was not so much the rewarding of partisans and the mass lopping off of rebellious heads that explained Regency success as it was the skilful, highly judicious manner in which the power was exercised. So carefully did the members consider the prejudices and feelings of local communities to be affected by their appointments, so thoroughly did they investigate the many and petty details connected with the distribution of the patronage, and so precisely thought out was each authorized removal that they steadily advanced over the years toward the full establishment of state-wide machine politics.

As soon as the Albany Regency began to operate, its members turned their attention to the judiciary as the surest and swiftest means to inaugurate their rule.[21] In each county there were a number of judges, masters and examiners in chancery, clerks, and others holding petty positions who were appointed by the legislature. In addition, the offices of justices of the peace also tended to be appointive, and because these were close to the people the men holding them exercised tremendous influence over the voters. The Regency therefore seized these positions at the very outset of their rule and converted them for their own special use. It became a strict rule that no man might occupy a seat upon the bench whose loyalty to the party was in any way questionable.

So the political affairs of the dominant party were engineered by a small number of persons acting in perfect accord. The central power in Albany, with its trusted friends outside, dictated every appointment made. Hence, if a man wanted an office at the hands of the governor, it was necessary that he should be on good terms with the county judges, be a straightout democrat, and a reliable friend of theirs. Except he would swear allegiance to the powers that be, it was useless for him to look for an appointment.[22]

Two techniques which the inner council developed to a high degree of proficiency in perfecting machine politics were the use of the official newspaper and of the legislative caucus. The Albany *Argus*, splendidly edited by Edwin Croswell and fully supplied with money received from printing state documents, served as the party organ and authoritatively laid down the party line on every major issue. Van Buren had always stressed the importance of a partisan newspaper which spoke with the force of the organization. With it, he said, we can endure a thousand "convulsions"; without it, we might as well "hang our harps on the willows." [23]

Use of the legislative caucus was the second technique, and it served many purposes. First, it was a convenient means of nomination. All fuss and bickering over the naming of candidates found expression on the caucus floor. But after that—after the majority had consented to the slate or revised it—opposition had to end. Nothing was carried beyond the chamber door except the single decision of the party. Second, it was a rubber stamp which affixed the label "Republican" to everything authorized by the Regency. Without this label the rank and file disregarded all proposals made to them. Finally, and most important of all, it was a whip to hold together an otherwise lax majority in the Assembly and Senate.[24] This singleness of purpose obviously gave the Bucktails greater strength. They were alive to sudden legislative maneuvers by the opposition and were prepared to counteract them with effective measures.

The Regency members would never tolerate dissension in the ranks. They acted firmly toward those who scoffed at "regular nominations" and "party discipline." [25] No mercy was shown to schismatics, waverers, backsliders, or "milk and water" Republicans. Said Silas Wright, Jr.: "Tell them [the Bucktails] they are safe if they face the enemy, but that the first man we see *step to the rear,* we *cut down.*" [26] Surprising as it may seem, it was not necessary to cut down many Republicans during the early years of Regency history. Van Buren had already seen to that.

Looking back to 1821, the year he left for Washington as Senator, Van Buren recalled in his *Autobiography* that his earlier political life had

been in general successful and in the end signally such. . . . I left the service of the State for that of the Federal Government with my friends in full and almost unquestioned possession of the State Government in all its branches, at peace with each other and over-flowing with kindly feelings towards myself, and not without hope that I might in the sequel of good conduct be able to realize similar results in the enlarged sphere of action to which I was called.[27]

Any person who knew Van Buren could scarcely doubt that he would indeed "realize similar results." He was no ordinary senator going to Washington for the first time. He was a man well schooled in politics, and possessed extraordinary powers of organization. He was a man who firmly believed in a united, caucus-ruled, and disciplined party. He could not abide anything less than this. He hated party division in any manner or shape for he had seen what it could do in New York. Let the national Republican party fall short of his hopes and he could be expected to reorganize it—or to make a valiant try.

Did the Regency begin sooner?

II: "THE MONROE HERESY"

THE GLORIFIED SWAMP that was the city of Washington had changed considerably since the last time Van Buren had seen it. On his previous visit in 1816 the charred remains left by the "arsonist" British were still in evidence and served as stark reminders of the price of liberty and the penalty of war. Now a bright new city was expanding in many directions. The White House was not yet completed but had been recently reoccupied by the President. It was clean and almost dazzling in the noonday sun. Although the outer walls had been rebuilt, both porticoes were still missing and the East Room had no floor, or plaster on the walls. President James Monroe was nonetheless content with his home—even if he had to go down into the basement to reach the garden.

The Capitol was in better shape. It had been rebuilt along the lines of the original, but costlier and more elaborate touches had been added. The colonnades, floors, and staircases were made of marble instead of freestone and brick. The capitals of all the pillars were carved in Italy, and Italian sculptors were brought over to supervise the work of installing them. In the rotunda, directly above a crypt intended for the body of George Washington but never occupied, were hung four new paintings by John Trumbull which depicted scenes of the American Revolution. The selections were wise but the way they were displayed was not: they were unprotected by railings or attendants, and consequently were at the mercy of the crowds who poked them with sticks and canes. Trumbull masterpiece or not, a taxpayer assumed the right to determine whether it was painted on the wall or on canvas.[1]

The social life of the capital had been seriously impaired a few years before when Mrs. Monroe refused to make or return courtesy calls. The great days of the vivacious and gracious Dolley Madison were over and it took a while before those affected could reconcile themselves to the change. Nevertheless, Mrs. Monroe was not a thoroughgoing reformer and continued the practice of holding receptions at the White House every Wednesday evening. For ten weeks, beginning in December, the cycle of dinners and balls was unending, and Washington society was as bright as any in the United States.[2]

Van Buren, a new arrival in Washington, was not long in acclimating himself to his new surroundings. He found for the first time in his life the milieu that best suited his unusual talents. His urbanity, his grace and manners, together with his cultivated command of polite conversation, made him a favorite among hostesses. What woman admired most about him was the great amount of attention he paid them at every social affair. Politeness was to be expected, but he went out of his way to be gallant.

His correspondence seems to indicate that Van Buren was a bit of a lady's man. He often asked his female acquaintances—regardless of their age, physical charms, or marital status—to write to him and told them how much pleasure he derived from their letters. Unfortunately, none of the responses he undoubtedly received has survived to the present, and it can be presumed that he himself destroyed them in his old age.

Van Buren may have been overly-attentive to the ladies, but he never violated the canons of good taste. Neither was he insincere or calculating in his flattery; he did not curry favor for some ulterior motive. This fact many biographers forget when they relate the Peggy Eaton episode, which occurred during Jackson's first administration. Some historians are convinced that Van Buren's pronounced interest in the woman was motivated solely by his desire to use her in a plot to discredit John C. Calhoun and thereby replace him as Jackson's successor to the presidency. They do him a great injustice. Mrs. Eaton was a woman of remarkable charm and beauty. These were qualities which Van Buren appreciated for their own sake, qualities which were in part the cause of his special attention.

One of the first social affairs he attended was an elaborate ball given by Colonel Henderson. Ellen Wayles Randolph was among the guests and, since she was one of *the* Randolphs, spent the entire evening surrounded by almost every bachelor and widower in Congress. However, when asked to name her favorite piece of music she showed her interest in Van Buren by requesting the song "Yellow-Haired Laddie." [3] Of course it is possible that the song really was her favorite, but observers chose to think otherwise. The incident could have been very embarrassing, but the New York widower who had four growing sons denied a "budding romance," and publicly silenced gossip by his tactful behavior in the future.

This was the first of his reported amorous adventures in Washington, but was by no means the last.

Van Buren's entrance upon the national scene as a United States Senator was what many of his enemies would regard as typical. Even before his official debut in the upper chamber of Congress he had become deeply embroiled in politics, patronage, and intrigue. The personalities involved were different from those in New York, but everything else was the same. His reputation as an artful politician had preceded him to Washington, and he fulfilled all expectations. Rufus King, the senior Senator from New York, predicted that within "two weeks Van Buren will become perfectly acquainted with the views and feelings of every member, yet no man will know his." [4] Obviously the statement is exaggerated, but it does underscore an important trait in Van Buren's personality. To speak freely about such matters of national importance as internal improvements, tariffs, and the banking system would be next to impossible, principally because in 1821 he had no fixed views upon them. Moreover, he never commented on any controversial subject until he had given it considerable study and had heard all sides. Thus many of his colleagues confused his circumspect approach toward vital issues with a refusal to commit himself.

Although he guarded his speech and tactfully sidestepped invitations to discuss questions about to be decided by Congress, his manner in private conversation was always so attentive and his curiosity so obviously sincere that he was able to draw out the people he talked with and get them to speak freely on those very matters he himself was careful about. Since he was not a greatly informed person and had to spend long hours gathering information on virtually every major subject, his methods of research seemed perfectly legitimate to him. But sometimes a congressman said too much, and instead of indulging in private self-recrimination he accused the New Yorker of clever and sinister cross-examination. Before long Van Buren was a convenient whipping boy for every stupid man in Washington, and no charge of base intrigue was too monstrous to level against him. To this day he is an easy victim for many biographers of men of the Jacksonian period.

But Van Buren was not lacking in views and principles, even if he did keep them to himself. He was a Jeffersonian, as he understood the term, and with the passing years his understanding of Jeffersonian principles grew. Not that he talked much about general concepts of government; on the contrary, his letters speak of people, elections, and votes. But his memoranda, notes, and other documentary fragments give him away. He was deeply concerned about the doctrines of his party. He wanted to emulate Thomas Jefferson, and he wanted to restore Republican principles to government.

With respect to some questions he was more than willing to speak openly and at great length. He proclaimed his faith in a united, caucus-ruled Republican party which would be sharply distinguished from any other political organization. On leaving for Washington, he reportedly told Harmanus Bleecker of his intention to "revive the old contest between federals and anti-federals and build up a party for himself on that." [5] If Bleecker correctly reported the conversation, it would appear that Van Buren headed for the capital with the declared intention of working a major political change that would effect the entire nation. Whether correct or not, however, it does point up something about which the Senator was quite certain: that Federalists, although disguised within Republican ranks, still rejected Jeffersonian principles. It was therefore imperative that they be identified and eliminated from the party, just as Clinton and his cohorts had been eliminated in New York.

In 1821, as he was beginning his senatorial term, Van Buren made his first identification. The culprit was the Speaker of the House of Representatives, John W. Taylor. The year before, Taylor, a New Yorker, had been chosen to his high office upon pledging his loyalty to the Republican party.[6] His many protestations of political orthodoxy notwithstanding, he had aided Clintonians in their race for the New York legislature. To Van Buren this was the act of a Federalist and therefore disqualified Taylor for reelection.[7] Without wasting time, the Senator decreed to all Bucktails in November, 1821, that Taylor *"could not be Speaker,"* [8] whereupon the New York representatives held a caucus and resolved that they would vote for "someone else." [9] Once this report was circulated, opposition to Taylor spread to representatives from other states. Part of the Pennsylvania and all of the Connecticut delegation in Congress came out against him.[10] The Secretary of War, John C. Calhoun, immediately chose a substitute candidate, and each contending group took "unwearied pains" to ensure Taylor's defeat.[11]

When the House convened in December, 1821, Caesar Rodney was one of the first men offered for the coveted place, but Southerners passed him over. Louis McLane was also found wanting, and General Samuel Smith of Maryland was disposed of almost as quickly as he was proposed. After lengthy debate Philip P. Barbour was nominated because he could unite the Virginia members against Taylor,[12] and to the surprise of most, he was elected by two votes.

Van Buren congratulated himself over the results; the

"trimmer" [13] had been ousted. He had no quarrel with the desire of Southern men to pick a successor and did not attempt to nominate a candidate of his own. All he wanted was the "Federalist's" removal. His "angry feelings" and those of the New York Bucktails were enough to doom Taylor's bid for reelection,[14] and consequently Van Buren was given credit for materially affecting the outcome of the most significant contest in Congress before he had officially begun his duties as Senator.

In the sprawling city of Washington, alive to the expansionist spirit gripping the nation, Van Buren found quarters in Strother's Hotel, at Pennsylvania Avenue and Fourteenth Street, where he joined the Congressional mess of John D. Dickinson. No sooner had he unpacked his bags and settled himself in his new lodgings than he was notified that he had a caller. He was undoubtedly surprised, but by no means displeased, to find John C. Calhoun waiting to see him. On the surface the visit was purely social, and nothing was said of any significance; but Van Buren used every moment of it to create a favorable impression on so outstanding a Southern leader.

Strange that Calhoun should make the first friendly gesture and that he should do so on Van Buren's first day in Washington. Probably he was anxious to see this "arch politician" and enlist his support in the coming presidential election before any of the other candidates approached him. Whatever his motive, he was especially cordial to the New Yorker, and their relationship began under the most favorable auspices.[15] Van Buren found Calhoun's company very "agreeable" and subsequently spent many evenings at the Southerner's home playing whist and informally discussing different issues.[16] But there was a basic political difference between the two men that was obvious to the New Yorker from the start. In the first few minutes of serious conversation he discovered that the Secretary entertained views of the Constitution which were far broader than any Jeffersonian had a right to hold. He detected a Federalist ring to Calhoun's words which greatly disturbed him— disturbed him for many years.[17]

Otherwise he got along famously with the people he met, and found Washington much to his liking. In February, 1822, he moved out of Strother's, which he said was "too gay" for his tastes, and followed Rufus King to Bradley's Hotel in Georgetown, where he remained for the next two years.[18] There he joined a mess including Stephen Van Rensselaer ("the Patroon"), Harrison Gray Otis, and Benjamin Gorham—as Federalist a group of Republicans as the city boasted—who welcomed his presence and disregarded his principles. Some gossiped that he was trying to break into the circle of "new fashioned aristocratic republicans," [19] but probably his real motive for moving to Georgetown was to save money by living in a less expensive hotel.

It may appear strange that a man who thoroughly despised Federalists could live with them. But Van Buren was so much the master of his emotions that he never permitted "corroding" political differences to mar his personal relationships. Only he could have managed the seemingly impossible feat of living with Federalists, enjoying their companionship and yet hating everything they stood for politically.

Van Buren intended to begin his term in office with as much dignity as befitted his high station. After a proper interval of time and after careful selection of a fitting topic, he would make his debut in the Senate. He aspired for recognition as a thoughtful congressman, but events and his own keen sense of political principle dictated otherwise. Instead of Washington being treated to the pleasant spectacle of a rising statesman just beginning his national career, it saw a New York politician in hot pursuit of the patronage. Less than two months after his arrival, Van Buren succeeded in involving the President, the Vice-President, the entire cabinet, and many senators and representatives in an unseemly affair that changed the course of the Republican party.

It all began innocently enough when the Postmaster General, Return Jonathan Meigs, decided to remove from office Solomon Southwick,[20] the postmaster of Albany, because he had become delinquent in his accounts and could not make the necessary restitution. A New York congressman and former Federalist, General Solomon Van Rensselaer, heard of the impending dismissal and began working to have himself appointed to the vacant office. He said he was weary of Washington and longed to return to the "comfort, peace and quietness" of his home.[21] Since Van Buren had been "very civil" to him and had spoken of him "in handsome terms," the General discounted all opposition to his plans. He would have been wiser had he gone to Van Buren and asked him for his consent. It would have been a gracious gesture toward the master of New York and might have saved Van Rensselaer many anxious moments in the future.

By the end of December, 1821, Van Rensselaer had made great strides in readying his application for approval by having secured the assistance of his friends Calhoun, Meigs, and a select number of congressmen from Ohio, New York, Kentucky, and Tennessee. To complete the list of endorsements, all he needed was a strong recommendation from Albany and the consent of Rufus King and Van Buren. The first of these he was promised, but the second he never received.[22]

When Van Buren learned of the vacancy and what was going on behind his back, he may have been a little piqued. He rejected Van Rensselaer's candidacy and gave as his reasons the General's past associations with Federalists and Clintonians. These were perfectly good and understandable motives, but there is a strong probability that he was also influenced by the General's presumptuousness in not consulting him beforehand. Why else would he choose as his own candidate for the post the aged chancellor and one-time member of the Constitutional Convention of 1787, John Lansing, and say that the "circumstances of the president's personal knowledge and regard for the chancellor is decisive with me as to the expediency of pressing him."[23] He was evidently angry enough with Van Rensselaer to pick any man, no matter how old or incapacitated, just as long as he could manage the appointment.

Van Rensselaer was shocked by Van Buren's attitude, but it did not alter his plans. He was advised to step up his campaign, however, and to exert pressure on the members of Congress before the Senator "engaged" them.[24] Any faltering on his part would eliminate him from the contest as well as discredit him in the eyes of his colleagues. Unless he hustled, and used every contact he had, he would be left far behind.

Van Buren, no idler himself, promptly went to the Postmaster General and submitted a letter signed by himself and Rufus King asking that a decision in the case be delayed to secure "a fit & full opportunity to make . . . representations to you on the subject." Since the post was one of the "principal distributing offices in the State," he did not think his request out of order.[25]

Such a letter from two senators in reference to an important position in their state should have given Meigs reason to pause, but when he received a petition in Van Rensselaer's favor signed by 22 members of the New York delegation, 11 of whom were Republicans, he made up his mind to offer the General the vacancy.[26] Not wanting to risk his own position, however, he went to the President with his troubles and was assured that he would be supported in whatever action he took. Meigs protected himself, but now he had involved Monroe in the affair.

Not content with a single letter of protest, Van Buren and King penned another. This time they talked the Vice-President and former governor of New York, Daniel D. Tompkins, into signing it with them. The three men insisted that Meigs do nothing for at least two weeks, so that the citizens of Albany might express their opinion.[27] Simultaneously, a hurried dispatch was sent to the Regency men asking them to "communicate as soon as possible the wishes of the republicans of Albany. . . ."[28]

For Van Buren only one step remained to ensure the success of his plan. He had to place the entire circumstances of the case before the President and directly advise him that Meig's action constituted a "Federalist" appointment. On January 5 he wrote to Monroe and asked that the Postmaster General's decision be suspended, explaining the seriousness of the request and enclosing letters from others to bolster his contention.[29] The moment he dispatched this letter he gambled on beginning his Washington career in splendid triumph or disappointing failure—and he was not one to countenance failure.

In the succeeding days Van Buren never ceased besieging poor Meigs; he fired one communication after the other at him and finally threatened, if his demands were not met, to "put the question on such political ground that the people of the United States may distinctly understand what principles prevail in that department of the government, and, may take the measures necessary to a wholesome reform." [30] He was not bluffing, for he knew that Van Rensselaer's appointment—a simple matter of Federalist preference at the expense of deserving Republicans—would certainly bring vigorous protests from party leaders. An official policy such as this was injurious to party discipline and if not repudiated at the outset could have terrible consequences. Obviously Van Buren was reducing the question to this one point and eliminating all other issues. To emphasize this he called upon all those Republicans who had endorsed Van Rensselaer's petition to meet him in caucus on January 6, 1822. By cracking the whip, by separating the Bucktails from the others, he was following a program already mapped out in brief to Harmanus Bleecker, that of reviving the "old contest between federals and anti-federals. . . ."

There is no recorded account of the caucus proceedings except that at their conclusion the delegation had been "persuaded" to "behave well," and Van Buren emerged holding a paper in his hand signed by a majority of members requesting that the President delay the appointment.[31] Now the Regency was instructed to get the citizens of Albany moving for Chancellor Lansing. In addition, Van Buren wanted his lieutenants Benjamin Knower, Roger Skinner, Moses I. Cantine, and others to send a memorandum to Monroe which would put their position on simple and straightforward grounds, but "with the utmost delicacy and respect." They were to reaffirm the contention that the dispute involved principle, and that they expected the administration to appoint Republicans, and only Republicans, to office. "I would present that question distinctly to the president," wrote Van Buren, "that we may know hereafter what we are to expect." If the petition, he added as an afterthought, "should in the least degree wear the aspect of threatening or scolding, it would be ruinous." He advised them to speak with firmness and politeness.[32]

As the whole problem reached the stage of absurdity, Monroe asked his cabinet on January 5 to restudy it with him and present their opinions. At the meeting subsequently held, the correspondence of the Vice-President and the two New York senators was examined again. Meigs defended his own decision while Smith Thompson, a New Yorker and Secretary of the Navy, attacked it by arguing for Lansing. Both William Wirt, the Attorney General, and William H. Crawford, the Secretary of the Treasury, chided the Postmaster General for involving the President when it was plainly a matter to be handled by his own department. John Q. Adams, the Secretary of State, and Calhoun disagreed with this view, however, and saw nothing in Meigs's behavior to warrant criticism.[33]

By the time the meeting broke up Monroe had finally come to a decision. As the officers rose to leave he asked Thompson to remain for a few last words. He made up his mind not to interfere, which meant that Van Rensselaer would fill the vacancy, but he wanted Thompson to understand his reasons for doing so. He explained that the post-office system as established by law vested all appointments in the head of the department "without reference to the President." And as he later reminded Van Buren, it had always been the uniform practice of the executive to avoid taking part in such questions.[34] On January 7, 1822, Meigs notified the old General that he was to replace Solomon Southwick as Postmaster of Albany.

Nevertheless, Tompkins and Van Buren continued their hopeless offensive in a spirit of never-say-die, referring to Van Rensselaer as a "warm, active and indefatigable opponent" of the Republican party and promising that the Bucktails would resist his appointment in every possible way.[35] But the matter was officially closed and no amount of threats could reopen it.

Van Buren was a poor loser, and perhaps few could blame him. The politician who failed to keep his party from awarding choice positions in his home state to members of the opposition was certainly not a master politician, was certainly not one with influence. At first his "shameful treatment" by Meigs seemed bad enough, but Monroe's later sanction of this injustice by his refusal to intervene was the worst blow of all.[36] Van Buren's efforts to advance the disagreement to a higher plane, to one of principle, were futile. But it gave him a splendid excuse—particularly when another former Federalist was later made marshal in the western district of Pennsylvania—to demand a reorganization of the Republican party.

The President of the United States, by his silence, was giving tacit approval to a pernicious doctrine, one which could eventually wreck the Republican organization. With a presidential contest approaching, factious splits were bound to appear unless discipline was reinstilled. "The disjointed state of parties here," Van Buren wrote, "the distractions which are produced by the approaching contest for president, and the general conviction in the minds of honest and prudent men, that a *radical reform* in the political feelings of this place has become necessary, render this the proper moment to commence the work of a *general resuscitation* of the *old democratic party.*"[37]

Van Buren had definite suggestions as to where and how the general resuscitation should begin. Obviously New York was "the source from which the good work ought to emanate." He recommended "prudence" and "firmness" and a "well-drawn resolution" by the state legislature. Finally he suggested that a correspondence committee be formed to communicate with Republicans of other state legislatures "to secure co-operation and unity of sentiment to affect a remedy." He warned that if the Bucktails "submit tamely to this decision you must expect hereafter . . . to get a republican preferred to a federalist by the government instead of that manly simplicity and characteristic boldness which distinguished the conduct of our public men in the early years of Mr. Jefferson's administration."[38]

Despite the Hartford Convention, the changing of names, and the reversing of party affiliations, Van Buren argued that the Federalists were still alive and active, were infiltrating the ranks of Republicans, were promoting disharmony by their continued insistence on Hamiltonian principles, and were waiting for the right moment to reassert their claim to national leadership. Monroe, in permitting Van Rensselaer's appointment, was negligent in failing to check this movement. Van Buren subsequently accused the President of trying to integrate the two parties and unite Americans into a single corps. One of the techniques of achieving this end, the Senator argued, was the impartial distribution of the patronage between Republicans and Federalists. With continued application of this technique, he said, the President hoped to fuse or amalgamate the two groups. The lines that had once separated them would be erased, and thus a genuine Era of Good Feelings would be inaugurated. Van Buren gave this policy a name. He called it "Monroe's fusion policy." [39] Later he stated his belief that the President consciously adopted it to break down the two-party system. He damned the policy and he damned the President, insisting that instead of reconciling conflicting interests Monroe had succeeded only in undermining the traditionally cohesive qualities that had originally united Jeffersonians.[40] Although at first the Senator hesitated to say so, he was forced to conclude that the President, by his "heretical" notions, was pulling the Republican party apart.

It may be unfair to accuse Monroe of consciously following a "fusion policy," [41] particularly when the only evidence that can be offered is his indifference to the long-standing feud between Federalists and Republicans. Nonetheless, he cannot escape the indictment that his silence during his second administration proved disastrous to the Republican cause in 1824. By failing to name his successor to the presidency—a traditional practice beginning with Jefferson—he is partly responsible for what occurred during the next election, when the party split into four separate groups. His policy, or lack of one if that is more correct, helped bring about the collapse of Republican harmony, discipline, and unity. Van Buren never forgave him for that.

In Albany the Regency men reacted boldly to their chief's suggestions, which were contained in his many letters to them. Meigs "must be denounced," they said, for his arbitrary treatment of Republicans and inexcusable behavior toward Federalists. And "through you," they told Van Buren, "retribution ought to reach him." [42] On January 21 they held a general meeting and passed a series of resolutions, all of which were forwarded to Washington, condemning the role of the national administration in appointing Van Rensselaer to office. [43] They charged the government with a conspiracy to keep New York in a state of confusion. [44] "O, Sir," the aroused William L. Marcy wrote to a friend, "it was as ungrateful not to know us at this trying period as it would have been not to have known us in 1814. . . ." [45]

This frontal assault on the administration, publicized in most of the other states, had obvious bearing on the next presidential election. Prospective candidates would either have to repudiate Monroe's policy and acknowledge Federalists as an ever-present threat to the Republican party, or suffer the loss of Bucktail votes in New York. Any indication that a candidate might sponsor the unification of the two parties, as the President seemed to be doing, would meet their wholehearted opposition. To them, the essential struggle between the major factions had to be kept alive if politics were to have any worthwhile meaning.

The Albany resolutions were disregarded when they reached Washington. Monroe, not one to be driven by such tactics, defended Meigs and refused to remove him from his post. [46] Those in Albany who favored Van Rensselaer's appointment held a meeting on January 25 and called Van Buren's interference "obtrusive" and "incompatible with official decorum. . . ." He and the Vice-President were accused of "exciting dissatisfaction with the national administration and producing an angry appeal to the people" which was nothing more than a "pernicious example of insubordination and contumely. . . ." [47]

A little discouraged by the setback, Van Buren nevertheless regarded the entire episode as useful from every point of view. The Republican newspapers, he wrote,

in every part of the Union came out loudly in our favor, the spirit which animates them is felt here & the aspirants for public favor [presidential candidates] who but a few months since placed their claims to confidence more on their character for liberality (if so the policy which has for its object the desertion of your friends & the purchase of their enemies may be called) than on their political stability & fidelity, are now looking in a different direction. The Presidential power has somewhat subsided but most measures still point in that direction. No one of the candidates have so decided a preference in public opinion as far as it can be gathered here, as to render the chance of success greater to him than to the others.[48]

The following year Meigs resigned as Postmaster General, and it was supposed then and later that he was dismissed at Van Buren's behest. Actually he left the cabinet because of his age, and "in terms of great kindness & respect for me," said Monroe, "which I reciprocated." [49]

The conclusion of the affair made Van Buren one of the most discussed young senators in Washington, despite the presidential rebuff. The attention of the nation was focused upon him, wrote Samuel A. Talcott, for conducting "the most prudent and best managed political measure" ever witnessed.[50] It cleared the air for some, alerting them to the pernicious ideas of the amalgamationists. They thanked the Little Magician— a man who had been in Washington less than two months and had succeeded in making quite a name for himself.

Having excited the fancy of the social and political world of the capital, Van Buren settled down to the serious business of beginning his official career on February 12, 1822, when he delivered his maiden speech in the Senate. A bill to confirm the title for thirty square leagues of land in Louisiana to a marquis was referred to the Judiciary Committee, of which Van Buren was a member. When the measure was brought to the floor for debate he obtained recognition from the chair and attacked the proposed legislation on the ground of fraud. While speaking, he was suddenly overcome by embarrassment and suffered a "breakdown." His debut was too much for him and, finding that he could proceed no further, he quickly retreated to his seat and tried to hold back the sense of shame and frustration that swept over him. He was well-prepared and should have acquitted himself with honor, but he was too intense and was much too impressed by the distinguished senators who sat clustered around him. Nevertheless the bill was defeated, and the venerable Nathaniel Macon of North Carolina complimented him for showing the dishonesty of the claim.[51] Later, when he had relaxed a little, he delivered his second speech, which more than made up for the inadequacies of the first.

As the Congressional session progressed, Van Buren took little part in the Senate debates. He listened, but paid closer attention to the talk in the cloakrooms. There the main topic of conversation was the coming presidential election. John Q. Adams, William H. Crawford, Henry Clay, William Lowndes, John C. Calhoun, and others were all mentioned as possible contenders. The problem was how to get the Republican party to narrow its choice down to one. For Van Buren there was no problem: a caucus was the only method for nomination.

In all likelihood Van Buren had favored Calhoun in 1821 and might have continued supporting him if in their talks together the War Secretary had refrained from expressing Federalist ideas when he discussed the powers of the government and the nature of the Union.[52] Considering his service to the nation and his Southern background, he would have made an ideal candidate, but this one fault outweighed all other advantages. For this reason the New York Senator dropped him and looked elsewhere for his candidate.

Of the other contenders, Van Buren apparently never con-

sidered Lowndes, who died shortly thereafter, and he ruled
against Adams on the ground that the Missouri Compromise,
which revealed strong Southern leanings among many Bucktails, had weakened his position in New York.[53]   Besides,
Adams was drab, colorless, and lacked sufficient popular appeal
to interest Van Buren seriously.

Henry Clay was of a different stripe, however, with many
glamorous attributes to attract a professional politician.   But
Van Buren wondered whether he could "stand the severe
ordeal of public opinion for two long years," despite the
"rather dashing" stand already taken by Missouri in his behalf.[54]   And since New York was going to back the winning
candidate in this election in order to "reform" the "old democratic party," Clay was passed over because his victory potential
was not judged to be strong enough.

Van Buren had always been interested in the South, and it is
certainly possible to interpret some of his statements, especially
those regarding the Missouri Compromise, as pro-Southern.
Crawford was the favorite from that section, and a few Bucktails were noticeably doing him homage in what looked like
the first overtures leading to an open declaration of support.
Mordecai M. Noah, editor of the *National Advocate* in New
York City, was one of the earliest converts, and the Washington
Republican erroneously concluded that Van Buren was behind
Noah's endorsement.[55]   Nevertheless, Van Buren showed a
"prudent reserve" when queried about it, and would not commit himself one way or the other.   But William Plumer, Jr.,
of New Hampshire, guessed what was going on when he informed his father that the majority of Bucktails, "with Van
Beuren [*sic*] at their head (who, by the way, is perhaps the
greatest manager here), had come on, in a body, to make their
fortunes by joining the strongest party, & that for the present
they declared for no one in particular, but were waiting, &
watching the progress of events." [56]

In March, 1822, Van Buren journeyed to the South; this was
the first in a series of trips that was begun, very possibly, with

a view to the "general resuscitation" of the Republican party through a strengthening of the Virginia-New York alliance— an alliance that had been successful in controlling the government since 1800. He had called for radical reform of the party, and he may have gone South to examine the climate of political opinion in that section and to discover on what basis the coalition might continue to operate. While on his journey he certainly spoke to a number of "bold" Republicans of the "old school," and heard much condemnation of the "course pursued by Mr. Monroe. . . ." [57] But whether this crystallized any of his thoughts and whether he met Thomas Ritchie, the editor of the Richmond *Enquirer* and chief of the Virginia Junto, cannot be positively stated.

Back in New York, the "dreadful design" of his trip was the subject of varied comment. "One set," reported a friend of his, "believed that there was a great plot to revive the republican party . . . and that Jefferson & Madison are to be engaged in it. The others said that the object of your journey was a beautiful & accomplished young lady, not distantly related to the Governor of Virginia, and that an alliance of portentous consequences was then to be formed between the 'ancient dominion' and this 'great state.' " [58]

Van Buren's actual intention in going to Richmond he guarded with scrupulous care, saying merely that he had been on a visit and had been treated with great kindness by all he met.[59] If he had any ideas about a political alliance of the old type, they lay buried in his mind. But a continued infiltration of Federalist principles into Republican dogma, a further decline in party morale, and a wider application of the "Monroe heresy" might translate his ideas into action.

III: OLD-FASHIONED JEFFERSONIAN REPUBLICANISM

VAN BUREN spent the summer and fall of 1822 attending to state politics, and enjoyed himself immensely in the process. Clinton begrudgingly retired to his home on Long Island and left the governor's chair vacant for the Bucktails to fill as they wished. The November election went off like clockwork, thanks to the Regency. Both houses of the legislature were filled with Bucktails, Judge Joseph C. Yates was elected governor, and by December the pleasant task of distributing the patronage to perpetuate Regency control of the state had begun.

With New York resting quietly in the hands of its masters, Van Buren returned to national problems in Washington. He had just reached his fortieth year as the second session of the Seventeenth Congress began in late 1822. One of the more pressing problems to come before this Congress involved the extension and improvement of that national road which stretched westward from Cumberland, Maryland. The year before, Congress had appropriated $9,000 for it, which Van Buren agreed to,[1] despite the fact that the road might someday stretch to the Mississippi River and compete with the Erie Canal. The $9,000 appropriation was vetoed by Monroe, however, on the grounds that it infringed on the police powers of the several states and was therefore not authorized by the Constitution.[2]

By January, 1823, the road was badly in need of repair and another bill was brought before Congress to provide the necessary funds to take care of it. In the debate over the bill, Van

Buren presented very practical reasons for favoring its passage. Unless something were done about repairs, he argued, the money already expended would be wasted. If the senators were opposed to its western extension, they could at least, he pleaded, preserve what was already constructed.[3] The bill was finally passed, and since it had been so phrased as to avoid all of Monroe's constitutional scruples, it became law.

Not much later Van Buren came to regret his vote, and publicly disavowed it. Internal improvements (which was part of Henry Clay's "American System,") was a Federalist doctrine —or so he said. That he could have endorsed it by his vote was, in his opinion, just another commentary on the depressed condition of the Republican party. By 1826 he was loudly denying that Congress had power under the Constitution to provide for internal improvements. His early vote of approval, he recorded in his *Autobiography*, was given "rather on the ground of its paternity . . . than from an examination of the subject." Afterwards, when he "thoroughly investigated" the matter, he claimed he found in it a basic conflict of jurisdiction between Federal and state authorities which might be removed only by an amendment to the Constitution.[4] Within a period of three years, after being further indoctrinated with the Jeffersonian philosophy of states' rights and especially after he found Republicans quarreling over the question, he became a conscientious and vocal opponent of government-sponsored internal improvements.

Legislatively speaking, the short session of Congress during 1822–23 was comparatively quiet; but politically speaking, those few winter months were marked by fierce in-fighting between the two Southern presidential candidates, Crawford and Calhoun. Their dislike for one another, which stretched back through their years in the cabinet together, now reached the stage of public knowledge—chiefly through the newspapers. They assaulted each other with every abusive word they knew.

Van Buren, who was ready to deliver New York's 36 electoral votes to the candidate of his choice, began moving closer toward the presidential battlefield. Then suddenly he pulled away. The cause of his abrupt behavior was a letter he received from the Secretary of the Navy, Smith Thompson, asking whether he would like to occupy the seat on the United States Supreme Court made vacant by the death of Brockholst Livingston. The offer sounded wonderful; the catch was that it came from the wrong man.

The President of the United States, not the Secretary of the Navy, appoints justices to the highest court, and Monroe had given no thought at all to Van Buren's possible candidacy. Rather he had invited Thompson to accept the job. But the Secretary, with vague prospects of becoming a presidential candidate in 1824, hesitated before giving Monroe his answer.[5] Instead, he wrote to Van Buren and said he was inclined to refuse the appointment for two reasons: poor health—he had the strange notion that a President's life was easier than a judge's—and ignorance of those branches of legal science dealt with by the Supreme Court. "Now my Dear Sir," he purred, "assuming that I am out of the question, will you permit me to offer your name to the President?" [6]

Van Buren was back in New York when this letter reached him, for Congress had adjourned on March 3, 1823. He should have disregarded the offer, considering the source, but as he thought it over he fancied the idea of sitting on the Supreme Court. Desire replaced good sense and when Rufus King counseled him to accept the position, he instructed Thompson to tell Monroe that should the President think his appointment "consistent with the public interest, and it is agreeable to him to make it, I will consider it my duty to accept it." Although he remembered that he had "on occasion opposed Monroe," he was sure the President knew there was nothing personal in it. As a final thought he added that if he were chosen to fill the vacancy, "I should consider a total abstinence from interference in party politics as a duty of the most imperious nature, and I feel entire confidence in my ability to withdraw entirely and forever, from the scenes in which for many years I have taken part." [7]

Only the year before he had said that he was *"abundantly satisfied"* with the office of senator and would not change it.[8] He even spoke freely of revitalizing the Republican party in view of its wretched state and the continued abandonment of its principles by certain government officers. But that was before a place on the Supreme Court of the United States had been temptingly placed before him. Now he was ready to convoke all his enemies and friends at Albany, give them an elegant dinner, treat them with champagne, and in a valedictory speech "bid farewell forever to politics and pledge himself to know no parties upon the bench." [9]

When Rufus King urged Van Buren to accept the judgeship he promised at the same time to write to the President and add his weight to Thompson's recommendation. His letters, written early in April, were extremely complimentary toward Van Buren, and without exaggerating he spoke praisingly of the Senator's "superior talents," legal acumen, public experience, and "uncommon sagacity. . . ." [10] To John Q. Adams he penned a note broadly implying that with Van Buren safely entombed on the bench, certain persons might find their positions in the presidential contest greatly improved.[11] The Secretary of State did not miss the inference, but he was clever enough to realize that while these maneuverings were in progress the best place for him was in his quiet study.[12]

Meanwhile, Monroe was suprised and a bit puzzled when these letters began reaching his desk. He had in no way encouraged Van Buren and could not imagine why anyone should think he would consider him for the court. Besides, he still believed that Thompson would eventually accept his offer.[13] But with the Navy Secretary strangely silent, Monroe petulantly decided to postpone the appointment, since the circuit duties of the Supreme Court were completed for the term.[14]

The postponement infuriated Van Buren, and he accused the President of behaving badly toward him. Was Monroe being deliberately vindictive? Whatever the reason, said the Senator, it was another example of the President's confused

mind—a mind softened by his habitual "indecision and intercourse with court parasites. . . ." [15]   How else could Van Buren
explain it?   How else could he explain the Federalist appointments?   How else could he explain the process of disintegra-
tion going on within the Republican party?

Turning to Thompson, the real culprit, Van Buren asked
him pointblank whether he had declined in such a way as to
leave no doubt in Monroe's mind of his intentions.   The Navy
Secretary meekly replied that he was not "absolutely" certain.[16]

Months passed, and the President did nothing.   He listened
to further recommendations and conjectured whether Thompson would accept the vacancy,[17] while Van Buren continued to
wail over the fact that such a pusillanimous idiot sat in the
White House.   Finally Van Buren said that he was convinced
Monroe would "sooner appoint an alligator than me." [18]   And
probably a Federalist alligator at that!

With the short respite given Thompson to examine his
future and think over the appointment at his leisure, he at
length concluded that the presidency was temporarily beyond
his reach.[19]   This settled, he decided to accept Monroe's offer.
But first he prepared a letter to Van Buren asking whether
"you think I could with propriety as it respects yourself take
the office." [20]

By now, resigned to his own failure, Van Buren had regained his composure.   He was inclined to tell Thompson to
do as he pleased, but King talked him into using sharper
language.[21]   Van Buren and Thompson had once been close
friends, and the Senator had named his youngest son Smith
Thompson after the Secretary.   But now Van Buren agreed
that the Secretary's little game had been a gross abuse of that
friendship,[22] and the relationship was abruptly ended.

As the judgeship drew further and further away from him,
Van Buren, quite naturally, returned to the question of the
presidential election.   The large number of candidates seeking
the office, some of whom had been campaigning since 1817,[23]
made the contest more fascinating for him.   Obviously a high

premium was placed on management, and he was courted in turn by each of the protagonists.

William H. Crawford, who unselfishly and foolishly withdrew as a caucus nominee in 1816, should have stood on "higher ground" than the others.[24] He had allowed Monroe to precede him, and one would think that the President would return the favor and designate him as his successor. Or at least designate someone. But Monroe remained silent and refused to interfere in the matter of selection. His refusal encouraged a large group of would-be candidates to disregard party unity. His refusal assured a breakup of Republican ranks.

It is quite probable that the President's failure to act as party chieftain, far more than his Federalist appointments, is the true reason for Van Buren's intense dislike of him. Monroe had a clear responsibility to the party by the very fact that he was the President of the United States, a responsibility he could not—indeed, dared not—disregard. But he did disregard it, under the mistaken belief that he could choose to be party leader or not, whatever he pleased. From that moment on Van Buren could not find a decent word to say about Monroe or his administration. As he grew older his language became sharper. The President, he wrote, had introduced no disturbing public questions. The tariff was not a problem; the issue of internal improvements was "speculative"; the United States Bank was going its separate way without regard for the government or the people; no embarrassing questions had arisen in foreign affairs. And yet the Republican party "was literally shattered into fragments. . . ." Monroe's sole accomplishment, Van Buren said, was to destroy the party that had given him his office. "In the place of two great parties arrayed against each other in a fair and open contest for the establishment of principles in the administration of Government which they respectively believed most conductive to the public interest, the country was overrun with personal factions." [25]

In the summer of 1822, the Tennessee legislature added a

fifth name to the ever-increasing list of contenders by nominating Andrew Jackson. The immediate reaction in the country to this proposal ran from disbelief to something bordering on horror.[26] Almost everyone was prepared to acknowledge that Jackson was a great military hero, the savior of his country, but they were not going to seat him in the White House on that account. He had little to offer the people except a short, inconspicuous term in Congress. He had a name, a reputation, but nothing else. Van Buren, like many others, paid no attention to his candidacy.

Of the remaining four aspirants, the New York Senator in December or January, 1822–23—just prior to the Supreme Court affair—narrowed his personal choice down to Crawford, the Secretary of the Treasury. Having "waited & watched" for over a year, he was now disposed to abandon his discreet noncommittalism and come out in open support of the candidate from Georgia. Crawford, he declared, was closest to his own political principles. He belonged to the states' rights school, was strict in his interpretation of the Constitution, and, most important, was dedicated to the maintenance of party harmony at all costs. "His friends," Van Buren reflected years later, "seemed more anxious to preserve the unity of the Republican party, and on that account I imbibed an early inclination to give him the preference."[27] Both the New Yorker and the Georgian had an unshakable faith in the value of a national caucus, regardless of the fact that it had lost public favor.[28] Van Buren viewed it as the most cohesive element in a party system of government. It engendered discipline, it separated loyal partisans from Federalists and vacillating independents. According to his reasoning, those who refused to abide by its decisions were traitors to the party and would succeed one day in destroying the organization and dissolving the bands holding the various sections of the country together.[29] When Calhoun pompously termed the caucus anachronistic and stated that he would not accept a nomination from it if offered, Van Buren coupled this with the South Carolinian's Federalist ideas and dismissed him as a potential candidate.

His [Calhoun's] views in regard to the construction of the Federal Constitution were latitudinarian in the extreme. Of these he gave us a striking and alarming illustration in his report as Secretary of War in favour of internal improvements by the general government. . . .[30] He was out of patience with Virginia politics and with the never-ceasing harping by her politicians upon the "doctrines of '98." If I had selected my Presidential candidate from personal preferences I might have chosen Mr. Calhoun, but the particular doctrines that were then so distasteful to him were in perfect harmony with my opinions and feelings. They constituted the creed of a political party to which I had belonged from the beginning and in whose ranks I hoped to remain to the last.[31]

Perhaps the strongest candidate in the Northeast, Van Buren would admit, was John Quincy Adams.[32] A superb Secretary of State, he nevertheless combined all of Calhoun's faults with a few of his own. The most disturbing feature of his political make-up, in Van Buren's opinion, was his obvious adherence to the Monroe heresy. Should Adams reach the White House, he would assuredly distribute the patronage to both Federalists and Republicans, basing his selections on the capabilities of an applicant alone rather than on his ability *plus* his strict devotion to the party. This "pernicious" policy was, as far as the Senator was concerned, the unforgivable sin. Because of it, and because of Adams's "political bias and opinions," Van Buren excluded him as a worthy successor to the presidency.

Henry Clay was possibly the most active nationalist of his day. His American System, which called for internal improvements, a protective tariff for manufactures, improved transportation, and home markets for the farmers, was little more than an elaboration of the ideas contained in Alexander Hamilton's report on public credit and manufactures. Yet Van Buren at this point failed to take notice of the System and liked the Kentuckian well enough to consider him for second place.[33] But that was as far as he would go, for he had doubts of Clay's ability to sustain himself during the long and bitter months ahead.

Almost as soon as Van Buren decided on Crawford he was at work planning the campaign. His many visits to Virginia during 1823 gave a fair indication of the energy he was willing to expend. Heretofore the New York-Virginia alliance had been unbeatable, electing in turn Jefferson, Madison, and Monroe. But Virginia always had the privilege of naming the president while New York had to be content with second place. All that would now be changed; instead of tamely following behind the Old Dominion, New York would lead the way. To continue this coalition, even in reverse order, was probably the cause of Van Buren's numerous trips to Virginia. The ever-observant Clay watched his movements and warned that this alliance might decide the election by drawing in Pennsylvania, New Jersey, and Maryland—leaving Adams isolated in New England.[34]

As early as February, 1823, Rufus King surmised that "V.B. *au fond,* is for Crawford; tho' he cannot be insensible of the difficulty of that labour." [35] King may have thought that the campaign would be an uphill struggle, but not Van Buren. He had faith in his own abilities and especially in the Congressional caucus which he would summon to nominate the Secretary of the Treasury. Once Crawford had been put before the people in the manner first employed by Jefferson, Van Buren expected the other candidates to withdraw. In the meantime he said nothing, especially when he learned that only a fraction of the New York legislators were inclined toward Crawford.[36] Most of the others were either divided between Adams and Calhoun,[37] or had not as yet made up their minds. But Erastus Root assured him that while indecision was rife, Republicans in the long run would not "consent to elevate to the first office any but a democrat, & Crawford is the only candidate on this side of the mountain who can rightfully claim that honorable distinction. He is called the *'radical'* candidate by way of derision. Jefferson was called the democrat or jacobinical candidate in '98 & '99 & by the same sort of people who now talk about *'radicals'.*" [38]

Before leaving Washington for home, Van Buren, in a long

conversation with the "Radical" Crawford "left little doubt that Crawford was authorized to conclude that V.B. was in his favor." [39] The two men agreed that nomination in caucus was essential as the best means to perpetuate the party in the traditional manner. Some people would call what they were about to do "radicalism," but the Senator regarded it as orthodox Republicanism. No action was to be taken for the time being, but when the campaign was well under way New York and Virginia would pool their respective strength, as they had in the past, and declare for the Georgian. Although certain people in Albany might balk at the idea, the Regency could be depended upon to drive them into line.

During the canvass preceding the great election "an open rupture" between Calhoun and Van Buren was barely avoided, but enough ill feeling was engendered to last a lifetime.[40] Conscious of the large faction in New York who favored him, the Secretary of War decided to intervene in the political affairs of the state in order to prevent Van Buren from giving Crawford New York's 36 electoral votes.[41] He got in touch with General Joseph G. Swift, Winfield Scott, Samuel L. Gouverneur (Monroe's son-in-law), and Henry Wheaton—his most outspoken supporters in the state—and urged them to "expose to the Union" the real character and history of such men as "Van Buren and the rest of the intriguers." [42] Crawford, he said, was reduced to complete dependency upon the Little Magician and could be "put down" only with "proper efforts" to restore the state to sound political conditions.[43]

Acting on Calhoun's advice, Wheaton, Scott, and Gouverneur, in May of 1823,[44] founded a newspaper, *The Patriot*, with which to begin the Herculean task of wrecking Van Buren's strength at home. Although the sheet was edited by Charles K. Gardner and Selleck Osborn, its most trenchant writing was done by Henry Wheaton. It did its best to expose "Van Buren and the rest of the intriguers," but its greatest service to the people of New York was its advocacy of a revised system of choosing presidential electors. According to the existing mode, the legislature made the choice, and with the

Bucktails in control of both the Assembly and Senate—"which no man knew how to wield better than Mr. Van Buren, though the Albany Regency"—the 36 votes of the state could be handed over to Crawford without the slightest difficulty.[45] To prevent this and to give Calhoun a fighting chance Wheaton and *The Patriot* demanded that the law be repealed and that the choice of electors be given to the people. In no time this cry was repeated by other newspapers, and then by the people. By the summer of 1823 the crusade was on.

All of Van Buren's plans for the coming election seemed to be under attack. The call to revise the electoral law was bad enough, but then he encountered open hostility on the part of most of the other states toward his intention of holding a Congressional caucus. If a caucus were held, Crawford's nomination was assured because of his popularity in Congress.[46] Friends of the other candidates were unwilling to sanction it for this reason, and they protested that the electorate had grown tired of such an outmoded and undemocratic system. They wanted the people themselves to choose between the contenders, and, if necessary, they would "intrigue & bargain" to bring this about.[47]

As Van Buren analyzed each new event and surveyed the national and local scenes, he could not shake off a sense of fear and foreboding. Everything was wrong. Only a few would listen to him, even though he believed he had the one solution to set matters right. Since the various Republican factions were unwilling to resolve their differences in a duly constituted caucus for the sake of the party, he predicted that a period was beginning "in which feelings of the most rancorous hostility are to have free scope." [48] Then the Federalists—in spirit if not in name—would return to power.

Late in the spring of 1823, Van Buren planned another trip to Virginia, "taking Monticello in my way." [49] But for some reason he did not get to visit his idol, Thomas Jefferson; he probably spent most of his time with Thomas Ritchie, the leading "Radical" in the Old Dominion. The exact date these two worthy politicians met is unknown, but the editor of the Rich-

mond *Enquirer* stated in 1838 that from "the first moment of
my acquaintance with you, I have been your personal & political friend." [50]   In his newspaper, beginning in January, 1823,
Ritchie repeatedly referred to the New Yorker and his friends
as "statesmen and patriots."   He went to great lengths to lavish
upon Van Buren all the journalistic encomiums he knew, and
their friendship became the subject of speculative comment in
and around Virginia. [51]   It was the beginning of what was to be
a union between the Albany Regency and the Richmond Junto.
The latter organization, save for its looseness of construction,
was similar to its New York counterpart, especially in that its
aim was control of the government of Virginia. [52]   "Between
the Regency at Albany and the junto at Richmond," exclaimed
Calhoun, "there is a vital connection. They give and receive
hope from each other, and confidently expect to govern this
nation." [53]

Like his opinions on so many other things, Calhoun was
only partly right.   All Van Buren wanted was a nation run by
the Republican party according to proper principles.   If the
party could be controlled by a New York-Virginia alliance, so
much the better.   Had this not been Jefferson's method of
operation?

By the summer of 1823 even Van Buren himself would have
to admit that the political horizon was none too bright.   In
New York the agitation for repeal of the electoral law had
swelled to enormous proportions and had finally given rise to
the so-called "People's Party."   Without reference to old principles that had always divided the electorate, this new movement cut across party lines and threatened to rework the political fabric of New York.

A rather strange aspect to the ever-increasing excitement in
New York was the indifference of some of the People's men to
the presidential candidates other than Crawford. [54]   Generally
speaking, they were simply against the caucus, against Crawford, and for repeal of the electoral law.   Since the issues were
local, some of the more practical Bucktails—who were still un-

questionably loyal to the Regency—wondered if it might not be politic, in view of the imminent November election, to advocate repeal of the existing law. Within each ward it became obvious that Republicans feared the issue and were willing to give it verbal approval or even more—rather than risk their own elections.[55] Jacob Barker told Benjamin Butler:

In our ward I had a hard hard contest . . . about giving advice to the Legislature in the shape of Resolutions to give to the people the choice of Electors. I never felt more at home than when I undertook to demonstrate that any alteration would be unwise. These magic words, *"the people"*, *"the people"*, *"the people,"* were rung through a thousand changes—but as we were not called together or authorized to manage *"the peoples"* affairs but simply the party's affairs, a vast majority of the meetings, after two hours dis-cussion, agreed indefinitely to defer the consideration of the subject. . . . You may rely upon it this universal Yankee notion will take out of the Republican ranks so many . . . [that] the Federalists, Clintonians & dissatisfied will unite & together make a majority.[56]

In the November state campaign many of the regularly nominated Bucktails, without any authorization, promised to support repeal and were thus elected.[57] No candidate "dared to avow his opposition to the measure," reported Jabez D. Hammond.[58] Years later, Van Buren agreed that the candidates had indeed been placed in a most "awkward" position.[59]

The majority of men chosen to sit in the legislature in November, 1823, were those who had openly promised to revise the existing law. Fortunately, a sufficient number of them were Van Buren men so that the Regency majorities in the Assembly and Senate were preserved intact. But their dilemma was immediately apparent: whether to cut their own throats by honoring their pledges, or break their promise and invite the people to cut their throats for them.

IV: THE SCHISM OF 1824

THE PROPOSAL in New York to revamp the electoral law was not nearly so destructive to Van Buren's plans as the sudden and overwhelming personal tragedy that befell William H. Crawford. While returning home from Washington late in the summer of 1823, the Secretary of the Treasury became feverish and found his skin acutely inflamed. He took to his bed and summoned a local physician, who immediately administered a large dose of lobelia to combat what was apparently a severe attack of erysipelas. The overdose of medicine precipitated a paralytic stroke, and Crawford was rendered sightless and dumb.[1] Paralyzed from the waist down, he was removed to the country, where he rallied and then slowly began to improve. Not until his sight and speech were partially restored was the news of his illness allowed to get abroad. Even then a full and complete account of his condition was suppressed lest it jeopardize his candidacy. For months only a few men knew the extent of his breakdown, and no one could guess how long it would keep him incapacitated.

Later that year in Washington, at the opening of the Eighteenth Congress, Van Buren listened intermittently to the reading of the President's annual message. Although brief, compared to some, and seemingly unimportant, the document constituted what eventually became known as the "Monroe Doctrine." The New Yorker, like others, missed its significance because he was too busy with other matters to be impressed by the words droned out by the clerk. He was totally preoccupied with the details of inducing congressmen to attend a caucus. Upon him rested "a great portion of the management" neces-

sary to bring it about, wrote Rufus King, and unless he exerted great pressure the caucus would never be summoned.[2]

Anxious to hold the meeting as soon as possible and thereby give Crawford's candidacy an "impulse" which would be
felt throughout the Union, Van Buren suggested to the Republicans that they convene at some time before Christmas.
Hopefully he added that it would end, once and for all, the
wrangling over the nomination. The usual procedure would
be followed, and the winning candidate would receive the support of the entire party. As a consequence, Republicans would
regain their old unity and harmony would be restored.

Van Buren found, however, that not more than sixty congressmen would consent to a caucus—less than a quarter of the
combined members of the two houses. Calhoun's partisans
held an "anti-caucus" caucus to agree to stay away from the
meeting; others thought of taking more drastic action.[3] The
House of Representatives debated going on record as disap-
proving the system altogether, and it was only checked when
the Radicals warned Clay that any "overt" act against a caucus
would cost him the support he might receive from them
should Crawford withdraw from the race on account of his
health. The Kentuckian respected the challenge, and advised
his friends to head off the proposal and say nothing more about
it.[4]

For his part, Van Buren was flabbergasted by the refusal of
Republicans to honor the time-hallowed, Jefferson-hallowed
institution of a national caucus. It seemed incredible to him
that they would abandon so much for the sake of their respective candidates. And, as might be expected, he blamed the
President for what happened. Monroe "pursued a course," he
wrote, "well designed to weaken the influence of the caucus
system, and to cause its abandonment."[5] Was any further
proof necessary to indict the President on the charge of deliberately wrecking the Republican party?

Nevertheless, Van Buren was shrewd enough to order a
postponement of his meeting until January or February, with

the expectation of enticing a more representative portion of the Congress to attend.[6] It was a futile gesture, but he could afford to wait.

With his campaign going from bad to worse, he tried to solve one of his problems by proposing an amendment to the Constitution. In the past there had been various motions to eliminate the Electoral College and establish a different mode of choosing the President. Since he was now the chairman of the Senate judiciary committee, he offered an amendment on December 29 which would give to the people—voting in districts created by the states—the right to choose the electors directly; the candidate receiving a majority of the electoral votes would become President. In the event that no one won a majority, the electors would meet a second time and vote between the two highest candidates. If a tie resulted, the choice would be thrown to the House of Representatives.[7]

In submitting his amendment, Van Buren spoke at length against a completely centralized government and affirmed his conviction that it should never be released from its dependence on the states. Then he proceeded to comment on the provisions of his amendment. His arguments sounded very democratic but his motives were purely political. He was attempting to provide an excellent answer to those in the states who were trying to anticipate Congressional action by amending their own electoral laws. The Regency might now appeal to New Yorkers to delay changing their law and allow the federal government to make the necessary revisions. Since it would take years to ratify an amendment, the election of 1824 would not be affected.

Although the Bucktails continued to debate the advisability of revising New York's electoral law, almost all of them firmly supported Van Buren's desire for a nominating caucus. This should be held, they said, "for the best good of the Rep. party & the State." Whoever opposed this, intoned Azariah C. Flagg, "is a scismatic [sic]. I wish to see a president" he continued, "who shall make the wishes of the republican party the rule of his conduct sufficiently seasoned with Democracy to stand by those who have stood by their country in hard times." [8]

The correspondence between the leaders of the Regency during the following weeks clearly indicates that their great fear concerned continued Republican unity. If a caucus were abandoned and many men were permitted to compete for the presidency, the great Jeffersonian organization would disintegrate into as many factions as there were candidates. The people would group themselves around individuals, and a series of personal parties would replace the present single party of principle. There were, of course, valid objections to a caucus, even Van Buren admitted that. But, as he said, it represented "the different quarters of the union," brought into "one body as perfect a representation as can be expected," and was "the best attainable mode of effecting the great object in view which has as yet been suggested." [9]

Thus, once the caucus convened and conferred upon Crawford its nomination, the Regency men would submit to him, no matter what their personal preference might be. "Unity among Republicans must be preserved," [10] argued Flagg, who was even prepared to support Clay or Calhoun to achieve this end. Therefore it is fair to state that if the caucus had nominated someone other than Crawford, Van Buren would have respected the party will.

By the beginning of 1824, the Regency cronies had come to regard electoral-law revision with a jaundiced eye. Any change jeopardized their plan to deliver New York's 36 votes to Crawford.[11] Under other circumstances they probably would have advocated revision. Instead, they condemned it and inveigled Governor Yates (by holding out the prospect of the vice-presidency before him [12]) into advising the legislature not to tamper with the present law until a uniform rule was adopted as an amendment to the Constitution of the United States, following Van Buren's proposal in Congress.[13] We "conspirators," Benjamin F. Butler trumpeted, labored incessantly, but "are hampered by premature commitments" made by many Bucktails. "Stick to principles," he exhorted them, "advocate the necessity of adhering to the old forms and established doctrines of the party and express the utmost readiness to submit individual preferences to the decision of the Caucus." [14]

Although working against increasingly difficult odds in Washington and New Work, and despite all the arguments he heard, Van Buren would not yield to prevailing sentiment in the nation by abandoning the idea of a general Republican meeting. Maryland, Alabama, and Tennessee had publicly condemned such a nomination, and an overwhelming number of people were known to be against it.[15] The friends of Clay, Jackson, Calhoun, and Adams, commented George McDuffie of South Carolina, "have a perfect understanding and are united in the determination to give the Caucus a death blow." [16] When these dire prophecies reached him, the New York Senator merely smiled pleasantly.[17] "V.B. puts a bold face upon affairs and speaks, however he thinks, that all is going on well both here and at Albany," commented the discerning Rufus King, "—tho', entre nous, I saw a letter that came by the morning's mail from General [Erastus] Root—saying *'we are here in trouble,* and *that there is not a majority of the members of the Legislature in favor of any of the Candidates.'* " [18] Van Buren scoffed at this rumor when he heard it. "I cannot help what . . . King may choose to infer from my looks, but the truth is that I have at no time doubted of our complete success." [19]

Early in February, more than half the members of Congress signed a statement declaring they would not attend a caucus. This information may have surprised some, but not Van Buren.[20] Many days before he had taken a private poll. The disappointing results in no way deterred him from issuing the caucus call on February 6. The notice, as printed in the *National Intelligencer,* was signed by 11 congressmen, but Van Buren's name was not among them. The meeting was to take place on Saturday, February 14, in the evening, and the members were to convene in the chamber of the House of Representatives.

On the designated evening, the gallery doors were opened to an awaiting throng of caucus friends and enemies. Within minutes all the available space for spectators was taken, and those who could find no seats swarmed through the corridors outside. Some sixty-six congressmen put in an appearance on the floor of the House, but it was a dismal showing. The New York, Virginia, North Carolina, and Georgia delegations were the largest; from the other states only two or three men, at the very most, acknowledged the summons. The severest blow was the absence of the representatives from Pennsylvania, since a New York-Virginia-Pennsylvania coalition, if it could have been built, would have been unbeatable in the election.

There was no need to account for the absentees; everyone knew where they were. "King Caucus is dead," had been their response to the invitation. And the many spectators who filled the galleries had come to give him a fitting burial.

In organizing the meeting Benjamin Ruggles of Ohio was chosen chairman and E. Calling, secretary. Despite the repeated cries for adjournment and a motion from one congressman that they postpone making any decision for six weeks, Van Buren, in his capacity as the Crawford leader and manager of the meeting, resisted all such demands. The caucus had already been postponed twice in the past few months. It was now or never.

The balloting began in a slow, measured tempo. Upon its completion the chairman announced, to the accompaniment of "heavy groans in the Gallery," that Crawford had received 62 votes.[21] Two were given to Adams and one apiece for Jackson and Nathaniel Macon. By proxy, two additional votes were awarded to the Treasury Secretary. Crawford was now in the company of Jefferson, Madison, and Monroe. All had been nominated by a Congressional caucus.

In the period preceding the meeting, Van Buren had hung on to a vain hope that Henry Clay would consent to run on the ticket as candidate for the vice-presidency. With "unwearied efforts" he tried to work out such an arrangement and communicated with Thomas Hart Benton, Senator from Mis-

souri, with whom he held "several conferences on the subject."
When the gist of these talks reached him, Clay let it be known
that he considered it his duty to seek the presidency, and would
not countenance any attempt to reduce him to second place on
the Radical ticket.[22]

Crawford, on the other hand, had favored Albert Gallatin
as his running mate. When Clay's rejection seemed irrevo-
cable, Van Buren was persuaded to accept Gallatin because of
the influence such a nomination might exert upon Pennsylvania.[23] It was presumed that there was still an outside chance
that this important state would join New York and Virginia
and thus insure the Crawford ticket against defeat.[24] Therefore, in January, 1824, Gallatin was "forced" to accept the offer
made to him [25] and he was duly nominated on February 14.
The vote was Gallatin, 57; Erastus Root, 2; Adams, 1; Benjamin Rush, 1; Samuel Smith, 1; William Eustis, 1; Walter
Lowndes, 1; John Todd, 1; Rufus King, 1.

Everything taken into account, the Van Buren conclave
proved three things. First, the Republican party was no longer
one; it was now divided into at least five separate parts. Second, that William H. Crawford was the most popular man in
Congress; no other aspirant could have attained as high a number of votes as he. Finally, that the caucus should never have
been held. It had outlived its usefulness and the people had
repudiated it. Nevertheless, Van Buren clung to it because
there was no other method available at that time which would
unite the party behind a single candiadte.

The Albany *Argus* spoke of Crawford as the "national"
candidate—which indeed he was—but more frequently newspapers referred to him as the Radical candidate who had destroyed all his prospects by accepting a congressional nomination.[26] "If the newspapers are to be regarded as indexes of
public opinion," reported *Niles' Weekly Register,* "never
was any political measure quite so unpopular in the United
States. . . ." [27]

Although a tactical mistake had been made, Van Buren
was not overly worried. Because of the number of candidates

it seemed unlikely that any one of them would receive a majority of electoral votes. The election would then go to the House of Representatives, and Crawford could still become president provided New York did not desert him. "Everything is here considered as depending upon New York," wrote Congressman William Plumer, Jr.[28] In a letter to the Regency Van Buren commented: "From a great variety of circumstances I am well satisfied myself that if N York does not repeal the electoral law & supports the caucus . . . Mr. Clay will retire & his friends will support Mr. Crawford." [29] Henry Clay saw this possibility but promised to prevent its fulfillment. "Mr. Crawford's friends," he noted, "will make an effort as long as they adhere to him, to exclude me from the House of Representatives, in the hope that my Western friends will take him, if they can not get me. They utterly deceive themselves. If they accomplish that object, and bring him into the house with Adams and Jackson, to my exclusion, he *can not* be elected." [30] Clay would make certain of that.

During the same month in which the last Congressional caucus was held, John C. Calhoun was eliminated as a presidential contender. For some time there had been signs that he would be forced to withdraw, and Van Buren informed the Regency of this on February 17, when he predicted that the Secretary of War was "on the eve of retiring in favour of Genl Jackson." At best, the South Carolinian had never been more than second choice with most Northern Republicans, except those in Pennsylvania. The Little Magician, perspicacious as ever and far ahead of the other managers, was already counting his candidate's blesssings once Calhoun was "thrown overboard." He prophesied that

If Jackson gets Pennsylvania Mr Clay *cannot get into the house* and will of course make an early & comparatively honorable retreat unless he should be prevented from doing so by the letters he gets from Albany holding out a hope that he may get that State which can never be realized. From this brief statement our friends will be made sensible of the extreme importance of their acting with energy & unanimity. Get some of the most prudent & confidential men together at your house & read them this letter. But for *strong reasons enjoin upon them not to speak of my name in connection with it.*[31]

Van Buren's one mistake was in thinking Clay's "honorable retreat" would be made in Crawford's direction.

Back in Pennsylvania, Jackson's popularity had grown to such an extent during the past few months that the position of the state's leaders who opposed him was visibly threatened.[32] Mass desertions into the ranks of the General's army followed. The political complexion of the state changed almost overnight, and the transformation was judged complete when George M. Dallas, Calhoun's most enthusiastic supporter, formally went over to Jackson on February 18. Ten days later, at the Harrisburg convention, Old Hickory was unanimously nominated for President, and Calhoun was designated as his running mate. Although his removal from the top of the ballot came as a shock, the South Carolinian accepted the verdict as final.[33] The precedent established in Pennsylvania was then followed by Maryland, New Jersey, North and South Carolina. This Jackson-Calhoun coalition, once formed, began moving at breakneck speed in capturing the votes of nonpartisans.

For Van Buren, Calhoun's demise as a candidate had two salutary effects: there was a possibility that Clay might retreat into the Radical camp, and the party was now split into four parts instead of five.

To Van Buren's lasting discredit it must be remembered that he labored intently to elect a man so ill as to be physically unfit to fill the office of President. He should have gone over to Clay, his second choice, or to Adams, in recognition of the preferences of New Yorkers.[34] Yet he would not abandon Crawford. The stricken Secretary was the only candidate who was a "Republican of the old school"; he was certain to win if the election went into the House and Clay was excluded, or so Van Buren thought; and, as President, he was the one man who would give the New York Senator the necessary power to end the schism of 1824, restore party harmony, and reconstitute the entire Republican organization along Jeffersonian lines.

Van Buren's all but silent participation in the affairs of Congress during this session indicates the amount of time he devoted to whipping a caucus together and to keeping Crawford in the forefront of the presidential race. His negotiations were widespread, and included, reported John Quincy Adams, a gesture of friendship by his party to the Massachusetts Federalists [35]—which is difficult to believe.

However, in January he did make a speech on the Senate floor concerning the power of the Federal government to construct roads and canals. The question, he said, was so unsettled and the opinions from different sections of the country were so "divergent" as to require constitutional amendment in order to give Congress the necessary power. The money to be raised for the internal improvements, he moved, should be apportioned among the several states according to population; although Congress would direct all such improvements, no construction would be undertaken within a state without the express consent of the legislature thereof.

Van Buren's amendment was formulated in accordance with his states' rights philosophy, and as such was a distinct disservice to the document which formed the basis of the American government. To belabor the Constitution by defining specific Congressional power was to hamper and restrict that instrument rather than enlarge and improve upon it. If Congress were reduced to passing amendments every time a question of its power arose, the government would cease operation. Fortunately, Van Buren's well-intentioned bill was killed.[36]

In similar manner, as chairman of the Judiciary Committee he reported two measures which were aimed at strengthening the states by altering and circumscribing the powers of the Supreme Court. He suggested that no state law be invalidated by the Court without the concurrence of at least five justices out of the seven. He also argued for an increase in the number of circuit courts, to be manned by a completely new set of judiciary officers who would have no other duties.[37] These bills, like his earlier one, made no impression on other congressmen, and they were allowed to die quietly.

In the spring of 1824 there was brought before the Senate a projected treaty with England, whereby the slave trade was to be condemned as piracy and both countries were to be given the right to search ships suspected of trafficking in humans. The Radicals were in immediate opposition to the treaty, fearing it would develop into a general agreement between Great Britain and the United States to destroy slavery in the South.[38] Van Buren was powerfully articulate during the debate, declaring he would vote against this treaty "in any shape" because it was bound to produce "collisions" which would give rise to uncontrollable agitation in the two countries. The right of search, he insisted, implied "the right to fire upon the vessel if she does not come to when ordered to do so." This he thought a most dangerous implication.[39] And so the Crawfordites, "with V. B. & Holmes [of Maine] at their head," belabored the proposal with "alterations" until they had succeeded in destroying it. As a result, said Rufus King, Crawford had a political hobbyhorse with which to ride through the South.[40]

The most interesting measure the Congress dealt with in this session was one to increase the tariff duties. After a brilliant debate between Henry Clay and Daniel Webster, the House, by a close vote, sent to the Senate a bill which boosted the duties on iron, woolens, cottons, hemp, wool, and cotton bagging. The arguments advanced in its favor were generally protective in nature, with only slight reference made to the revenue it would bring.

Andrew Jackson, who had been elected to the Senate from Tennessee the previous October and sat directly in front of Van Buren, reportedly favored a tariff provided it was "judicious." [41] Clay, when he heard the remark, tried to "scandalize" its ambiguity. Well, "by——," he snapped, "I am in favor of the *in*judicious tariff." [42] Van Buren himself said nothing during the Senate discussion of this bill and, interestingly enough, did not attempt to make it a campaign issue. He was ignorant of the broader aspects of the question and had not decided whether he wished to subscribe to the protective system or not. He had no particular love for the manufacturer, but was only too willing to aid the farmer in any way possible. Consequently he acted in deference to the wishes of New York by voting for each provision of the measure, with one exception. The duty on cotton bagging he resented because it disproportionately advanced the interests of Kentucky and was obnoxious to the cotton-growing states of Georgia, Alabama, the Carolinas, and Mississippi, whose electoral votes were very important.[43] Nevertheless, this particular increase was passed over his objection by the count of 24 to 23.

When Jackson, who had supported the entire tariff, saw the New Yorker switch his vote on this one section, he turned around and said: "You give way, Sir!"

"No, sir," Van Buren replied—as he later recorded the conversation—"I have been from the beginning opposed to this clause . . . unless the duty was greatly reduced. Subsequent reflection led me to regard this provision as an exceedingly exceptionable one and I finally determined to oppose it in any shape. . . ." [44]

Although it sounds unlikely, Van Buren reports that on the following day he spoke to Jackson about the political effect the cotton-bagging provision would have on Southern states. He predicted that the motion would be brought up again because the vote had been close, and urged the General to help in striking it out.[45] As anticipated, five days later the clause was reintroduced by Nathaniel Macon and this time was defeated, with Jackson reversing his previous vote.[46]

The Senate then passed the remainder of this mildly protective tariff on May 13, and Monroe added his signature a few weeks later. Although the rates imposed by the law were not too high, Southerners condemned them because they believed a general price rise would result. A system which forced them to buy on a closed market and sell on an open one they termed unfair. Later they used stronger terms and warned that a tariff might precipitate the dismemberment of the Federal Union.

The Middle and Northwestern states, consisting of New

Jersey, Pennsylvania, New York, Indiana, Ohio, and Illinois, were united in supporting the bill.[47] New England and the border states were divided. Missouri, Tennessee, Kentucky, Connecticut, and Vermont voted for the measure, while Massachusetts, Maryland, and Delaware were opposed. New Hampshire and Maine split.[48] By and large, the agricultural and manufacturing areas voted with the majority and the commercial and navigating areas with the minority.

Because of the proximity of their seats in the upper house, Jackson and Van Buren came to know each other very well during these months together. Each later agreed that his earlier opinion of the other underwent sharp revision. Thinking back to 1824, Jackson said:

I had heard . . . about Mr Van Buren, especially about his *non-committalism*. I made up my mind that I would take an early opportunity to hear him and judge for myself. One day an important subject was under debate in the Senate. I noticed that Mr Van Buren was taking notes while one of the Senators was speaking. I judged from this that he intended to reply, and I determined to be in my seat when he spoke. His turn came, and he rose and made a clear, straightforward argument, which, to my mind, disposed of the whole subject. I turned to my colleague, Major Eaton, who sat next to me: "Major," said I, "is there anything non-committal about that?" "No, sir," said the Major.[49]

With Van Buren in Washington, unable to oversee affairs in Albany, his cronies soon found themselves submerged in the murky waters of New York politics. Without his advice, tact, counsel, and "sober second thought" to rely on, the members of the Regency proceeded to commit a blunder of the first magnitude. By an act of incredible folly they removed De Witt Clinton from his presidency of the Canal Board.

The former Governor's continued presence on this board— for which he received no salary—was a fitting acknowledgment of the state's appreciation for his past promotion of the Erie Canal. However, there were some who envied him this honor and were intent on kicking him even though he lay prostrate and possessed no power with which to harm them. Early in 1824, Marcy informed Van Buren of the continued irritation the situation provoked, but added that it was slowly diminishing. "Judge Skinner behaves quite well; now and then he indulges his spleen against *certain persons* for keeping Clinton in the board of canal commissioners—but that is seldom. These fits come to him less frequently than one would expect considering the very bad weather we have here." [50]

The condition might have remained static had not Skinner suddenly decided that he could execute a scheme worthy of his distinguished master. In April, 1824, he convinced the Regency brethren that by ousting Clinton they could "entrap the people's party." [51] Since removal required the consent of the legislature, Skinner argued, the People's men would have to indicate by a show of hands whether they approved of the dismissal or not. If they voted in the affirmative they would lose the support of the die-hard Clintonians. If they voted against removal they would lose what little standing they had with independent Republicans. In either case the Bucktails would gain ground.

Fear of their long-standing enemy, a desire to help Van Buren in the presidential campaign, and the necessity of discrediting the People's party convinced the Regency leaders that Skinner's plan was worth a try. The possibility of failure was obscured by their enthusiasm, and incautiously they moved toward their nebulous goal.

On the last day of the legislative session, a "significant consultation" went on in the Assembly. When the conference ended one of the men went to the Senate and delivered a message to Silas Wright. The latter then opened the drawer of his desk, removed a slip of paper, and handed it to Senator John Bowman. After reading it, Bowman obtained recognition from the chair and submitted a resolution to expel De Witt Clinton from the office of canal commissioner. Cries of horror rent the air, but when the vote was taken the People's party men supported Skinner's anti-Clinton move, and the motion was overwhelmingly passed.[52] In the Assembly the result was the same, where by a vote of 65 to 34 the People's men agreed to the dismissal and were caught in "the trap successfully, if not wisely, baited for them." [53] The legislature then adjourned to meet on the first Monday in November.

The "outrage," perpetrated without notice or specific complaint against the incumbent commissioner, operated like "an electric shock in the whole community." [54] Eight to ten thousand citizens in New York City and Albany held mass meetings and passed resolutions against this "flagrant and wanton violation of public trust." [55] The Regency had gone too far in the exercise of its power, they cried. In instance after instance the junto had brazenly defied what was known to be the will of the people. Charles G. Haines, addressing "many thousands" in front of City Hall in New York, said that a small body of politicians, "against the wishes of a million and a half of people," had combined to sweep Clinton from an honorary post "without daring to tell why; without daring to attempt palliation." [56] This cowardly act, he insisted, would not go unpunished. The removal, intoned *Niles Weekly Register,* was a "mere political *ruse de guerre* to operate on the presidential election." [57] The New York *Evening Post* called it "envenomed malignity. . . ." [58]

Thus Clinton, the underdog, became a hero; and Skinner's perfect plan boomeranged.

V: THE RESCUER OF HIS COUNTRY

As PART OF the campaign to discredit Crawford before the electorate, a renewed attack was begun in the spring of 1824 upon his ability to discharge his duties as Secretary of the Treasury. The previous year, on January 20, 1823, a letter signed "A.B." appeared in the Washington *Republican,* charging that a Treasury report concerning the deposit of funds in Western banks had omitted certain necessary documents. A subsequent investigation by the House exonerated Crawford from all implications of intended deception, but the mysterious "A.B.," in successive issues of the *Republican,* continued accusing the Secretary of mismanaging public funds.[1] The storm subsided for a year until Senator Ninian Edwards of Illinois—the suspected author of the letters, although he denied it in testimony before a House committee—was nominated by Monroe as minister to Mexico. With perfect timing, the Radicals waited until his appointment had been confirmed in 1824 and he had left for his post before they charged him with lying. Edwards heard the report while en route to Mexico and dispatched an immediate answer to the House of Representatives. He acknowledged his perjury by admitting to the authorship of the letters, but also repeated his many accusations against Crawford.[2]

The House immediately appointed a committee of seven, whose principal members were John Floyd, Daniel Webster, John Randolph, John W. Taylor, and Edward Livingston, to reinvestigate the charges. Monroe, whose conduct now appeared hostile to Crawford's presidential aspirations, considered recalling Edwards,[3] but the committee relieved him of this duty by sending the Sergeant at Arms after the minister and ordering his return to Washington.

Van Buren, incensed by the attack upon his candidate, was nonetheless sanguine that the general temper of the capital was opposed to Edwards. "Our friends need not fear," he wrote the Regency, "that he [Crawford] will suffer any thing that his enemies can do agt him. . . . I have just left him & am more & more pleased with the man. Edwards will probably be retained in the country & those who expect better things from Mr Monroe than I do believe that he will forth with remove the man Edwards." [4]

The committee continued hearing testimony long after Congress adjourned, and at length reported that the charges against Crawford were unsubstantiated. It refrained from expressing any opinion against Edwards but an adverse implication could scarcely be missed. Although Adams asserted that political expediency alone decided the case, Edwards had discredited himself by originally denying his part in writing the "A.B." papers.[5] When the report was submitted to the President on June 21, Monroe prepared to dismiss the minister. However, he was wisely counseled by Adams and others to take the easier course and allow Edwards to resign. The President begrudgingly consented, and Edwards, without permitting a day to lapse, tendered his resignation.

Fortunately Van Buren had little to do with the "A.B." plot and left Washington before the investigating committee had made its report. In May, immediately after Congress adjourned, he took another trip to Virginia: this time his goal was Monticello. Adams noted down the departure in his *Diary*, stating that there was "much speculation" as to the object of the journey.[6] The watchful Henry Clay erroneously conjectured it to be the first step in withdrawing Crawford from the presidential contest,[7] and Jackson received identical information from a friend in Virginia. "It seems that Mr. Van Buren, not content with the exercise of his talents for intrigue in his own state, must try his powers with [the] *ancient Dominion,* a place I can assure him where his intrigues will receive no nourishment, but must form abortions, or if born, will wither and die." [8]

Accompanied by Governor Mahlon Dickerson, the Senator was received with "unaffected cordiality" by Jefferson when he arrived at the former president's home.[9] For Van Buren it was more than a first meeting with a "great man." Considering himself one of the few orthodox Republicans left in the country, he came to pay his respects to a statesman whose principles of government he greatly revered. In speeches without number he referred to various statements made by the Virginian, offering them as unassailable truths. His own ideas on internal improvements, states' rights, and the caucus system were all, he thought, basically Jeffersonian.

During the subsequent days of his visit, Van Buren took early-morning drives about the neighborhood with his host, soaking up the purest form of Republicanism. ". . . It may well be imagined," he afterwards wrote, "with how much satisfaction I listened to Mr. Jefferson's conversation. His imposing appearance as he sat uncovered—never wearing his hat except when he left the carriage and often not then—and the earnest and the impressive manner in which he spoke of men and things, are yet as fresh in my recollection as if they were experiences of yesterday." [10]

In many respects the two men were alike, differing only in degree. John Q. Adams was impressed by this fact, but concluded that Van Buren more nearly resembled James Madison in calmness, gentleness of manner, discretion, and aptitude in avoiding personal collisions. In "profound dissimulation and duplicity," Adams added as an afterthought, the Little Magician took after Jefferson. But his "fawning servility" belonged to neither of the past Presidents.[11]

Disregarding the abusive language (the hallmark of Adams's Diary), it is interesting that the New Englander should even attempt a comparison of Jefferson and Van Buren. He probably noted that the New Yorker tried to imitate the Virginian in many different ways. Both men in their day were master politicians, with the Senator having a slight edge in this regard. In their relations with the Republican party, however, Jefferson, as its founder, molded it in the beginning to conform to his ideas of democratic government; whereas Van Buren, in the later period, reformed and restored the party to its earlier vigor. To the Virginian, the party was an instrument for the attainment of better government; to the Little Magician, the party often—but not always—was an end in itself. Not until his thinking matured further and he realized that the party was a device—although an all-important device—and no more, did he discard the mantle of a partisan politician and assume the garb of a respected statesman.

In his concepts of government, the Senator followed Jefferson. There was nothing original in his thinking; its content was all secondhand, and tempered with a sense of the all-hallowed party. He believed that democracy and liberty were best attained through a party system, which could protect and defend as well as aid and comfort the people of the United States. He believed that liberty was in inverse proportion to the amount of government exercised by a central authority.

Jefferson discussed with Van Buren a wide range of subjects during the latter's visit to Monticello. The older man recalled the stormy period of John Adams's administration, when Mahlon Dickerson and Thomas Cooper, both victims of the Alien and Sedition Acts, walked "arm in arm" to prison.[12] Jefferson had not the slightest reserve in referring to his political contemporaries, but what impressed Van Buren most was the "absence of personal prejudice which characterized his observations upon the conduct & views of his opponents. . . ."[13]

The New Yorker's position as chairman of the Senate judiciary committee provided the former President with an opportunity to discuss the court system as it was then constituted. Jefferson remarked that the life tenure enjoyed by the members of the Supreme Court tended to subvert republican principles of government. He thought a definite change in this instance was necessary, and personally advocated annual appointments, as practiced in New England, although he admitted a four- or six-year tenure might prove more practical. Van Buren recalled that he was shocked by these "extremely radical" views but later in life he came to "subscribe to their general correctness." [14]

As to the powerful Second National Bank of the United States, Jefferson was "much disturbed by the sanctions which its pretensions received from the decisions of the Supreme Court, under the lead of Chief Justice Marshall. . . ." [15] Van Buren himself wasted no affection on banks but as yet held no special grievance against the largest of them. He criticized the court, however, for what he later called its "latitudinarian constructions of the constitution in support of enormous corporate pretensions." [16] He contended that the judiciary branch would sooner or later defy the popular will, misuse its power, and excite distrust. The only remedy he could see was to amend the Constitution and make the offices elective. He fought for years to restrict government in all of its branches, but he kept returning to the one solution: amend the Constitution. And this was no solution at all.

Van Buren's short visit to Monticello cleared his mind of much of its fuzziness on almost every vital issue of the day. The seeds of Jeffersonianism were sown deep in his mind. Henceforth he was a most pronounced champion of the states and their prerogatives. His resistance to federally sponsored internal improvements stiffened. His dislike of tariffs for the manufacturer's exclusive benefit became fixed, and he was more conscious of the need to check government activity outside those fields defined by the narrowest interpretation of the Constitution. No other man, with the exception of Andrew Jackson, had as great an influence on Van Buren's life as Thomas Jefferson. To the Senator, the conduct, character, and principles of the Virginian formed his *beau ideal* of thorough patriotism and accomplished statesmanship." [17]

The aged and penniless former President urged his guest to stay longer than he had originally intended, but Van Buren was anxious to return to Washington and learn the results of the committee investigating the "A.B." affair. He was asked as a favor if he would send by mail a recently published pamphlet by Timothy Pickering, former Secretary of State under Washington and Adams, said to be hotly critical of Jefferson.[18] Van Buren was only too glad to be of service, and once back in the capital he procured a copy of the brochure and sent it to Monticello. He accompanied it with a letter in which he asked a question that had been on his mind for many months. He wanted to know what his idol thought of Monroe's policy to amalgamate the Republican and Federalist parties.[19]

In a letter which occupies 27 pages in printed form, Jefferson briefly noted Van Buren's question and devoted the remainder of the communication to throwing "light on history," amusing the New York Senator with "anecdotes not known to every one." Actually the letter was a reply to Pickering's "elaborate philippic" against himself and the older Adams. Toward the end of the letter he briefly alluded to the Monroe heresy and assured his correspondent that it was "an amalgamation of name but not of principle. Tories are Tories still, by whatever name they may be called." [20]

To Van Buren these words were everything he expected. They justified his entire stand with respect to the caucus. After all, he was only trying to alert Republicans to the danger of joining Federalists in support of certain candidates not of the "old school," to get them to see the need of perpetually standing guard over their principles and remaining united in order to meet every challenge to their power by their natural enemies. Jefferson's words, therefore, were those of encouragement, and Van Buren profusely thanked him for them. "You may rest assured," he added, "that the numbers of those [Republicans] is yet large sufficiently so I hope to rescue their country from misrule. . . ." [21]

All through the campaign of 1824, Van Buren and other caucus-minded Republicans were engaged in a losing battle. A great deal depended on Virginia, Pennsylvania, and New York, and the signs pointed to sure defeat for Crawford in at

least two of these states. When Gallatin was nominated for the
vice-presidency he was expected to bring Pennsylvania into the
New York-Virginia alliance. But Jackson's entrance on the
field paralyzed those schemes and Gallatin now hung like "a
dead weight on the caucus ticket." [22]

In New York the Radicals were reeling under blow after
blow. "We *whack* them on the [Assembly] floor," chuckled
Henry Wheaton, "& they are obliged to Caucus *all night* to
make up for what they lose in the day time." [23] The controversy over the electoral law was still raging, and Clinton's sum-
mary dismissal had made him a martyr. Worse, the boorish
Governor, Joseph Yates, had failed to obtain renomination for
his office, and out of spite and "a most deep-rooted hatred for
Mr. V.B.," called a special session of the legislature to meet in
August to revise the state's electoral system.[24]

Van Buren hurried home to meet the new attack on his
organization, and immediately began "exerting his utmost" to
sidetrack the legislature from respecting the Governor's demand.[25] Clinton predicted that without a new law Crawford's
chances of capturing New York in the presidential contest were
"good." Appreciating the Little Magician's methods, he had
grave doubts that any reform would be made before November.[26]

When the special session met, despite the presence of a
large number of People's men, the Regency quickly seized control of the proceedings and never relinquished it. After a
"respectable" interval of four days, the legislature adjourned
without accomplishing a thing, except to condemn the Governor for having called the session in the first place.[27] Here
was a splendid example of the steamroller tactics the inner
council could employ so well. It was also a foul abuse of
delegated power.

Despite his success in the extra session, Van Buren recognized the danger that his Regency faced. Growing resentment
against the organization was bound to find a normal outlet in
the November election. His only salvation lay in Crawford's

election, which would counteract any temporary loss of popularity and control. As the "rescuer of his country" he would then give the people what they wanted.

But there was more than the presidency at stake. The temper of the times made it appear very probable that Clinton would return to active politics. It also seemed likely that the legislature would pass to the control of the People's party. Only by renewed and heroic efforts on his part could Van Buren sustain both Crawford and the Regency during the next three months. Slowly, therefore, the idea of a new coalition forced its way into his mind. Toying with the notion at first, he finally reasoned that this was the only means of halting the Radical party's steady decline. If he could persuade Henry Clay to withdraw as a presidential candidate and join Crawford by running for the vice-presidency, Van Buren would immediately improve the Bucktail position in New York, where the Kentuckian had a large following, and might also attract a sufficiently large number of votes from the West to compensate for the loss of Pennsylvania.[28] In addition, should the election go to the House of Representatives for a decision, Clay would be "all important" with himself out of the running.[29]

Writing to Benjamin Ruggles of Ohio three weeks after the New York legislature had adjourned, Van Buren outlined his project. It was a "matter of great interest," he stated, to effect a "cooperation" between the friends of the two candidates. The fusion of Clay supporters in the West with the Crawfordites in the East and South "would make a great & powerful party capable of sustaining the interest of the country. . . ." Would not the office of Vice-President, he asked, be more agreeable to Clay "I had reason last winter to think so that it would.. If we could now *know* with absolute certainty that the friends of Crawford & Clay in the Electoral College would *at a proper time* unite the necessary previous arrangement could I am persuaded be easily made."

It is important to note that Van Buren wanted the alliance to be brought about "by the electors." Such a coalition, executed at the last moment, would, he said, "make a party like the old Republican Party of the Union & one I would be willing to stand or fall with." [30]

Van Buren expected Ruggles to help with the coalition and yet give the impression that the movement was spontaneous. Meanwhile, the Senator circulated the report that Clay's partisans would vote for Crawford in the New York legislature.[31] And such was the "influence of the V. B. party," the Kentuckian was advised, "that many of *your* friends appear to 'cow' under it." [32]

Over and above the fact that this intended alliance would improve Crawford's position, the Radical party was suffering in the South by the candidacy of Albert Gallatin. Nominated the previous February, Gallatin had added very little to the ticket. His own state of Pennsylvania had declared for Jackson, and in Virginia he was spoken of as a dead "weight on Mr Cr." During September, Van Buren, who had never completely endorsed Gallatin, was repeatedly advised that Crawford's partisans were "certain of having their numbers much diminished by the nomination of Mr G." Gallatin's voluntary withdrawal *"in a proper manner* could not fail to promote the cause both here [Virginia] & elsewhere." Only Clay, in the opinion of some, could "unite all the friends of Mr Cr. . . ." [33] The Radical group in Pennsylvania itself realized that "Gallatin is a great injury & that the feeling against him is general." [34] William Smith of South Carolina, whose hatred for Calhoun bordered on the violent, declared that a more fortunate choice for Vice President should have been made.[35] His resignation, said Louis McLane, would also "relieve our fds. in N.C. . . ." [36]

While Van Buren considered asking Gallatin to withdraw, Clay was informed of the suggested alliance with Crawford by Josiah S. Johnston of Louisiana. His reply to the offer was elusive and lacked his customary straightforwardness.[37] He did not care for the second place, but he did not reject it outright. Johnston pressed for a clearer answer and emphatically stressed the point that the Crawfordites were "very anxious" to make him Vice President. "They say Gallatin would not be in the way." [38]

Clay's second letter was nearer a formal refusal and Johnston understood it as such, but other Radicals were not so discerning and kept up their plans to engineer a coalition.[39] They did not object to the Kentuckian's hesitation, reasoning that a few Western States might turn to Jackson if they believed Clay had withdrawn from the race.[40] This was perhaps Van Buren's motive in suggesting that the switch to Crawford should be made in the Electoral College and not before.

Another reason for the necessity of strengthening the ticket was Crawford's continued illness. Joseph Gales and William W. Seaton, editors of the Washington *National Intelligencer,* saw the Secretary and reported that "every function of his body was impaired, unless perhaps his hearing." The distortion of the mouth, they averred, had disappeared.

His eyesight & the use of his pen-hand are not yet perfect, but sufficiently so. Using glasses, he is able to read the small print of a newspaper, which is almost a miraculous restoration of that organ. His *mind* & *memory* are perfectly *sound, vigorous* & *active.* . . . His limbs have not regained all their flecibility [*sic*], nor his speech all its distinctness. . . . On the whole, when we recollect that for 12 months Mr C has been in the Doctor's hands, bled to the verge of death, difitalised [*sic*] into fits, and stylazied to infantine helplessness, we have reason to be more than satisfied at his recovery.[41]

Although Crawford was making excellent progress, his physical condition was still serious.

On September 8, Van Buren ruled that Gallatin must go even if Clay refused to take his place. Writing to Lacock and Lowrie, both of Pennsylvania, he instructed them to consult with Gallatin and obtain his formal resignation as candidate for the vice-presidency. After that, Lacock was to journey to Lexington, Kentucky, and offer the vacancy to Clay. Although the two emissaries complained of the "burden" placed upon them and the lack of time to accomplish their mission, they promised to do their best.[42]

On September 29, the unsuspecting Gallatin was handed a letter written by Lowrie. It was brutally frank, saying that his chances of election were hopeless and that the party wished to make an "arrangement" with Clay in order to improve Crawford's position.[43] He was therefore asked to withdraw. With a sigh of relief, Gallatin obligingly consented to retire from the contest. To Van Buren, the manipulator of this unwholesome affair, he penned a friendly note explaining that since "the continuation of my name was injurious to the Republican electoral ticket in some quarters, & that my withdrawing would facilitate a plan you had in view of substituting another candidate . . . I enclose . . . my resignation." [44]

The actions of the New York Senator during the fall of 1824 showed him to be a desperate man clutching at every straw to stave off impending disaster. His own state stirred restlessly and verged on outright revolt against Bucktail rule.[45] Covering as best he could the numerous rifts which were breaking out in the party and the legislature, Van Buren blandly told friends that he expected Clay to accept his offer of second place.[46] It showed that he was beset with real doubts about winning New York's entire electoral vote for Crawford. And in a pessimistic frame of mind, or perhaps owing to practical necessity, he contemplated dividing the vote with another candidate.

Because of the large number of contenders, many politicians had predicted from the beginning that the election would go to the House of Representatives, where the President would be chosen from among the three candidates with the highest electoral count. This early prediction soon developed into an obvious fact, and it became imperative for each manager to secure enough votes to place his man among the first three contenders, in order to be eligible for possible selection. With this much reasonably certain, Van Buren altered his strategy in October and began concentrating on insuring Crawford's inclusion among the three candidates to come before the House. At one time he controlled New York's 36 votes, but that was no longer certain because of the electoral-law excitement. He was therefore obliged to consider sharing votes with other candidates in order to keep as many as possible. Since Clay was still uncommitted to the alliance and very much in the race, Van Buren was afraid that the Kentuckian's friends held "the balance in their hands" as far as New York was concerned. But rival managers were just as perceiving as Van Buren and each mulled over various schemes to get their candidates into the House and yet prevent others from doing the same. Henry Storrs reported to Clay:

I have lately heard a suggestion that the friends of Mr. Adams, with the view of excluding you from the House of Reps. may perhaps give to Mr. Crawford the entire tickett [sic] of Electors [in New York] if they find they cannot carry their own. I have no doubt they would do so, if they cannot elect their own, unless they should be deterred by the fear of actually electing Mr. Crawford by that very course. They would take any step short of actually electing Mr. Crawford, which should exclude you from the House.[47]

With rumors such as these to confuse the situation further and invite intrigue, and not knowing with certainty the position of Clay, Van Buren wrote to Joseph Gales asking what he thought of dividing "the votes of New York with Mr Clay or Mr. Adams." The editor of the *National Intelligencer* had a ready answer. If Massachusetts voted for Adams, he said, and "it is necessary to split the apple, the half had better be given to Mr Clay than to Mr Adams—for I begin to believe he will lose Ohio, where the People appear to be getting Jackson-mad!"[48] Nine days later, however, Gales changed his mind and advised his friend that a portion of the votes should go to Adams "as the least dangerous candidate of the two." He liked Clay "less and less" because of his "indefatigable efforts to work into the Ho of Reps to get himself . . . elected to the first place. . . ."[49] Van Buren might have been inclined to say more but his tongue was silenced when word arrived from Kentucky that Henry Clay had emphatically declined to run with Crawford.[50] The Senator had no claim on the Kentuckian, but he maintained to his dying day that Clay had thus made one of his greatest political mistakes—a mistake that kept him forever from the presidency.

From then on, the Radical party allowed each state to write in its own favorite for Vice President, but Crawford, Gales, and Samuel Smith believed that Van Buren's "conduct" entitled him to a preference. Although the Virginia "central committee" was informed of this, there was no general movement to place the New Yorker on the ballot.[51]

The final Bucktail humiliation was the return of De Witt Clinton to political life. His dismissal from the Canal Board as a victim of Regency tyranny made him the only candidate for the gubernatorial nomination by the People's party. On September 22, 1824, at Utica, he was duly nominated, and in an address issued to the electorate, the People's men called for the reform of the electoral law, the end of caucus nominations, and the destruction of the Albany Regency.[52] They declared that if democracy were to continue to advance within the state the Van Buren candidate for governor, Colonel Samuel Young, along with the entire Radical faction, would have to be defeated.

By the middle of 1824 the leaders of the People's party, along with most New Yorkers, had shaken off their indifference to the presidential election since it was now so closely allied to their local interests and, over the months, had come to favor John Q. Adams.[53] Clinton, on the other hand, was a confirmed Jacksonian, and had very decided opinions as to the worth of the other candidates. Calhoun, he said, was "treacherous"; Crawford was "as hardened a ruffian as Burr"; Clay he discounted; and Adams "in politics was an apostate, and in private life a pedagogue, and every thing but amiable and honest. . . ." Jackson was one of the few men in public life to escape his criticism. Governor Yates he termed "perfidious and weak," while Samuel Young was "much of an imbecile." Although Erastus Root was merely a "bad man," Martin Van Buren was the "Prince of Villains," a "coward," a "scoundrel of the first magnitude" and a "confirmed knave." [54]

Only in New York politics, it would seem, could a gubernatorial candidate who favored one presidential hopeful be
backed by a party favoring another.

Despite his battering, Van Buren tried to be optimistic.
"We shall undoubtedly elect Col. Young, by a very large majority," he remarked to a friend, "& when once in the chair of
State, his course will be plain & easy. You should not be discouraged by occasional delinquencies. They occur in all
parties. Our systems, as long as they are preserved, will purify
the body politic, & keep matters well." [55] The Senator did not
rely on words alone to buoy up his spirit. "Arrangements" in
the different wards were being completed with zeal and
unanimity.[56]

However, those who watched the political events as they
transpired in New York could not but agree with Henry R.
Storrs when he wrote:

[There is nothing] relating to our own State which can honor our
political character abroad. The profligacy of the times, the thirst
for public office and emolument and the unwearied and artfull
efforts to corrupt and purchase others have truly sunk our state in
public estimation. If there is any virtue or honor or pride of
character or firmness left in the State which can operate on our
legislature I do not by any means despair of an honorable result at
their meeting in November.[57]

VI: "TREASON BY G——"

ON ELECTION DAY in November of 1824, Van Buren was given a taste of the rancor that had been building up in the state against himself and his lieutenants. When he appeared at the polls to cast his vote he was immediately recognized. A small crowd gathered around him and started shouting in unison, "Regency! Regency!" A dozen or so Clintonians pushed through the mob and challenged his vote on various technicalities. The efforts of a few less emotional bystanders to have the challenges withdrawn proved futile, and Van Buren was required to take the prescribed oath before casting his ballot.[1] The Senator mistakenly attributed the demonstration to Clinton's removal from his position as canal commissioner and found solace in the thought that he personally had taken no part in it.

The state election results indicated how far the Regency had fallen from public favor. From the very first returns received, Van Buren knew that the final result would be decisively anti-Bucktail.[2] By the following morning he conceded that his forces had been "completely routed." In the words of one contemporary, it was a "tornado." [3] Clinton was elected to the office of governor by a majority of 17,000 votes, and in six out of eight senatorial districts the anti-Regency ticket was victorious. However, the upper house was still "safe for another year at least," sighed Butler with heartfelt relief, because of the large number of holdovers from the previous election.[4] But in the Assembly the Radicals were exterminated by the dozens. Clintonians and People's party men now comprised two thirds of that body. "Panic" broke out among the

Bucktails, and they besought Van Buren to throw his "whole influence into the scale for Jackson & do it promptly & openly & boldly," thereby undoing some of the mistakes of the past.[5] But it was too late to correct past errors. In any case, shifting to Jackson was certainly not the answer.

As the final results of this crushing defeat came in, Van Buren sat in his office eating breakfast and brooding over Clinton's dismissal. Judge Roger Skinner, the author of that scheme, stood by the window looking down at State Street and nervously tapping the glass with his fingers. Then, suddenly, Van Buren lashed out angrily: "I hope, Judge, you are now satisfied that there is such a thing in politics as *killing a man too dead!*" Skinner turned around, a pained expression on his face, and without saying a word rushed from the room. Knowing that the rebuke climaxed the Judge's misery, the Senator raced after him and humbly begged his forgiveness. But the hurt went deeper than a few sharp words. No one had to remind Skinner that he had played a large part in reviving Clinton to political life. This "pang inflicted on his heart," Van Buren later recorded, undermined Skinner's health and "he died not long after in my arms." [6]

In the midst of the turbulence that marked the low point in early Regency history, the New York state legislature convened on November 2 to choose presidential electors. According to the law, each house was to draw up a list of 36 electors. The two lists were then compared, and if they agreed exactly no further action was required. When they differed—as was often the case—the Assembly and Senate met together and on a joint ballot selected the electors from the names contained on the two lists.

Because it had become obvious that the final selection of a President would take place in Congress, New York's vote was rated one of the most important factors in determining whether Crawford or Clay would be the third candidate to go into the House of Representatives.[7] As a result, managers in Albany resorted to every political trick to control the outcome. Promises were made and broken in an instant. Threats were commonplace. Underhanded schemes were boldly essayed because only the highest form of intrigue could decide the issue.

The members of the legislature were slow in arriving at Albany on the day appointed for the election, and the voting was postponed until November 10. Meanwhile, the Bucktails, under the command of the Regency, were herded together in a caucus on November 5 to choose their 36 electors. Only 80 men took part, including a number of Clay partisans who "were disposed to take up Mr. Crawford as their second choice" should the Kentuckian bow out of the contest.[8] They felt that they had a right to attend the meeting and they were well advised that Van Buren would acknowledge any gesture of friendship from them as a possible sign of their willingness to participate in a last-minute alliance. Indeed, the magnanimous Senator was prepared to give a small percentage of the electoral ticket to Clay as an inducement for them to vote for the remaining Crawford candidates.

Once admitted to the caucus, however, they gave little indication that they were on the verge of deserting their choice. On the contrary, at the first opportunity they called upon the other members to abandon Crawford and unite behind Clay. They ascribed the recent defeat at the polls to Regency stubbornness over support of the Treasury Secretary and predicted an even worse disaster for the party when the legislature balloted for presidential electors. They had not come like poor relations to accept whatever might be offered them. They wanted a sizable share of the ticket.[9]

The verbal brawl that followed was cut short by the calm words of Silas Wright, who refuted the claims of the Clay men and chided their presumptuousness. "The arrogance of a little faction of perhaps 10 men," wrote the enraged Butler, "in demanding from 70 the surrender of their opinions, produced a happy influence on the minds of our men, & the proposition was voted down almost unanimously without a division."[10] Instead, a ticket was adopted consisting of 29 Crawford men and seven moderate Clay sympathizers. This arrangement, claimed the Radicals, was reasonable, just, and sufficient to both candidates. After the final vote, only three or four dissenters withdrew from the meeting, but it was said by one Clay partisan that they did not leave voluntarily, that they "were in affect expelled. . . . They were treated with the most insulting contumely, and threatened with the high displeasure of the name & style of the 'Albany Regency.' " [11]

Although Van Buren had been anxious to compromise with Clay's friends, he did not believe at any time during the caucus that it was "practical" to do so. The impertinent offers made by the minority, he asserted, "came from sources on which no sort of reliance could be placed & were in themselves extremely equivocal." [12] He would wait. The time was not yet ripe.

On November 10 the legislature at last got down to the suspensive business of choosing the presidental electors. In the upper house, no sooner had the chairman's gavel sounded to announce the presence of a quorum than the Bucktails outvoted their opponents and nominated the Crawford electoral ticket precisely as it had been drawn up in caucus. Seven places out of the 36 were reserved for Clay. "We could not avoid taking them on also," Van Buren told the Secretary of the Treasury one week later, "as they came from districts which were entirely agt us. . . . We could not do without their votes & therefore had no discretion on the subject. The assurance given was that if the rest of our ticket prevailed they would *certainly* vote with us & *probably* if it did not." [13] Thus the seven votes did not constitute a "compromise" or a settlement, but rather a necessary gesture of friendship. It was understood, and there was "assurance given," that if the Crawford ticket triumphed in New York the seven would cast their ballots in the Electoral College for the Radical candidate.

In the Assembly, on the other hand, there was such division between the Crawford, Clay, and Adams factions that no one ticket could muster a majority despite several days of balloting. This was enough to convince the Adams supporters, who were the most numerous in the lower house, that they had to share their ballot. So, rather timidly, they approached the friends of Clay and invited them to a series of caucus meetings.[14] Preliminary discussions were held but differences of opinion immediately arose as to the exact number of votes to be conceded. Consequently nothing was settled during the initial stage of the conferences.

Then the Regency made the last in a long series of great mistakes. Van Buren, unbelievably inept, gambled on winning or losing a majority of the 36 votes for Crawford. There is almost no way to account for his temporary loss of political astuteness. His action was senseless and certain to fail in its object. His knowledge of human nature completely failed him and he deserved the beating he took.

According to a scheme that he must have pulled from Judge Skinner's bag of tricks, he advised the Bucktails in the Assembly to vote for the Adams ticket. At once the deadlock would be broken and the legislature would immediately proceed to a joint ballot.[15] By reducing the candidates to Adams and Crawford, Van Buren presumed that the friends of Clay would vote for the Radical candidate, to form a winning majority, since they had promised to do so once the Kentuckian was excluded. He had an "assurance" of this, but to make doubly certain of it he was prepared to offer them as high as 15 votes for their support. These votes would be given to Clay by the Crawford men in the Electoral College.

The Regency, as obtuse of their chief, went one step further and decided to spring their little plan on the Assembly floor as a surprise. On November 12, the appointed day, the lower house had just completed another trial of strength among the three factions when Flagg rose and announced his "determination to vote for the *Adams ticket* in order to bring the two houses to a joint ballot. . . ." The shocking suddenness of the move and its obvious intent "threw the Clay party into convulsions, & McClure, Mallet & Tillotson made some inflammatory remarks, which were answered very dispassionately by Flagg & Waterman."[16] Someone then moved for an adjournment, and the motion was unanimously carried.

That evening the Albany Regency officially promised 15 votes to the Clay men if they would agree to the scheme. "The offer was considered, talked about but no step taken by them to secure its acceptance." However, Van Buren was reasonably certain when the meeting broke up that a few of them were willing to go along with the plan.[17] Or so he thought from their reactions.

When the Assembly met on the following day, the Adams ticket was nominated. Both the Clay and Crawford factions voted with the majority. A joint meeting of the two houses should have ensued but it was postponed over the weekend to "give time for reflection." [18]

With unwarranted optimism Van Buren proclaimed that the worst part of the struggle was over. He had, he said, "the most positive assurance that when the Clay ticket was out of the way," Clay's partisans "would vote with us & we went into the ballot with a *certainty* that if they did we could not be beaten & the best reason to *believe* that we would succeed without them." [19] But Van Buren was never more wrong. The Clay men were moved to near violence when the leaders of the Bucktails "corruptly & wickedly determined to vote for the Adams ticket in the lower house, so as to reduce the question to Crawford & to Adams." A "fouler" and more "dishonorable piece of management," wrote Ralph Lockwood, "could not in my estimation be adopted." [20]

As the supporters of Clay left the Assembly hall, seething with rage over their betrayal by the Regency, they were met by a number of People's men, including Thurlow Weed, Henry Wheaton, and James Tallmadge, who persuaded them to attend a conference that evening with the friends of Adams. There, they were told, they might avenge their wrongs as well as gather a few votes for their candidate. Without hesitation the invitation was snapped up. The Clay men, in their existing frame of mind, were amenable to any scheme which would humble Van Buren and repay him for his treachery.

When the conference convened clandestinely that night there was one difficulty that had to be resolved before any agreement could be worked out. The legislators, upon reassembling Monday morning, would only be able to vote for the men whose names were contained on either the Senate or Assembly electoral list. The upper house had chosen a ticket consisting of seven Clay men and 29 Crawfordites; the lower house had selected 36 Adams electors. For the friends of Clay to elect their seven men on the joint ballot they were forced to vote the Radical ticket.

Although the problem seemed insurmountable at first, it was soon overcome to the satisfaction of all. With a boldness characteristic of Van Buren in his better days, they agreed to print a third ballot or split ticket containing the names of men taken from the two lists. The Clay men would be removed from the Crawford ticket and added to a group of men taken from the Adams list. In addition, Tallmadge and Wheaton pledged themselves to exert an "influence" upon the electors "to induce them to give to Mr Clay a sufficient number of votes to ensure his return to the House of Representatives." [21] There was a tacit understanding that at least eight votes would go to the Kentuckian one way or another, and while it was considerably less than Van Buren's offer of 15, Clay's followers deemed it high enough to bring them eventual victory and revenge.

When the idea of a third ticket was finally accepted by the conferees, strictest secrecy was enjoined on all. To Thurlow Weed went the task of printing this split ballot, which would be quietly distributed on Monday to the members of the Adams-Clay coalition. The editors of the *Daily Advertiser,* who may have been privy to the plot, obligingly gave Weed permission to use their offices. On Sunday morning the young newspaperman locked himself in and "worked off the ticket." [22] After the ballots had been printed, those intended for the Clay members of the legislature were given to Peter B. Porter for distribution, while Wheaton and Tallmadge looked after the needs of the Adams men.

Recognizing that the split ticket might be elected by a small majority, making each vote momentously important, Weed thought it imperative to check the loyalty of every anti-Crawford legislator. In his wanderings he came across evidence proving that three so-called friends of Adams had been "persuaded" to switch to the Radical candidate. Weed, accompanied by James Tallmadge and Henry Wheaton, confronted the treacherous trio and informed them that their duplicity was known. An investigation would be demanded, Tallmadge said menacingly, unless they agreed to vote an electoral ballot which was endorsed with his own or Wheaton's initials. Their ballots would be examined during the canvass, and if the three men followed instructions, all would be forgotten; otherwise, the evidence Weed had against them would be made public. There was no choice but to accept Tallmadge's offer, and thus another Regency plot was vitiated.[23]

On Monday, November 15, the two houses of the New York state legislature met together in a joint session with 157 members present and voting.[24] After a short delay in bringing the large body to order, the balloting was begun, attended by feverish excitement and nerve-racking suspense. All the anti-Radicals were jittery, while the Van Buren faction, outmaneuvered and outfoxed, was naively confident of success, innocent of what was going on about them. When all the ballots were finally collected, the Lieutenant Governor, Erastus Root, began to canvass the votes.

He drew the first split ballot from the box. As he looked at it, his mouth popped open and his face twisted in agonizing pain. "A printed split ticket!" he exclaimed in a horrified tone.

"Treason by G——!" shouted Perley Keyes, a member of the Regency, springing to his feet. General confusion followed, accompanied by the "awful" groans of the Bucktails. Above the din the voice of James Tallmadge could be heard calling for order. "I demand," he cried, "under the authority of the Constitution of the United States, under the Constitution of the State of New York, in the name of the whole American people, that this joint meeting of the two Houses of the Legislature shall not be interrupted in the discharge of a high and a sacred trust. I demand further that the great business of the nation shall now proceed in order to its completion." [25]

Presumably these words had a quieting effect upon the members and order was eventually restored. The counting of ballots was continued and upon its completion the presiding officer announced that seven Clay electors had received 95 votes; 25 men on the Adams ticket had 78 ballots cast in their favor; the Crawford ticket received 76 votes, and there were 3 blanks.[26] As soon as the result of the canvass was promulgated the Crawfordites voiced the objection that a majority of all the members present was necessary for a choice and since 79 constituted a majority only seven electors had been selected. The Adams party countered by insisting that the three blanks were lost and that 78 comprised a majority. The president, Erastus Root, who knew what the outcome would be, refused to put the question to a vote and in disgust left the chamber accompanied by a strong contingent of Regency men.[27] The remaining members agreed that 25 Adams and seven Clay electors had been chosen and then adjourned, planning to meet the next day and complete the ballot.

By the time the initial shock wore off it was simple enough for Van Buren to understand what had happened. The Clay men, he said, had lulled him into a drowsy feebleness with worthless promises, intending all the while to "deceive" him. In return for what they thought was his vile attempt to eliminate Clay, they voted for Adams.[28]

But their "double-dealing" had yet to complete its cycle. On the following day, when the legislature met to select the last four remaining candidates, they reversed their ground and voted with the Crawford party. This was done to prevent Adams from receiving so many votes as to destroy the possibility of the election going to the House of Representatives. Their "double-double-cross" split the 36 votes of New York among three candidates. Adams had a majority of 25, Clay came next with seven, and Crawford last with four.

The anti-caucus, anti-Crawford, anti-Van Buren, and anti-

Regency factions celebrated long into the night over the results of the contest. The Little Magician had been so badly defeated that his enemies were volunteering as pallbearers to help lower him into his political grave.[29] "Van Buren and his invincibles are beaten at last," wrote one, "and Waterloo was not more fatal to Napoleon and his followers than the result of this day are to them." [30] "Van B. looks like a wilted cabbage," said Henry Wheaton in a fit of laughter, "& poor Judge Skinner has quite lost his voice." [31] "I feel a pride," said the meddling Calhoun, "in reflecting that the victory in your great State is almost wholly owing to the wisdom, firmness and disinterestedness of our friends." [32]

The day after the election Van Buren settled down to the unpleasant task of reciting to William Crawford the events that had taken place in New York and had ended so disastrously. In a long letter he gave full vent to his wrath against the friends of Clay. *They deceived us,* he cried "although they still . . . pretend that they voted with us. The next day the rogues who had cheated us under a sense of shame & apparent contrition voted with us to elect four more of our ticket." He readily admitted, however, that "the great responsibility assumed by our friends in refusing to pass the electoral law" had been a basic cause of defeat. Nevertheless, he thought he had assurances from the Clay men that they would act with the Regency to nullify this disadvantage. With a highly moral tone, he concluded:

Upon a review of the whole, I do not find any thing to regret except the result. Our conduct was simply this: Both the other parties saw their interest in depriving the State of its vote & were willing to do it; we had no interest in such a result & under the circumstances were bound to prevent it. . . . As it is all other feelings are mingled in those of indignation agt the base instruments through which we have been destroyed.[33]

No one familiar with New York politics ever supposed that the election was over on November 16. "Van B's intrigues will not cease," warned Henry Wheaton, "so long as there is the slightest glimmering of hope & he must be looked after." [34] There was a two-week interval before the Electoral College would meet and anything could happen before then, as the friends of Clay were about to discover. Under the absurd notion that they had seven votes safely tucked away in their pockets, with a promise of an additional vote, Porter, Clark, and the other Clay sympathizers commended themselves for having "punished" Van Buren and his Regency and having placed Henry Clay in the House of Representatives. But they failed to reckon with Thurlow Weed, who had no intention of permitting Clay to get that far. Pressure from all quarters was exerted on the 36 electors to induce them to change their votes, and Van Buren and Marcy were just as active in this respect as Weed or anyone else. [35]

It is futile to guess what took place during these two short weeks, but when the New York College of Electors met on December 1, two of the Clay men were unaccountably absent. The remaining members of the College filled the two vacancies by appointing John Taylor and William Maner. Both these men voted for Adams instead of Clay. A third elector, Pierre E. Barker, was subjected to so many threats that out of stubbornness and on the advice of friends he finally decided to cast his ballot for Jackson. The Regency was not outdone, needless to say, and succeeded in convincing an original Adams elector to switch to Crawford. When the ballots were tabulated, New York gave Adams 26 votes; Crawford 5; Clay 4; Jackson 1.

Thurlow Weed contends that both he and his party acted in good faith, despite their failure to supply Clay with the additional four votes. He admits that a pledge had been given, but only on the condition that Louisiana should also vote for the Kentuckian. And since "Louisiana voted for General Jackson," he wrote at a later date, ". . . that left our friends free to vote for Mr. Adams." [36] He told this boldfaced lie to hide the fact that the votes were deliberately withheld to exclude Clay from the House contest. The New York electors met on December 1, while the vote of Louisiana was not known in the East until December 15 at the earliest. [37]

When the total electoral ballots in the nation were counted, Jackson received 99, compared to 84 for Adams, 41 for Crawford, and 37 for Clay. Jackson's greatest strength came from the Southern states, Pennsylvania, New Jersey, Indiana, and Illinois. New England and most of New York went for Adams; Crawford carried Virginia and Georgia; and Clay took Kentucky, Ohio, and Missouri. It is important to note that the West was divided between Jackson and Clay.

Although Andrew Jackson led all the other candidates in the Electoral College, and had piled up a decisive popular vote in those states where the electors were chosen by the people,[38] he was not elected President. No one possessed a majority, and so the final choice rested with the House of Representatives where the excluded Clay was reputedly lord and master.[39] In the vice-presidential race, Calhoun won hands down. He polled 182 votes, while his nearest rival, Nathan Sanford, received only 30. Out of appreciation for his efforts in behalf of Crawford, Georgia nominated Van Buren for second place.[40] Joseph Gales, when he heard of this *beau geste,* remarked to the New Yorker that it "may be some satisfaction to you to know, let things go as they may, that your honor, integrity, & fidelity in this crisis have been appreciated by your friends & associates as they deserve." [41]

But it was little consolation, and in later years Van Buren felt this election was the final proof that the Republican party had completely disintegrated.

There was no difference in the political condition of the country between 1816—when Mr. Monroe received a caucus nomination, on a close vote between Mr. Crawford and himself, and was elected— and 1824, when the caucus system was appealed to by the supporters of Mr. Crawford, which called for its abandonment. . . . Mr. Monroe and a majority of his cabinet were unfortunately influenced by different views, and pursued a course well designed to weaken the influence of the caucus system, and to cause its abandonment. Mr. Crawford was the only candidate who, it was believed, could be benefited by adhering to it, and the friends of all the others sustained the policy of the administration. Those of

Jackson, Adams, Clay, and Calhoun, united in an address to the
people condemning the practice of caucus nominations, and an-
nouncing their determination to disregard them. Already weakened through the adverse influence of the administration, the
agency which had so long preserved the unity of the Republican
party did not retain sufficient strength to resist the combined assault that was made upon it, and was overthrown. Mr. Crawford
and his friends adhered to it to the last, and fell with it.[42]

VII: A FEDERALIST-REPUBLICAN

WHEN Van Buren left Albany to return to Washington he said he was "as completely broken down a politician as my bitterest enemies could desire." [1] On board a steamer lazily descending the Hudson River, one of the passengers advised him to settle his differences with Clinton; but he was in no mood for jokes. He remained in New York City only long enough to pay the bets he had lost in the state election—he invariably gambled on elections—and then continued on his journey to Washington. Upon reaching the capital he took a furnished house with Stephen Van Rensselaer ("the Patroon"), Louis McLane of Delaware, and Alfred Cuthbert of Georgia.

Despite his many reversals, the Senator was not as broken-down a politician as he may have thought. When he read the returns from Louisiana and knew that Crawford was one of the candidates to go to the House he regained some of his earlier optimism. Crawford's "prospects as to the election," he informed the Regency, "are far, very far, from desparate [sic], & are believed to be every day improving. . . . If Crawford had got the votes of New York his success would have been next to certain, as it is his prospects are good. His friends here are determined to stand by him & should no where waver." [2]

Despite the claims of some historians,[3] Van Buren never for a moment considered repudiating Crawford. In the first place it was impractical; in the second, he liked neither Adams nor Jackson. As with other moderate men in Washington, he found the military chieftain from Tennessee to be "unsafe." [4] Old Hickory, warned John Williams, the ex-Senator from Tennessee, has " a perfect understanding [with] . . . Clinton.

. . . And if J. is made **Prest Clinton** will be his *premier*." [5]
The possibility of the New York Governor attaining high office
in Jackson's cabinet was a terrifying prospect, and Van Buren
backed away from the Hero of New Orleans in frightened
alarm. Adams, on the other hand, may have been the favorite
of the manufacturing and farming groups in New York, but to
the Regency chief he was tainted with the Monroe heresy.[6]
In fact the New Englander has assured Daniel Webster that if
elected his administration would "be just and liberal towards
Federalists. . . ." [7] If elected he would be that choicest of hy-
brids—a Federalist-Republican—and surely Van Buren could
never support him.

Almost as soon as the official returns from Louisiana were
published, Van Buren had mapped out a plan of strategy.
Under no circumstance did he want a choice to be made in the
House on the first ballot. Only with repeated and fruitless
attempts to choose a President could he bargain his candidate
into the executive chair.[8] "Crawford's friends," wrote one
representative, "wish to come in, & have it said that they made
the President, but not on the first ballot, nor till they have
shown, by the state of votes, that Crawford is clearly out of the
case." [9]

As the election day drew closer, and while Van Buren coasted
along on a well-charted course, every one else was talking of
"plots" and "bargains." [10] Henry Clay, who more than any
other man could decide the contest, was beset by offers from
the managers of each candidate.[11] He could not remain neutral for long, and on January 8 he finally fixed his choice upon
Adams. In his estimation Crawford was too ill to assume the
presidency, and Jackson, a military chief, "would lead the Republic to ruin." [12] Two weeks later he made his decision
public.

In what was to have been a general movement into the
ranks of the dour New Englander, agents were sent to leading
congressmen urging them to follow Clay's lead. One of them,
Francis Johnson of Kentucky, called on Van Buren and asked
him to help in lifting Adams to the presidency. The New

Yorker refused, without giving his reasons, and no amount of persuasion could force him to change his mind. As Johnson turned to leave, after failing in his mission, he haughtily remarked that Adams would be elected with or without Van Buren's aid. The Senator candidly replied: "I think that very possible, but, Mr. Johnson, I beg you to remember what I now say to you—if you do so you sign Mr. Clay's political death warrant. He will never become President be your motives as pure as you claim them to be." [13]

One of the first responses to the announcement of the Adams-Clay alliance was the publication of an unsigned letter in the *Columbian Observer* of Philadelphia, charging that the Kentuckian had sold his support in return for the post of Secretary of State.[14] The impetuous Clay immediately published a "card" in the *National Intelligencer* demanding that the author "unveil himself" and give satisfaction. When the innocuous and ridiculous representative from Pennsylvania, George Kremer, came forward, Clay's indignant behavior seemed laughable. Nevertheless the Kentuckian insisted on an investigation and although a committee was eventually chosen, nothing ever came of it.[15]

Meanwhile, in the best tradition of intrigue, the Jacksonians began courting the friends of Crawford. It was rumored that the General himself had visited the ailing Radical and "made very humble submissions, & profered [*sic*] him any terms which he might ask as the price of his cooperation & support." [16] Van Buren, too, fished in troubled waters. Giving the appearance of a manager about to sell out, he asked Adams to appoint a friend to a consular post in South America. The Secretary of State, anxious to please, made a personal visit to the Senator's lodgings and assured him that should his friend mention a specific port he would recommend the appointment to Monroe. Later, on second thought, the cagey Adams told Van Buren that the nomination could not be made until after the election.[17]

With bribery the order of the day, and with many persons engaged in the game of President-making, the Little Magician could take comfort in the fact that at least he was not buying and selling votes like so many of the others. His plan of opera-tion was straightforward and direct. With each state possessing one vote in the House election scheduled for February 9, 1825, and a majority of 13 required for a choice, he figured that Adams had no more than 12 votes, while Jackson could count on seven and Crawford four.[18] True enough, the Secretary of State actually did have 12 states lined up for the first ballot, thanks to Clay, including Maryland and Louisiana, both of which he held by the margin of a single vote.[19] But it had been "ascertained that one of the Maryland delegation would, on the second ballot, vote for Gen. Jackson, and would con-tinue to do so." [20] Therefore, Van Buren reckoned, if Adams could be kept from winning the thirteenth state and was dead-locked with Jackson over a long enough period of time, Craw-ford might then become a rallying point and eventually take the presidency. "It will depend on slight circumstances how the matter goes after the first ballot," he said. "Mr Crawford's chance in the house will then be better than it has been at any period. His friends adhere to their determination to abide by him." [21]

The key to the scheme lay in holding the thirteenth state in abeyance. And that state turned out to be New York.

Rival managers were quick to observe that the New York delegation was split right down the middle. This was just what Van Buren wanted. The more split delegations the better; at least it would keep Adams from tallying up the remaining state he needed for election.

Of the 34 New York votes within the delegation, the Little Magician controlled 17 and Adams controlled 17.[22] The only difficulty that might lead to trouble was that one of the men whom Van Buren counted on as part of his strength, Stephen Van Rensselaer, was inclined toward Jackson. To convince him to vote for the Radical candidate became the Senator's only serious problem. Since the two men were messmates, Van Buren had many occasions to speak to him; here he was aided by others. Several conferences were held in which every argument was exhausted. Under this constant hammering, week after week, Van Rensselaer finally gave in. He promised, before witnesses, that he would vote for Crawford and under no circumstances would he cast his ballot for Adams.[23] Now, with New York deadlocked, no candidate would have the necessary majority and the balloting would go on and on until one side gave in. Everything, it seemed, depended on the well-meaning, pious, and kindly Van Rensselaer.[24]

On the morning of February 9, the day of the election, the old Patroon left his boarding house after reassuring Van Buren that he would "adhere" to Crawford. But when he arrived at the Capitol, Henry Clay and Daniel Webster were waiting for him and hustled him into the Speaker's room, where they plied him with every conceivable argument to force him to retract his promise and vote for Adams.[25] Staggered "by the representations of those gentlemen," Van Rensselaer, moments later, stumbled from the room. As he proceeded to the House chamber he was met by Louis McLane, who noted unmistakable signs of hesitation and indecision in the old man's appearance. McLane sent word to Van Buren in the Senate to drop whatever he was doing and come to the House.[26] At first the request was refused but when it was repeated the Little Magician raced to answer the summons. On entering the hall he had only a vague idea what was happening, but Cuthbert of Georgia stepped up to him and briefed him on the action of the past few minutes. The Patroon, he said, had just given further assurances of his loyalty and there was no need to do anything more. Relieved by this news, the Senator remained to see the voting but was "pained to witness Mr. Van Rensselaer's obvious agitation and distress." [27]

At noon on February 9, in the domed lower chamber of Congress, equipped with everything from a canopied dais to spittoons, sofas, and snuffboxes, the electoral votes of the nation were counted in the presence of both houses and a packed gallery. John C. Calhoun was declared the new Vice-President, but no one, it was announced, had received a majority of votes for President.   The senators filed out of the room, leaving the representatives behind to name Monroe's successor.   Henry Clay, solemn and dignified, assumed the Speaker's chair and directed each state to poll its members.

Van Buren stood near one of the entrances, his eyes staring fixedly at the ballot box as it was passed among the members of the New York delegation.   When it neared Van Rensselaer's desk the old man trembled with misgiving.   He kept remembering the words of Clay and Webster who had warned him that the "disorganization of the Government" might be the consequence of his vote.   They had strongly impressed upon him what "preservation of order" meant in terms of his large landed estates.[28]   Tortured by doubts he dropped his head to the edge of his desk and prayed to the Almighty for guidance. When, at length, the ballot box reached him, he removed his hands from his eyes, and slowly lifted his head.   As he did so he saw a ticket on the floor bearing the name of John Quincy Adams.   No one with Van Rensselaer's faith needed further proof that God Himself had interceded and answered his prayer.   He dutifully picked up the ballot and thrust it into the box.[29]   Adams won New York and with it the presidency.[30] When the final result was announced, Adams had received the votes of 13 states, Jackson of seven, and Crawford four.[31]

The anti-Adams men took their defeat with little grace. Clay, as the President-maker, was the target of most of the angry epithets, but the Patroon came in for his share of them.   "Genl. V. R. has for two years been one of our mess," stormed McLane. "He has betrayed those with whom he broke bread." [32]

Back at the boardinghouse, the Patroon begged his friends to forgive his weakness, but he was met with icy stares.   They allowed him to remain at the house and eat at the same table with them, but no one, including Van Buren, would speak to him.[33]

The Regency chieftain was "greatly dissapointed [sic]" at the outcome, wrote Henry Wheaton.   "He expected the contest would last several days, & then *he* would come in & decide it." [34]

Had we been able to prevent "the election of Mr. Adams on the first ballot," explained Walter Lowrie, "we had great hopes that we could have elected Mr. Crawford." [35]

Adams's election brought no great cry of indignation from the country as a whole until it was announced that he had offered Henry Clay the office of Secretary of State. To the Jacksonians the action proved the charges of corruption made prior to the election. It sealed a bargain—a wicked bargain— to keep Old Hickory out of the White House. Some wondered whether any prudent men would now dare to identify themselves with the new administration. [36] "Was there ever witnessed such bare faced corruption?" asked Jackson. Judas, he concluded, had received his "thirty pieces of silver." [37]

Clay, after accepting the nomination, justified his action by declaring that he could not elect a man and then refuse to serve under him. Such behavior would tend to discredit his motives in voting for Adams. It might indicate that he had a low opinion of the new President and therefore had done the country a distinct disservice. [38] Instead, by accepting, he would not only endorse the administration but help formulate its policies as well.

As was to be expected, Van Buren observed a discreet silence after the election. He did not rush to join the opposition even though he suspected the chief executive of adhering to the Monroe heresy. He waited for proof. The rumors that Adams intended to offer Clinton the post of minister to the Court of St. James did not perceptibly disturb him, probably because he did not believe the report, considering the Governor's pro-Jackson position during the election. [39] He maintained a friendly disposition toward the President and his Secretary of State, voting to confirm the nomination of the latter despite opposition from the Jacksonians and a large number of Radicals. [40] In fact, his relations with Clay during the following weeks improved to such an extent that in a moment of weakness he reportedly admitted to him that he had "committed a great error in not withdrawing" Crawford from the presidential contest in May of 1824. [41]

But some of the members of the Albany Regency were jittery about Adams, particularly when they kept hearing that he was prepared "to amalgamate & breakdown party lines." Lot Clark thought the Radical party should join the opposition immediately. He had information on good authority that the "patronage in N. Y. will be given to the federal party." Adams, he contended, was "deadly hostile" to the Radicals. "On the whole sir," he wrote, "we have got him to fight & we may as well buckle on our armour now as at any other period. The Old Republican party of the Union will be rallied. They are alarmed. All regret that they did not go to caucus. If they had, a Republican with Federalist sympathies would not now be President of the United States." [42]

To men like Clark, open and immediate hostility to the Federalist-Republican seemed the only way to revive the old party.

On the day of the inauguration, Van Buren joined "the immense throng" at Adams's house and paid his respects. He may have seen the Marquis de Lafayette there, for the beloved Frenchman was just beginning an extended return visit to America. After taking his leave the Senator decided that good manners—which no one could ever say he lacked—required a visit to the retiring President. He found Monroe alone, "and was as usual kindly received." Although the relationship between the two men had never been "confidential" and Van Buren had no respect for Monroe's talents, nevertheless they conversed amiably for an hour.[43] But to the head of the Regency, the former President personified everything he dreaded most in politics. He blamed Monroe for bringing discord and schism to the "Old Republican party of the Union." The election itself and the abolition of the caucus system were the direct results of his "fusion" or "amalgamation" policy. Let Adams follow a similar course and all Van Buren's pent-up anger and frustration would burst in on him and bring havoc to his administration.

VIII: SHIFTING LOYALTIES

THE EIGHTEENTH CONGRESS in its second session elected a President, but did little else. Tortuous arguments over abolishing imprisonment for debt and suppressing piracy in the West Indies wasted valuable time without accomplishing anything. The proceedings were enlivened, however, when the "kingly" John Quincy Adams on March 7 sent his cabinet nominations to the Senate. That of Clay headed the list, and after the Jacksonians got off a few choice remarks about a "corrupt bargain," it was confirmed, along with those of James Barbour as Secretary of War and Richard Rush as Secretary of the Treasury. Adams had asked Crawford to remain in the cabinet but was refused.[1] Southard, Wirt, and McLean responded to the President's invitation and continued in their respective positions as Secretary of the Navy, Attorney General, and Postmaster General.

The tenseness of the Washington scene during the past winter had kept Van Buren from looking in on New York.[2] Flagg, Marcy, and Skinner made periodic reports and did their best to cope with the triumphant People's party and the new governor, but they were resigned to the fact that this was to be a "belt-tightening" year.

Almost immediately after the disastrous November election, the New York Senate and Assembly passed the necessary legislation allowing the people to decide on the method of choosing presidential electors. The voters were asked whether they wanted them selected by districts or on a general ticket; and if the latter whether by plurality or by majority vote.

Clinton was not satisfied, however, and in his annual message of January, 1825, asked the legislature for more definite action.[3] The Regency favored the democratic districting system by which the electors would be appointed throughout the state according to the number of congressmen representing each district; those men chosen would in turn select two additional electors corresponding to the two senators in Congress.[4] Silas Wright wrote:

We think the plan rather cunning as it is sound in principle [and] peoplish in its character. . . . All our friends must take at once the district ground, as that is the democratic ground beyond all question. You will think this is contrary to my ground of last winter. It is, but it is more democratic, and the keeping of the vote of the State together anyway, when dishonest men try to divide it, is impracticable. On the district ground we shall, at the ballot-boxes, whip the Clintonians, as they will take the *general ticket plurality ground.*[5]

Wright was certainly not in Van Buren's class when it came to political analysis, and very often, as this instance when he endeavored to outguess the opposition, he was wrong. The Clintonians committed themselves to the districting method, and in response to the Governor's plea enacted it into law on March 15, 1825. The following November the people ratified it.

Shortly after becoming President, Adams invited De Witt Clinton to accept the post of minister to Great Britain. In the months prior to the presidential contest certain people in Congress had been busy spreading the story that the Governor was uncommitted.[6] Later, after Adams was elected, rumor had it that Clinton was making friendly overtures to the administration.[7] However, the President offered this important position to the Governor in recognition of the "claims of New York, & particularly of the party" which gave him the votes of the state.[8] But some of the Regency members pounced upon it as a sure indication of the President's intention to "breakdown party lines." [9] Silas Wright termed it "the unkindest cut of all." [10] Others, especially when the "corrupt bargain" charge reached its peak in March, accused Adams of "systematic exertion" to "conciliate" the New York Governor.

Clinton, whose comments on the President could rival anything Adams ever wrote in his *Diary* about other men, rejected the offer when he received it. Although by temperament they seemed ideally suited to one another, Clinton, a Jacksonian, would have none of Adams and told him so. The rejection, commented Marcy, was emphatic and delivered "in such a manner as to leave no reasonable doubt that he means to embark in an opposition to Mr. A. I am of opinion nothing need be feared from this opposition if a cordial union could be formed among the friends of Mr. A, Mr Crawford & Mr Clay." While Marcy was instinctively thinking of "union," he tempered his judgment in a closing paragraph. "The republican party of this state," he wrote, "will not however embark with much zeal in favor of Mr. A. until some thing has occured [*sic*] to warrant them in believing that he had not a congeniality of feeling with Mr C[linton] in regard to this party, when the offer was made or if he then had he has not now." [11]

The post was then forced upon the aged Rufus King, whose confirmation by the Senate was almost automatic.[12] As the new minister prepared to leave for England, Van Buren wrote a letter wishing him health, happiness, and honor, but King's sons had reason to believe that the Senator considered the appointment "ill judged & unpopular." [13] Thurlow Weed could not imagine any reason strong enough to justify the selection.

But the worst was yet to come. When Roger Skinner died shortly thereafter, the President appointed Alfred Conkling, a Clintonian, to succeed him as United States Judge for the Northern District of New York. The Governor, quite naturally, was delighted, the Regency horrified, and Weed dumbfounded by Adams's political stupidity.[14] From Buffalo, Peter B. Porter wrote a letter to Henry Clay warning him that Clinton was no friend of the administration and any patronage accorded him was wasted. He might also have added that such action could easily provoke the Regency into declaring all-out war on the President.   The letter was put before Adams but did not prevent Conkling's appointment.   Clay tried unsuccessfully to cover up his chief's ineptness by insisting that the selection had *not* been made "upon the strength of Mr. Clinton's recommendation alone, but upon that of others also." [15] Nevertheless, explanations could not hide the obvious fact that Adams was committed to the Monroe heresy.   Succeeding appointments proved it.

The Congressional session over, Van Buren returned to his home in Albany for a short but well-earned rest.   His unsuccessful labors in a cause which from start to finish ran counter to the wishes of the people at large and for which he himself demonstrated a slight contrition at the end, had drained much of his energy.   He had failed to save his country, and the party still lay prostrate, divided, and disorganized.   He had alienated himself from a large segment of the electorate of New York, and his only means of reinstating himself and blotting out his recent mistakes was to become once again a grass-roots politician and tour the hinterlands.   Perhaps he could "revive" in the hearts of New Yorkers a love for the "Old Republican party of the Union."

For the remainder of the spring and summer he worked with "holy zeal" to regain the confidence of the masses.   He went from county to county, speaking to local leaders and exciting their interest in himself and his organization.   To the members of the Regency he gave explicit orders: under no circumstances were they to discuss the next presidential election.   State and national issues had to be kept separate.   That was one lesson he had clearly learned in 1824.   They should studiously avoid commenting upon Adams's present administration.   "Non-committalism" was the key word, and his orders were to be obeyed to the letter.[16]   The practical problem of winning additional seats in the Assembly of New York was the immediate concern of all, and to that end the Regency was directed to turn its complete attention.   With organization and leadership, two advantages lacking among Clintonians, the Bucktails reckoned they could fight their way back into power.

All things considered, one could not expect the people of New York to reverse their political position in less than a year's time and return to the Republican fold. Yet that is precisely what they did. Clinton's removal as canal commissioner and the electoral-law revision ceased to be live issues by early fall of 1825.[17] The Regency endorsed the districting system and thereby obliterated the turbulent question of whether the legislature should continue to name the presidential electors. Once this controversy was eliminated, the people returned to the Bucktail party.

Since New York's Constitution had been amended in 1821 to broaden the suffrage right, democracy had made notable strides within the state. Farmers in the western counties, small landowners throughout New York, mechanics, shopkeepers, and merchants had all despised the aristocracy for depriving them of their voting rights during so many years. They united under the Republican banner, exercised their voting privilege, and lent their support to pull down the citadel of New York aristocracy—the Federalist party. When the Clintonian faction replaced that stronghold, the people did not relax their opposition. Yet with all their determination to oppose the aristocrats, on such issues as the electoral controversy—which was essentially a battle for increased democracy at home—they were capable of bolting the Bucktail party and voting against it. Once the irritant was removed, however, they could not escape the realization that the Clintonians were the political descendants and heirs of the Federalists, with whom they had no business associating.

In addition to the fact that the Bucktails were generally in step with the advance of democracy and symbolized the perpetual struggle against the old aristocracy in all its forms, their attitude on such questions as banks, internal improvements, and state finances also won the sympathies of the rank and file. Regarding banks, the position of the Van Buren Republicans was clear. They were naturally suspicious of large financial concerns and were chary in handing out charters for the incorporation of new banks. They could not abide any institution which stimulated overexpansion and made possible wild, speculative schemes. The depression of 1819–21 had impressed this strongly on their minds, for this was a lesson in conservatism that crystallized their earlier opinions of keeping the number of banks at the absolute minimum required by the needs of a community. After many years—toward 1829—they gradually adopted the belief that the legislature ought to regulate a portion of the operations of the state's banking system. Perhaps this was out of keeping with the spirit of the age of individualism that pervaded the country, but regulation was the only means, the Bucktails reasoned, of eliminating "wildcat" banks which sapped the state's economic vitality.[18]

The Bucktails made a sharp distinction with respect to internal improvements. They agreed with Van Buren in insisting that this was a matter for state jurisdiction alone, according to the Constitution, but they denied that it should be interpreted as an open invitation to sponsor one canal and state road after the other.[19] They were tightfisted about appropriations and stubborn about approving new ideas to better transportation facilities in New York. Because of the popularity of expansionist ideas, theirs was a continuous battle against local politicians with hair-brained schemes to lay new taxes for additional improvements. The dictum of the economy-minded Bucktails was that the state had to be kept out of debt.[20] Therefore no enterprise would receive their blessing unless it would accord with a strict financial program of regulated expenditures and would give sufficient indication that when completed it would earn money. Van Buren summed up their position precisely when he wrote: "No consideration, however imposing, should lead us to commit the interest and character of the state to the promotion of any undertaking, in the practicability of which there is not the clearest reason to confide, or which, when accomplished, would be of doubtful utility." [21] The Republicans always asked: Can the state afford it? Can the development earn money?

Thus it was no surprise to find the Bucktails rapidly regaining their status as the party of the people late in 1825. Not even the elaborate ceremonies that marked the opening of the Erie Canal on November 2 slowed them down, although the success of the canal during the next few years heralded the conversion of many Western farmers to the Clintonian program of increased improvements. This tremendous waterway, traversing a distance of 363 miles from Troy to Buffalo, had cost over $7½ million to build. In the last week of October, 1825, accompanied by a group of leading citizens—not including Van Buren—Clinton boarded a canal boat at Buffalo and ten days later arrived in New York City, where he poured a barrel of water taken from Lake Erie into the Atlantic Ocean. The canal, however, did more than link the Atlantic with the Erie—it linked the East with the West. The states of Ohio, Illinois, Indiana, and the Territory of Michigan now had a quick and relatively inexpensive means of transportation for their exportable farm surpluses. The burdens of immigration westward were lightened. At the same time, the value of real and personal property in New York City rose 60 per cent in five years, and the canal was said to earn $700,000 annually.[22]

Van Buren celebrated his forty-third birthday on December 5, 1825, the day the Nineteenth Congress convened. What should have been a happy occasion was marred by the fact that the administration forces in the House of Representatives, led by Daniel Webster of the persuasive tongue, had elected John W. Taylor as Speaker by the narrow majority of five votes. Van Buren had hoped to humble Taylor, a Clintonian, but the Adams-Clay party was a trifle too strong. In the Senate, neither the combined followers of Jackson and Calhoun nor the partisans of the administration held a clear majority; therefore the success of the President's term in office depended upon the Crawfordites. Van Buren temporarily remained neutral.

The Jacksonians—minus their leader, who had resigned from his Senate seat the previous October—were "of course looking out for the weak points in the enemies lines," the Regency chief noted, and were "ready for the assault when opportunity offeres. We of the Crawford school lay upon our oares and will not lightly commit ourselves except in deference of old principles." [23]

It was therefore with particular interest that the Congress listened to the President's annual address delivered on December 6. One of the most powerfully nationalistic state papers of its time, Adams's declaration of future policy opened with a discussion of the approaching congress of South American nations to be held in Panama. An invitation already tended the United States had been accepted, and ministers were shortly to be named. The message also made reference to a bankruptcy law, the improved condition of the finances, and the needs of the army and navy.

Then Adams launched into the heart of his address. "The great object of the institution of civil government," he said, "is the improvement of the condition of those who are parties to the social compact. . . . Roads and canals, by multiplying and facilitating the communications and intercourse between distant regions and multitudes of men, are among the most important means of improvement." He urged that political and intellectual institutions be founded as well, advocating the establishment of a national university and an astronomical observatory ("light-houses of the skies"). He called for the construction of waterway and harbor installations. "The spirit of improvement is abroad upon the earth," he proclaimed.

We have seen under the persevering and enlightened enterprise of another State the waters of our Western lakes mingle with those of the ocean. If undertakings like these have been accomplished in the compass of our Confederation, can we, the representative authorities of the whole Union, fall behind our fellow-servants in the exercise of the trust committed to us for the benefit of our common sovereign . . . ? [24]

The opposition's reaction to the message was, from the start, emphatically hostile. Ridiculing the proposals as an unwarranted and grossly exaggerated interpretation of the powers of the Federal government, its newspapers rang out with critical denunciation. Many neutrals were also appalled by the pronouncement. Thomas Ritchie in his *Richmond Enquirer* asked: "Are we really reading a state paper, or a school boy's Thesis?" [25] Willie P. Mangum, congressman from North Carolina, stated his objections in a different manner: "Sir, this administration I verily believe will be conducted upon as corrupt principles indeed more corrupt, than any that has preceded it. Bargain & compromise will be the order of the day—I came here hoping that I might be able to lend to it a frank support—The Crawford party will have to stand aloof, they will not be able I fear to support this administration." [26] Thomas Hart Benton later reflected that the address furnished a "topic" against Adams and "went to the reconstruction of parties on the old line of strict . . . construction of the constitution." [27] Jefferson said some of the President's doctrines were unconstitutional. A Western editor named Francis P. Blair, upon reading them, deserted Clay and joined Jackson.[28]

The Albany *Argus,* however, refrained from comment. In reprinting the message, Edwin Croswell prefaced it briefly with the words: "It will be perceived no doubt with satisfaction that the offer of the Southern Republics, for the attendance of republics in the congress of Panama, has been accepted by our government, and that ministers will be commissioned to attend." [29] In the succeeding weeks the Regency organ remained peculiarly evasive regarding the other features of the address, except to reprint a few unfriendly editorials from other journals. Van Buren was not so sure this was wise, but Marcy assured him that editor Croswell had not been "incautious." [30]

Van Buren's personal reaction to the presidential communication was violently hostile, although he did not reveal it immediately. He had always believed in the "least-government-possible" doctrine and for the past two years he had become more and more alarmed by those who would stretch the Constitution in an effort to enlarge the powers of Congress.[31] Adams's message was clearly a Federalist pronouncement, and Van Buren later criticised it as

filled with well-wrought encomiums on the Federal Constitution, plausible definitions of the grants and limits of powers between the General and State Governments, and eloquent injunctions in favor of their faithful observance; and yet not one of the followers of the old Republican faith—no intelligent friend of the reserved rights of the states could fail to see in them the most ultra latitudinarian doctrines.[32]

The party with principles had to challenge the party with the program. As a true Jeffersonian, Van Buren could not accede to Adams's definition of the responsibilities of the American government. As a superb politician, hoping to revive the old party of the Union, he wanted a little more time before publicly joining the opposition.

Two weeks later, on the floor of the Senate, he stated his objections to Federal-sponsored internal improvements in a speech that was heavily loaded with the dogmas of Jefferson. He went as far as to propose a constitutional amendment, although he meant it only as a ruse to scare Clay and Adams off the question. He began by reading two resolutions.

Resolved, That Congress does not possess the power to make Roads and Canals within the respective States.

Resolved, That a select committee be appointed with instructions to prepare and report a Joint Resolution, for an amendment of the Constitution, prescribing and defining the power Congress shall have over the subject of Internal Improvements, and subjecting the same to such restrictions as shall effectively protect the sovereignty of the respective States. . . . [33]

From the first discussion of this power, Van Buren remarked in elaboration, there had been an "unbroken, and, frequently, angry and unpleasant controversy." Different and mutually hostile opinions existed upon the subject which could only be eliminated by the democratic process of constitutional amendment. "As early as 1808, the propriety of an appeal to the States upon the point in question, had been suggested by Mr. Jefferson, in his last message to Congress." Since John Quincy Adams had seen fit to revive the controversy, the Senate should take action to settle it.[34]

Certainly Van Buren's resolutions were not in keeping with the true spirit of the Constitution. In effect he was again proposing its amendment simply to quell a disagreement over Congressional powers. His proposals would fail to solve the problem and in fact would create new ones. They did not touch the basis of the difficulty, and therefore were not likely to receive approval. Van Buren knew this, for he wrote to the Regency:

The debate on my Resolutions will be extensive & probably lead to a review of what has been & to soundings to see where we are now. It is supposed by some that we shall have a majority but I am not so sanguine. The West wants roads & canals & must have them, rightfully if they can otherwise if they must. I believe however that we shall be able in the end to break up all interference on the part of the Genl Govent without a previous amendment of the Constitution. It is strange that our people are so indifferent upon this subject. There is no State in the Union that has so much interest in it as ours; growing out of our past expenditures & liability to future contributions for like works in other States. The administration are intent upon sustaining themselves & it appears to be immaterial whether they derive their aid from Jew or Gentile or whoever else can help.[35]

In other words the resolutions were not intended to be passed by Congress. They were merely a reply, couched in negative terms, to the President's request.

Back in Albany, the Regency men were celebrating. They had won the November election and were presently feasting on the offices denied them the previous year. The clerkish but highly efficient Flagg was elected secretary of state; Nathan Sanford was elected United States Senator to replace Rufus

King; William L. Marcy was reelected comptroller; Samuel Talcott became the attorney general; and Samuel Young was chosen speaker of the Assembly.

Coordinating their activities to a greater degree than was possible before, Van Buren in Washington and the Regency in Albany provided each other with helpful advice and vocal support. Late in January, to bolster the Senator's position on internal improvements, Silas Wright introduced two resolutions in the New York Senate placing the state on record as favoring popular election of the President by the district system and denying that Congress had the power to construct roads, bridges, and lighthouses. "All this," James Tallmadge confided to John W. Taylor, "is in persuance of orders from Washington." [36] When Van Buren received a copy of the resolutions he turned them over to his friends Gales and Seaton, editors of the *National Intelligencer*. "I wish you would republish [them]," he wrote, ". . . in your paper of Monday." [37] He did not add that the reason for his request was to serve notice that he was about to begin a full-scale attack on the administration. Although Van Buren did not publicize his intentions, they were well known. "A Senator from this State," declared Tallmadge,, "*is soon* to make a speech. It is to be a great effort & in due time the adminisration *is to be* charged as advancing federalists etc etc & the Democratic party is to be aroused etc etc." [38]

Two months had passed since Van Buren first heard Adams's message. His neutrality had come to an end.

The skirmishes between the Adams and Jackson parties up to this point were minor compared to the furor aroused by the Panama mission; at the same time Van Buren edged closer to the opposition faction. Having observed the President's policies for the past year—especially since December—he concluded regretfully that both Adams and Clay were guilty of promoting "Monroe's fusion policy. . . ." [39] Their appointments could not be explained any other way. Furthermore, Adams in his annual address had revealed himself to be closer to the Hamiltonian than to the Jeffersonian principles of government. For the sake of the party and preservation of Republican ideals, Van Buren could no longer remain silent.

The Panama mission, which he regarded as blatantly unconstitutional and at variance with the foreign policy established by Washington and Jefferson, provided the occasion for his first major blast against the administration. On that issue he intended to call a halt to Adams's entire program. What had held him back from this course during these past months was his fear of the repercussions such a move would have on New York and the Regency. He was still worried, despite the November election. New York was safe, but he wanted to keep it that way. So, to prevent a repetition of the 1824 fiasco and yet "reprove" Adams's policies, he decided to act as an independent critic of the administration and not involve his state. Later, at a more propitious moment, this could be changed; but not now. Never doubting that the "speedy reunion of the Republican party" was at hand,[40] he felt he could help it by acting alone.

Curious to know the Jacksonian position on the Panama question, he sought out Vice-President Calhoun in his home at Georgetown. Because of their relationship during the last election the conversation between the two men was highly formal. Calhoun was guilty of continually stirring up opposition in New York to overthrow the Little Magician and his machine. If any man had cause to complain it was Van Buren, but it was he who made the first overture toward a reconciliation.

After the required pleasantries, the Vice-President frankly told his visitor that the Panama mission would constitute the first major struggle between the administration and the Jackson party. Delighted by this information, Van Buren acknowledged his own opposition to the measure and told Calhoun that he could be counted on to lend his support in defeating it. Not a word passed regarding an alliance. Van Buren offered his own services and nothing more. Although an understanding or agreement of some sort would eventually be reached, for the present it was best left unsaid. (One thing Van Buren did do was instruct the editor of the *Argus* "to send his coun-

try paper to Mr. Calhoun as a permanent subscription.") [41]
The interview was short and to the point, and was the first step
leading Van Buren into the Jackson camp.

The Panama congress was, on the whole, very popular
throughout the country. The destruction of Spanish power
in the New World and the erection of independent republics
in South America had received the cordial approbation of citizens of the United States. They applauded the suggestion that
the free states in the Western Hemisphere should meet in
Panama to discuss matters of mutual interest, and immediately
contrasted this proposed congress with the hated Holy Alliance
of Europe, the enemy of liberty and the protector of despots.[42]
To Adams the congress was a "grain of mustard-seed." [43] Perhaps its very popularity strengthened Henry Clay's conviction
that the United States should participate in it. In any event
both he and the President went ahead with all the arrangements for sending ministers to Panama.

The opposition in Congress, once having agreed to attack
the mission, was somewhat at a loss as to the correct and most
efficacious method to conduct the campaign. But after Van
Buren's interview with Calhoun, the Jacksonians suddenly experienced the heartening effect of the New Yorker's powers of
organization. They were summoned to caucus meetings and,
upon his advice, resolved to use delaying tactics to defeat the
mission and to begin their assault in the Senate, over the
nomination of ministers, rather than in the House, over the
appropriation of their salaries. This was the wiser course,
since the administration had a greater majority of votes in the
lower chamber. Adams suspected "a union of Crawford,
Calhoun and Jackson partisans" when the House took up the
question and called for some important papers, but he was sure
of it when the Senate began debating the nominations.[44]
There, on February 15, Van Buren signaled the commencement of hostilities by proposing that the Senate, in its deliberations, "ought to act with open doors; unless it shall appear that
the publication of documents, necessary to be referred to in
debate, will be prejudicial to existing negotiations." He also

moved, with malice aforethought, that the President be asked whether such an objection existed. By a close vote of 23 to 20, the upper house passed both resolutions and the battle was on.

After a few days' delay Adams responded testily that the "communications from me to the Senate . . . have been made, like all other communications upon Executive business, in *confidence.* . . ." He deemed it "my indispensable duty to leave to the Senate itself the decision of a question, involving a departure . . . from that usage, and upon the motives for which . . . I do not feel myself competent to decide." [45]

This crusty reply only antagonized a few neutral senators and gave the opposition a chance to introduce further dilatory motions, each requiring the taking of a separate vote. Thus the Senate, with studied deliberation, lumbered along at a maddeningly slow pace and wasted as much time as possible. The climax of this farce was reached when the upper house drew the shroud of mystery around itself and conferred secretly for three weeks in order to examine and study Adam's communications. These defiant, procrastinating tactics could not go on indefinitely, however, and the climax came on March 14.

Van Buren had just moved that the Constitution did not authorize the sending of representatives to an assembly of nations to serve as mere deputies without diplomatic character. He submitted a resolution that it was not in the power of the Federal government to appoint ministers to the Panama congress and that to do so would be a departure from the traditional foreign policy of the United States. With this, the senators who supported the administration, their patience almost exhausted, finally stiffened. They defeated the proposal by 24 to 19. They then went on to confirm the nominations of Richard C. Anderson and John Sergeant as ministers, and William B. Rochester as secretary.[46]

Van Buren's actions during these trying weeks caused much speculation within the ranks of the three major Republican factions, especially since he seemed to be acting without his Radical friends. "Will you do me the favour," Peter B. Porter anxiously asked Clay, "to inform me what Van Buren is doing at Washington. Is he leagued with the V. President? and, if so, has this combination yet avowed or disclosed any distinct ulterior object, beyond that of breaking down the administration? Are Clinton's friends acting with him?" [47] In his reply Clay gave a fairly accurate estimate of political conditions in the capital and described what he and Adams were up against. The House, he exclaimed, was safe, but the Senate was infested with 15 or 16 members who were the antagonists of the administration at all times. Eight or ten more were "secretly inclined" to opposition and when they united the two groups formed a majority. Despite their "display of tactics" the Panama mission would, continued Clay, receive Senate approval.

You would be astonished at the shifts and variations to which they have resorted to procrastinate the final decision. I hope the veil will be removed. I let the nation see, in all the nakedness and the deformity, faction and its workings. Your Senator (Mr. Van Buren) goes along with the faction, on this affair, with as much zeal as the most zealous of them. . . . I imagine that the V. Pres, V. Buren and their associates have not yet agreed upon the terms of this most strange ———. Opposition for the present, with an understanding that they will here after endeavor to settle matters probably are all the conditions yet settled. V. Buren came here at the commencement of the cession [sic] with unfriendly purposes, to which he was stimulated by the success you had in N. York in your elections last fall.[48]

Meanwhile Van Buren was preparing a speech that was to be his great effort against this "ill-advised" mission. As was often the case when he was so inspired, he worked long hours, doing an unusual amount of research and making himself certain of his facts. His singularly accurate and discerning mind then arranged those facts in a precise, logical form. He subsequently wrote out his material, corrected it, and re-corrected it. When finally satisfied, he practiced his method of delivery before a full-length mirror to acquire the proper gestures. On March 22, 1826, he added the final touches to his Panama address. The pleasure he felt in its completion he shared with the Regency. "I have this moment finished the last sheet of my speech on the Panama question. When you see it you will have a view of the whole ground & see that we have neither laboured wrongly or in vain." [49]

Van Buren's speech was part of an organized program of debate to enumerate and explain the arguments of the opposition and if possible to discredit the mission. Thomas Hart Benton of Missouri, Robert Y. Hayne of South Carolina, John M. Berrien of Georgia, and John Holmes of Maine were the senators entrusted with the duty of carrying out the main lines of that attack, and each was given a specific feature of the conference with which to deal. Hayne voiced the Southern fear that the mission would discuss the suppression of the slave trade and the independence of Haiti. He asked whether Americans would deign to meet with representatives of an island controlled by Negroes. Then he answered his question: not while there were Southern votes in the Congress to prevent it! [50]

Van Buren followed—according to the schedule they had worked out beforehand—and spoke with greater conviction. His bland and smiling countenance placed everyone at ease but did not soften the force of his powerful arguments. No political tirade this, but the eloquent plea of an isolationist.

He began by stating that the question was not whether the United States should take part in the advantages to be gained from an assembly of American states, but rather should it *"be of the character, and in the form proposed."* This was the heart of the matter. What had been suggested by the President, and the methods he proposed to realize that suggestion, Van Buren averred, revealed highhanded, reckless contempt of the Constitution and of the power of Congress. A simple case in point involved the documents required by the Senate, which had been denied it for a number of weeks. Then, he said, instead of receiving "full and explicit communications, a portion only of the requisite information is sparingly doled out—just enough to satisfy the successive calls of the Senate." [51]

Turning to the Panama congress itself, Van Buren asked his

listeners whether they believed that the delegates attending the meeting would assume legislative powers or merely act in an advisory capacity. As far as he was concerned, after carefully reading the treaties between the various South American republics establishing the assembly, he thought it was undeniably evident that the members planned to take action. And by what authority could the United States take part in such a conference that was at variance with the loosest interpretation of the Constitution? He said that they had been asked to join a confederation which by its nature would supersede the powers of Congress. There were some who claimed that the Monroe Doctrine compelled this country to participate in the proposed meeting. Such an interpretation, Van Buren declared, distorted the true meaning of that declaration. The former President had asserted correct principles but at the same time "left us free to act or not in enforcing them." Now the Secretary of State demanded that the Senate "fulfill the alleged *pledge* of Mr. Monroe, in his message of December, 1823." They were not so pledged, insisted Van Buren. What Adams apparently had in mind, the Senator continued, was an agreement with the member nations at the congress whereby the United States would assist these nations should the "powers of Europe make common cause with Spain or otherwise attempt the subjugation of Spanish America. . . ." Furthermore, the United States was to pledge itself to resist any effort by Europe "to colonize any portion of this Continent." Was the Senate willing to sanction this? "No—thank Heaven—a policy so opposite to all the feelings of the American People; so adverse, as I firmly believe it to be, to its true interests, has no friend, at least no advocate on this floor." If there were to be an alliance or agreement, the Senate members themselves should undertake the responsibilities of bringing it about and not a motley group of foreign delegates whose one object was to force the United States into assisting them in warding off an attack by Spain. No government had the right to ask aid in an effort to change the condition of the world. The proposed congress was a *"political connexion,* at war with the established policy of our Govern-

ment." Washington's *Farewell Address* pointed out the true
national direction in foreign affairs. So too did the many
state papers of Thomas Jefferson. If those principles were
abandoned in favor of this Panama congress, the United States
would be placed in the same category with the Holy Alliance.
"But I am against all alliances," Van Buren concluded,
"against all army confederacies, or confederacies of any sort. I
care not how specious, or how disguised; come in what shape
they may, I oppose them." [52]

All agreed, enemy as well as friend, that this was one of
Van Buren's finest efforts as an orator. The speech, wrote
James Kent, contained arguments against the mission which
were strong and impressive.[53] Benjamin Butler said that it
gave great satisfaction to Van Buren's friends, and "great an-
noyance to those who think 'the kings name [John Q. Adams] a
tower of strength.' Need I add that it has conferred new
honors on yourself? . . . I confess I was not prepared to expect
so triumphant an exposition of the grounds of opposition." [54]
Ambrose Spencer, an old political foe, thought "the minority
in the Senate were put in the wrong on the Panama Mission
by the Pres' message but having seen your speech & Col Hayne's
I must admit my first impressions are weakened & that you had
made a very plausible if not full case against the Mission." [55]
The *Albany Argus* came out with an extra edition reprinting
the speech in full. Although some readers might disagree with
Van Buren's views, the editor commented, they would have to
admit that the address was "very clear," "statesmanlike," and
marked the "beginning of a policy, not recognized by the previous practice of our government." [56]

For many months the *Argus* had refused to take a positive
stand on either the mission, Adams's annual address, or the
next presidential election. With respect to the latter, Croswell
stated in his newspaper on April 3 that the "republicans of
this state have no immediate interest in the question." [57] He
enlarged upon this idea in a personal letter to Van Buren, in-
forming him that although there was an "increasing aversion
towards Mr. Adams" among New Yorkers, there was an equal

aversion to any "collision" with the administration which would drive them to the support of Governor Clinton. "They prefer, *for the present, at least,* to stand in the capacity of lookers on. . . ." For this reason and because it was believed that a "very great evil" would result from a contrary course, "we propose to let the National politics alone." [58] Years later, Van Buren explained that this was the "origin of the non-committal" charges made against him, even though he himself had nothing to do with the editorial.[59] His protests to the contrary notwithstanding, it is perfectly clear that he was in accord with the policy of separating national and state politics during the early part of Adams's administration. For the remainder of the year 1826 the *Argus* was nonpartisan—a course of action which could not have been maintained without Van Buren's express consent.

Berrien, Benton, and Holmes, all of whom followed the Little Magician in denouncing the Panama mission in the Senate, argued the strictly constitutional point of view. Their speeches were closely reasoned and extremely long, but it remained for John Randolph, the new senator from Virginia, to climax the debate with verbal pyrotechnics. While the Senate was considering a resolution introduced by John Branch of North Carolina contesting the competency of the President to appoint ministers to Panama without the consent of the upper house, Randolph rose, allegedly to contribute a few well-chosen opinions. What took place, however, was far worse. Half crazed, but with talents that had earlier distinguished him in the House of Representatives, John Randolph of Roanoke could still deliver a six-hour address—provided a sufficient amount of porter was on hand—and send his enemies running for cover. Replete with lively historical and classical references, his usually aimless and rambling remarks delighted the spectators as much as they appalled his colleagues. On this occasion, however, he knew exactly where he was going. Using the Panama mission as a point of departure, he launched into a blistering personal rebuke of Adams and Clay and compared their coalition to that of "Blifil and Black George . . . of the puritan with the blackleg." [60]

Clay, bristling with indignation and highly sensitive to the bargain charge, challenged Randolph to a duel in defense of his honor. The Virginian, with the fearlessness of one deranged, readily accepted, and on April 8, 1826, gave the Secretary of State the satisfaction he demanded. Thomas Hart Benton, a witness of the proceedings, declared that while Clay fired with intent to kill, the lunatic Senator threw his shots away.[61] "I will never make a widow & orphans," said Randolph in stentorian tones. "It is agt. my principles." [62]

Fortunately, neither man was injured, but the Virginian left the field with a bullet hole in his coat. Clay ended the *opéra bouffe* by replacing the damaged garment. The episode, however, did not silence the Senator nor did it convince a large portion of Americans that Clay had not indeed sold out to the New England "puritan." Said one Radical: "The Administration are both weak & wicked I fear,—and the present prospect is that the Members of Congress from the south of Washington will unite to put down Adams, & if they can get no better, they will take up Genl Jackson for that purpose." [63]

IX: THE MASTER OF NEW YORK

FURTHER DEBATE on the Panama issue was suspended when a bill revising the Federal judiciary system was introduced from the House. Calling for the addition of three judges to the Supreme Court and for three new circuits in the West, the measure was a blind, according to Van Buren—an elaborate scheme on the part of Henry Clay and Daniel Webster to create a post to which the obnoxious Postmaster General, John Mc-Lean, might be elevated.[1] Van Buren, chairman of the Judiciary Committee, brought the House bill to the Senate floor on April 7, 1826, but he added a few important amendments. By deft manipulation he was able to exclude McLean from possible consideration for any of the proposed judgeships. He fought for the emasculated bill as though it were one of the most important pieces of legislation to come before Congress that session, and when the amendments finally came to a vote, the Senate overwhelmingly passed them. The House rejected the changes, however, and the measure was lost.

During the debates Van Buren indulged in a few interesting remarks on the nature of the judicial branch of the national government, all of which harked back to a number of basic ideas he had taken from Jefferson. In the first place he was decidedly opposed to relieving the judges of the Supreme Court from their circuit duties. Furthermore, he accused the Court of encroaching upon the rights of the states in dealing with cases arising out of the contract clause of the Constitution. He deprecated the nullification of "statutes of powerful States, which had received the deliberate sanction, not only of their legislatures, but of their highest judicatories. . . ." But in many ways what was most obnoxious to him was the near "idolatry" accorded the Supreme Court, requiring "not a little share of firmness in a public man ... to express sentiments that conflict with it." To the belief which claimed "for the court the character of being the safest depository of political power, I do not subscribe. . . . I believe that the judges . . . are subject to the same infirmities, influenced by the same passions, and operated upon by the same causes that good and great men are in other situations." [2]

In every respect Van Buren's remarks showed how disgruntled he was with the course of American politics. He harped on the question of governmental powers and worried over increased centralization of authority in Washington. His quarreling with Adams and Clay began over principle, not politics. He wanted to do something about the Republican party, to revitalize it, and if the President had not subscribed to the "wrong" philosophy of government he might never have opposed him. Van Buren had "bottom" (to use Marcy's word), that is, depth, integrity—always did have for those willing to ignore preconceived prejudices in assessing his character.

About the middle of April, Van Buren's position was no longer in doubt. By word and deed he had relegated himself to the side of the opposition. Although he was not as yet a regular member of the Jackson party, he was the most prominent antiadministration man in the Senate, and for the remainder of the session he sparked almost every debate which would embarrass the President and the Secretary of State. By and large the disputes were petty, but finally a bill was received from the House authorizing the necessary appropriations for the Panama mission. It steeled both sides for a final test of strength. The Jackson men were immediately on hand with amendments to weaken the measure, but they were outvoted by the same margin—24 to 19—that had killed Van Buren's earlier resolution to declare the mission inexpedient. On May 3 the upper house approved the appropriations bill and the first round in the battle against a reawakened Federalism came to an end.

The opposition leaders could claim little satisfaction from these developments. While they had successfully delayed the mission for months, they failed to talk a single senator into reversing his position once the debate began. From February to May, Clay had held the line against them until the final count was taken. Earlier predilections favoring the conference prevailed and were never overcome.

Many years later it was reported "that a Senator—understood to be Mr. Van Buren—on being rallied on the triumph of the administration party on the Panama mission, replied, '*Yes; they have beaten us by a few votes, after a hard battle;* But if they had taken the other side, and refused the mission, we should have had them!'" Someone may have made the statement, but not Van Buren.[3] He honestly opposed the mission for sound reasons and could not have made the remark, even in a joking way. Men of this era had a simple rule to go by when they wrote their reminiscences fifty and sixty years later: if they could not remember who had made a particular statement, and if it were blatantly political, then the author was necessarily Van Buren.

The administration suffered an unexpected setback some weeks later, when word reached Washington that the Panama congress had adjourned before the United States delegates had arrived. The congress itself failed to justify Clay's hopes and to some extent discredited the persons who had predicted its success. Only then where the Jacksonians rewarded for their long and arduous labors, but it was hardly the prize they wanted.

In May the Congressional session had almost reached its end, but still no quarter was given to the harassed Adams. His power to appoint foreign ministers was challenged, and the Senate considered a motion to regulate and reduce the executive patronage. The proposal was accompanied by six bills, each specially written to restrict the President's prerogatives. One bill would have prevented Adams from designating newspapers for the publication of laws and advertisements. The others would have virtually transferred from the President to Congress the power of appointing midshipmen, cadets, postmasters, and revenue collectors. The measures were so flagrantly partisan that the administration men easily had them tabled.

Despite the articulate objections to their program, Adams and Clay pushed ahead with it nonetheless. Several bills were dropped into the legislative hopper which would transform the American System into a body of law. Unperturbed by Van Buren's constitutional amendments, which were designed to block Congressional consideration of internal improvements, they sponsored two measures dealing with the building of the Dismal Swamp Canal and the repairing of the Cumberland Road. When these bills reached the Senate, Van Buren cautioned his colleagues against them. The creed of the old Republican party, he insisted, denied that the "Government possessed the Constitutional power to make these roads and canals, or to grant the money to make them." [4] But in neither case could he break the administration majority or convince the Westerners that his arguments were valid; and so the bills passed.

With this last defeat for Van Buren the session closed. Although Clay and Adams had walked off with most of the laurels —bedraggled as they were—an opposition had been formed, along rather indefinite lines, which was ready to challenge every move the administration made. As yet no one had come forward to reunite the shattered fragments of Jefferson's old party and give this movement greater force and direction. Some spoke of turning to Old Hickory, but their words lacked conviction.[5] None of the important Congressional leaders—including Van Buren—had made any specific arrangement with Jackson or his principal advisers, and consequently the three factions comprising the opposition lacked essential unity of action. To a certain degree this accounted for the failures of the past session. Unless something were done to correct the situation, the administration would continue to defeat the opposition at every turn. Journeying back to Albany, Van Buren had a few days to think deeply on these matters, and by the time he arrived home he had a fairly definite idea about what should be done.

If all the forces opposing Adams and Clay were to be united to form a single party, he reasoned, the members would have to be taught discipline. That was a primary consideration. And, as he knew from his experiences in New York, one of the best methods of achieving discipline was an officially sponsored newspaper. Before leaving Washington he had discussed with the Vice-President the possibility of establishing such a newspaper, but the idea was coldly received. The ambitious Southerner argued that the *United States Telegraph,* under the editorship of Duff Green, was already doing a very creditable job of annoying Adams and Clay, and there was no need to establish another journal to compete with it. Van Buren disagreed with him because the *Telegraph* was not a strictly *party* newspaper, representing all the antiadministration factions. He knew, although he could not say so, that it was a Calhoun organ, dedicated to Calhoun's ascendancy, his ideas, his glorification. Instead, the Senator wanted Thomas Ritchie to come to Washington and begin a paper which all Republicans could regard as authoritative.

From Albany, Van Buren continued pressing his arguments on the Vice-President and enclosed letters from others to support his points. Still he was refused. In his reply Calhoun was very friendly, discussing the recent illness of his own son and rather hypocritically congratulating the "intriguer," as he once called him, on the splendid unanimity of New York Republicans. Regarding another newspaper, however, he was adamant:

A paper is already in existence, and it does seem to me that two on the same side must distract and excite jealousy. Each will have its partisans. To make a new arrangement on the existing establishment is not without difficulties. The consent of the proprietor must be had. He has entered with zeal on his duties, and is sanguine of success. The circulation of his paper is said to be rapidly increasing.

The importance of the exchange of letters lies not so much in what appears to be Van Buren's attempt to whittle away at Calhoun's prestige, or in the Vice-President's expressions of friendship, but rather that this was the first outward sign that the Senator was seriously considering the reestablishment of a national party. He was thinking of the three opposition factions loosely bound together through a newspaper that would speak for all of them. Calhoun failed to see this and he took the defensive when he thought his influence was at stake.

The Vice-President's letter had additional significance. It revealed that both he and Van Buren had reached further agreements since the debate over the Panama mission. "I entirely concur with you as to our course," wrote Calhoun. "Our liberty and happiness depend on maintaining with inflexible firmness, but with moderation and temper, republican grounds and republican principles." [6] The Vice-President was now speaking Van Buren's language!

July 4, 1826, was a milestone in the history of the United States. It was the fiftieth anniversary of the signing of the Declaration of Independence, and the nation observed it by paying heartfelt tribute to the great men of the past. A few days later the newspapers, with large black borders, announced the deaths of Thomas Jefferson and John Adams on the very day the anniversary was celebrated. Bells tolled mournfully, and the black crape displayed everywhere was an unwanted reminder that the "giants" were disappearing one by one and might never be replaced.

Having lost his political mentor, Van Buren turned for counsel to James Madison, and began a short correspondence that failed to achieve its main object. The former President was gracious but not very helpful. The Senator had invited his comments on the power of Congress over internal improvements, but Madison hedged and merely pointed out the dangers of giving the power to either the national government or the states. Whether the Constitution was explicit in defining jurisdiction, he refused to say. Van Buren thanked him for his letter and injected the rather illogical note that he believed George Washington opposed internal improvements since he never brought the subject before Congress.[7]

The Senator kept thinking about the party throughout that summer. In a sense his letter to Madison was an indication of this. He hated the administration of John Quincy Adams and wanted to "reprobate" its heresies, yet he had done nothing but make speeches. The newspaper he had proposed to establish was a dead issue and would remain so. Perhaps all along he had been deluding himself as to its efficacy. Fundamentally, as he well knew, only a single party built around Andrew Jackson, and taking every advantage of his enormous popularity among the people, could successfully challenge the administration. Let the Hero then declare himself a strict Republican of the old school and Van Buren would immediately begin the reorganization of the party. In a letter written in November, 1826, to P. N. Nicholas of the Richmond Junto, Van Buren was quite explicit. "If Gen Jackson & his friends," he said, "will put his election on old party grounds, preserve the old systems, avoid if not condemn the practices of the last campaign we can by adding his personal popularity to the yet remaining force of old party feeling, not only succeed in electing him but our success when achieved will be worth something. We shall see what they are willing to do." [8]

Within four months he could wait no longer, for by that time the Democratic party was taking shape.

For the remainder of 1826 Van Buren concerned himself with local matters in New York, and when he was done he had regained complete mastery of the state. In one of the shrewdest schemes he ever conceived—a tribute to his daring, ingenuity, and knowledge of men—he succeeded in crushing the Clintonian party.

Fearlessly he ordered the Regency to nominate as its candidate for governor in the next election the recent secretary to the Panama congress, William B. Rochester. Because he was a friend of the administration and because the Bucktails were not yet committed to Jackson, Rochester would attract a considerable number of votes that would normally go to Clinton, who was seeking reelection. The Governor's natural reaction would be to blame Adams and Clay for the defection and accuse them of plotting his downfall. In turn, the entire body of Adams supporters would desert Clinton after the election, the Governor's party would collapse, and the Bucktails would strengthen their grip on the state.[9]

This was an intricate game that Van Buren was playing, and one not entirely in line with his celebrated principles. Silas Wright and some of the other lieutenants were very skeptical about it, but the Little Magician convinced them they had nothing to worry about.[10] To the amazement of many, his scheme worked perfectly. Supposedly good Clintonians, who were more faithful to the President than to the Governor, voted for Rochester in the November election, believing that they were helping to sustain the national administration. For days the outcome was in doubt, so close had been the balloting. But in other elections it was a thumping Republican victory. These results, crowed the *Argus,* were due to the "union and energy" of all, but especially to the "young men." [11]

On the Sunday following the election Van Buren was preparing to leave for church when he heard a signal notifying the townspeople that the steamboat from New York had arrived in the harbor. Shortly thereafter a "busy friend" of Clinton's raced past Van Buren's window, his face aglow with excitement. The Senator turned to Marcy, who was with him, and remarked that the ship had undoubtedly brought the news of the Governor's reelection. A little later, at church, Mr. and Mrs. Clinton arrived and took their seats a few pews in front of Van Buren and Marcy. No sooner had they settled themselves when Mrs. Clinton turned around and "favored" the Regency pair with a "look," prompting Marcy to whisper to his friend that the election was indeed lost.[12] The vote was very close, however, for the Governor had won by a scant majority of three and a half thousand.

The strange course of events at first baffled Clinton and then roused him to a magnificent rage. Although he had been returned to the executive mansion, he had lost more than he gained. He reacted just as Van Buren predicted, blaming Adams for trying to defeat him. "The late election," he wrote, "so far as it can be viewed at present was managed to a great extent by a most profligate coalition between the Bucktails and the several administration men. The latter have failed in their main object which was to crush me. . . ." [13]

Clintonians everywhere were disgusted and ashamed, the objects of pity and ridicule. "I am decidedly of opinion," ventured Ambrose Spencer, "that the party attached to Mr. C[linton] is entirely dissolved, & that were an election to come on tomorrow & Mr C. a candidate for Governor against any decent man, he would lose his election by thousands." His friends, Spencer continued, consider themselves "politically deserted & destroyed." The Bucktails "have now the game in their own hands," for which Clinton must assume sole responsibility. Had the Governor, Spencer concluded, "come out openly in favor of Mr. Adams, he would have kept his friends united, & maintained a rallying point, & gained a large accession from the other party; but we now have no standard erected, nor any rallying point." [14]

For the trifling price of the governorship, therefore, Van Buren severely damaged the pro-administration, pro-Clinton faction in New York and was practically assured of directing the state's electoral vote in the next presidential contest to the candidate he chose. He could now mix state and national politics if he so desired, without worrying too much about the consequences. Early in December, the *Argus* indicated that a change in policy was not too distant.[15]

Sadly, John Quincy Adams noted in his *Diary* that the state of New York was in the hands of Martin Van Buren.[16]

X: THE MAKING OF THE DEMOCRATIC PARTY

JACKSONIANS interpreted the fall elections throughout the country as a decided trend away from the administration, and included the results in New York as part of this general picture. Although they had added to the House of Representatives a number of new men from Ohio, Virginia, Kentucky, and Illinois, this did not indicate a repudiation of Adams and Clay by the people, since few of the candidates waged their campaign battles over national issues.

As the second session of the Nineteenth Congress got under way on December 4, 1826, of all the active politicians in Washington, Van Buren was the greatest enigma. Not even the vain and ambitious Calhoun—the Senator's liaison with the Jacksonians—could define his exact position. About all one could say was that Van Buren was decidedly anti-Adams without being clearly pro-Jackson.[1] Clay, with his great fund of information, claimed to know the "game" the New Yorker was playing, and described it as "inculcating Neutrality" regarding the "general administration, which means ultimate hostility to be gradually approached." [2] But the Secretary of State guessed wrong this time; the Senator was much further along in his "game" than that. By December-January, 1826–27, he had already begun—as he had promised himself—the process of reconstituting the Republican party along the traditional lines laid down by Jefferson. It was to be achieved through the election of Andrew Jackson in 1828.

For a number of reasons Van Buren discarded his older notion of waiting until the General pledged himself to "old

party grounds" before he organized the undisciplined Jacksonians. (Although there is some indication that he believed
he had received the assurances.[3]) There was the possibility that
Jackson might never give those assurances; and a delay in shaping a national party would allow the administration extra time
to mend its broken fences in the several states—particularly in
New York. Unquestionably what impressed the Senator with
even greater force was the knowledge that his intentions did
not require Jackson's immediate authorization, provided that
the Hero ultimately accepted what was done. And Old
Hickory could not help but league himself with the only national antiadministration organization once it was formed,
especially since it would be dedicated to his election to the
presidency.

Some historians are of the general opinion that the Republican party split into two groups along clearly discernible lines
shortly after Adams's election: that the antiadministration
forces rallied around Jackson and eventually called themselves
Democrats, while the pro-administration faction united behind
Adams and Clay and referred to themselves as National Republicans.[4] True, a cleavage among Republicans did appear as
early as 1826, but it was not a sharp division, and few contemporaries regarded it as irreconcilable. All opponents of
Adams did not rush into the Jackson camp. Many of them,
especially the Radicals, were perplexed and did nothing but
grumble.[5]

Van Buren was one of the very few who insisted that the
break was a throwback to the old division between Jefferson
and Hamilton. He had said this repeatedly, thinking the Republicans would wake up to political reality. When they did
not, when they continued regrouping themselves along arti-
ficial, personal lines, he undertook the task of making the
break permanent, which necessitated, of course, redefining
party principles and reestablishing party organization.

The making of the Democratic party—or, more precisely,
the revamping of the Republican party—was largely the work
of Martin Van Buren. While he was aided and abetted by

many—among whom were John H. Eaton, Hugh Lawson White, William B. Lewis, Francis Preston Blair, James Buchanan, Thomas Ritchie, Isaac Hill, Amos Kendall, and Thomas Hart Benton [6]—he alone discharged the tremendous task of basic reorganization. It took him two years to accomplish his ends and not until well into 1828 did the "Democratic party" finally emerge. Andrew Jackson naturally contributed an indispensable element to the work by lending his name and popularity to the movement, although he himself remained silent and inactive in Tennessee.[7] Moreover, there had already begun a movement in a few states away from personal factions and toward something approaching national politics.[8] But it was Van Buren who joined together the different sections of the country and united the followers of Calhoun and Crawford with the Jacksonians. It was he who tried to draw the East and West closer together. It was he who renewed the alliance between the North and South that lasted until 1860.[9]

Apart from his conscious effort to unite the Jackson groups, Van Buren forced a stronger states' rights doctrine into the party platform, insisted that the activity of the Federal government be reduced, and, in short, demanded that Jacksonians become doctrinaire Jeffersonians.

It has been pointed out by recent historians that in several respects Jackson's election to the presidency in 1828 is somewhat similar to Franklin D. Roosevelt's election in 1932. A few of these historians argue that the politicians surrounding these two men were interested primarily in electing their man, and only secondarily in creating a party or establishing political principles. The man came first; the principles would be found afterward.

Whatever truth there may be to this thesis regarding the politicians of either period, it can not be applied to Van Buren. He had been arguing principles long before he became a Jacksonian; and they were the same principles *after* he became a Jacksonian. With him the issues and the party came first; then he found his candidate.

Unlike so many other politicians who were driven to Jackson's support because of local conditions in their states, Van Buren's motives were different. He was the master of New York; he did not need a popular national cause or personality to reclaim a lost position. But had he been motivated by a concern for the New York situation he would never have gone over to the General. De Witt Clinton had been aboard the Jackson bandwagon long before the Senator showed any serious interest in the Tennessean. By shifting to Jackson, Van Buren was deliberately complicating the New York political scene; at the same time, he was placing the General in the awkward position of having to accept support from two long-standing enemies from the same state.

Nevertheless, Van Buren turned to Jackson. He did so because he could use the General to reform the party, eliminate Federalist principles from the national government, and oust Adams from office. He needed Jackson, more so than Jackson needed him. Yet, despite the need, and before joining the General's party, he asked for assurances that the "old systems" would be preserved. After joining, he did not hesitate to warn Jackson against avowing *"any opinion upon Constitutional questions at war with the doctrines of the Jeffersonian School."* [10] And Van Buren had a very clear idea of what those doctrines were.

The regard Jackson had for Van Buren's opinion and judgment on all the major issues during his eight years as President is proof that the New Yorker was not a politician who had to be taught what to believe and what side of an issue he was expected to support. Jackson was no fool; neither was he hypnotized by a wily magician. He appreciated Van Buren's solid worth as a statesman and political strategist.

To state that the Democratic party would never have appeared without Van Buren is nonsense. The services he rendered could have been performed by another equally skilled as a political theorist and professional politician. As a matter of fact, he himself never fully realized the long-range extent of his labors, and yet the alliances he concluded and the creed of government he borrowed constituted for many years the basic structure of the new organization. What he did was instinctive of a master politician.

As was to be expected, he approached his target rather indirectly at first. Toward the end of December, 1826, he wrote a long and confidential letter to Azariah C. Flagg, asserting that both he and the Regency might play an important role in the future affairs of the nation by the simple expedients of continued opposition in Congress and firmness in New York.

What I write to you is so far only confidential that you may in your best discretion communicate it to such of our friends as you think necessary. Mr. Wright will soon be with you as well as [Perley] Keyes and [Jonas] Earl. From them and our immediate friends in Albany Knower, Marcy and Croswell you know I have no secrets. The strong impressions previously made on the minds of Mr Adams & his Secretary etc as to Mr Clinton's views have been confirmed. . . . They now look upon him as an adversary on his own account. Without N. York they cannot make battle & to it every eye is directed. To secure so inconsiderable a personage even as myself has been deemed a matter of moment but I believe they are satisfied that that is out of the question & I am convinced *that John A King (who left here this morning) carries instructions to the liegemen to resist . . . my election* [to the Senate]. Under these circumstances they have determined to build up a party in N York to be led by Taylor Porter & Young & to be continued and sustained by the Genl Administration. . . . The federalists here are quieted by Taylor & Webster with assurances that a few Bucktail appointments are necessary & that after the next election Mr Adams will manifest his respect for the Federalists & his gratitude for their support in a suitable & strong manner. *I have ample means of knowing what is going on & the inducements for every step of consequence.* Depend upon it my dear Sir that there never existed a Cabinet that conducted the affairs of the Country upon so degrading a scale as the present. Every thing is made to bend to the election, & without any fixed principle of action or rule of conduct, the effect of every measure or appointment upon that single subject, is the controlling consideration. If the attempt now making have to please all parties by an equal distribution of favours amongst them succeed, it will certainly be the first time. I am morally certain that the present administration must go down & I firmly believe that such ought to be the case. To say this in my place before the election is with me a great consideration but I will be governed by the advice of my friends.

Immediately after the commencement of the session you must put your heads together & let me know precisely how the land lays. I would of course do it respectfully & on a subject on which the feelings of the State would be on my side viz the power of Congress over internal improvements. I approve Mr Croswell's course in keeping the party together but feel very solicitous that he should not enable Clinton & his friends to prejudice us abroad by insinuations that we at home are for the administration. No one knows better than himself how this is to be avoided without running counter to his general object. If we are discrete [*sic*] & wise we can play a great part in the coming contest. My language here to our friends is that we will support no man who does not come forward on the principles & in the form in which Jefferson & Madison were brought forward & this they will in the end all assent.[11]

In another letter, written to Benjamin F. Butler a week after the commencement of the Congressional session, the Senator pursued his point about delivering a "constitutional speech & therein reprobate strongly but respectfully the heresies of Messrs Adams & Clay on the subject of the power of the Federal government. . . ." [12] Fortunately he later dropped the matter, because he knew that to "play a great part" in the election he would have to act far more vigorously. Instead of continuing a long-drawn-out campaign in the Senate against the administration, he decided to attempt the unification of the opposition and thereby restore the party to the position it occupied before 1824.[13] The effect upon Adams, Clay, and the country at large would be far greater than any speech he might make. It meant that he had definitely and irrevocably abandoned his noncommittalism and had gone over to the Jacksonians. What he had in mind was not an agreement on a single issue such as he had made with Calhoun over the Panama question, but rather a strong and concrete coalition to last for years. No longer apprehensive of its effects at home, he brought New York along with him as his price of admission into the Jackson camp. He promptly advised the Regency, and editor Croswell was instructed "to do what was needful." From then on the *Argus* was to focus its guns on the White House. But the editor, always a cautious man, was slow in bringing his victims within range, and while a few desultory shots were aimed at Clay in February, 1827, not until March did the firing become systematic.

The speed with which Van Buren suddenly turned to Jackson was immediately communicated to the General, and Sam Houston stated peremptorily that the New Yorker's conversion was "in all good faith. I have not spoken to him only in the way of politeness since we met, but your friends who know him best are satisfied as to his course, and pleased with it." [14] The Hero too was probably pleased, although he did not break his silence to say so.

Van Buren's first step in the execution of his elaborate plan of uniting the several factions was to win over the Vice-President. The initiative for this first alliance seems to have come from the New Yorker, not the South Carolinian. So the Senator left Washington in December, 1826, accompanied by Stephen Van Rensselaer, and spent the Christmas holidays conferring with Calhoun at the home of William H. Fitzhugh of Virginia. Their conversations went unreported, but their final agreement was definitely known. Van Buren, speaking for many Radicals—although not all—and Calhoun, representing his own loyal group, agreed to join forces to promote Jackson's election in 1828. But what assurances were there that the former Crawfordites would respect this alliance? The Senator replied that as a start he would write to Thomas Ritchie, one of the foremost Southern leaders of the Radical group, and secure his support for the venture. Whereupon Calhoun set aside his doubts and the two men "united heart and hand" to defeat John Quincy Adams.[15]

To reconcile past differences between the new allies and also to keep the number of candidates down to a maximum of two—which would tend to reassert the two-party system—

Van Buren and Calhoun agreed to sponsor a national nominating convention. The idea was in accord with popular sentiment, and besides winning additional backing for their candidate it would cause favorite sons to refrain from seeking local nominations.

Van Buren discussed the possibility of a national convention with Samuel D. Ingham of Pennsylvania, and later with members of the Regency. On January 9, 1827, an editorial appeared in the Albany *Argus* reporting that a convention was under advisement in Washington but that nothing would be decided until popular reception of the idea had been ascertained.

Meanwhile Van Buren went ahead with his letter to Thomas Ritchie, and upon its completion submitted it to Calhoun and Ingham for their approval. Since they had no suggestions to make, it was forwarded to Richmond as written.

Ostensibly the Senator was arguing for a convention to be held in Jackson's favor, but more particularly he revealed to Ritchie his plan to reorganize the Republican party and to revive the alliance between the North and the South—or as he termed it, the alliance between the planters of the South and the plain Republicans of the North.

At the very beginning of his letter he admitted to his correspondent that he was "not tenacious whether we have a congressional caucus or a general convention, so that we have either." But he thought the convention had certain advantages. First of all it would concentrate the entire vote behind Jackson and achieve "what is of still greater importance, the *substantial reorganization of the old Republican Party."* [16] It would remove the "embarrassment" of those who had "scruples" regarding a caucus and would be "more in unison with the spirit of the times. . . . "

The only possible way to eliminate Adams, the letter continued, and restore "a better state of things" was to combine "Genl Jacksons personal popularity with the portion of old party feeling yet remaining." And since Adams would never submit his name to a convention, the Jacksonians could sponsor a meeting which of its very nature would tend to *"draw anew"* [17] the old Party lines. . . ." The subsequent election "would reestablish them; state nominations alone would fall far short of that object."

His plan, Van Buren said, would greatly improve the condition of Republicans in the Northern and Middle states by "substituting *party principle* for *personal preference* as one of the leading points in the contest." At the same time the fear of sectional rivalry would be greatly diminished. "Instead of the question being between a northern and Southern man, it would be whether or not the ties, which have heretofore bound together a great political party should be severed. The difference between the two questions would be found to be immense in the elective field. Altho this is a mere party consideration, it is not on that account less likely to be effectual."

All over the nation, he went on, even in New England, the divisions between Republicans and Federalists were still being maintained. He thought that this should be continued at all costs. Party distinctions should always be maintained, he argued, "and the old ones are the best of which the nature of the case admits. Political combinations between the inhabitants of the different states are unavoidable & the most natural & beneficial to the country is that between the planters of the South and the plain Republicans of the North. The country has once flourished under a party thus constituted & may again."

This letter of Van Buren's admits of no doubt that he was intent on "forming" the Democratic party. He said he wanted to produce a coalition between the great sections of the country, substitute principles for personalities, and "draw anew old Party lines" based on the natural divisions between the followers of Hamilton and those of Jefferson. It would take an enormous amount of work to engineer this plan, including much talk, convincing argument, and political maneuvering, but he thought that he was suited to the task.

Continuing his letter to Ritchie, Van Buren wondered aloud whether Americans would ever face up to the fact that the party system was the best and only means of eliminating prejudice between the free and slave states. "It would take longer than our lives," he mused "(even if it were practicable) to create new party feelings to keep those masses together. If the old ones are suppressed, geographical divisions founded on local interests or what is more, prejudices between free and slave-holding states will inevitably take their place." In the past, he declared, party attachments furnished an antidote to sectional prejudices "by producing counteracting feelings." Only when those attachments were "broken down" was it possible for "the clamour against the Southern Influence and African Slavery" to make headway in the North. "Formerly attacks upon Southern Republicans were regarded by those of the north as assaults upon their political brethren & resented accordingly. This all powerful sympathy has been much weakened, if not, destroyed by the amalgamating policy of Mr. Monroe." This sympathy can and should be revived, he said, and the proposed convention would be "eminently serviceable in effecting that object. The failure of the last caucus furnishes no argument agt a convention nor would it against another caucus.[18] The condition of things is essentially different. Then the South was divided, now it is united. Then we had several parties now we have in substance but two. . . ."

It would be a mistake to interpret Van Buren's words as a defense of the slave system of the South. He simply recognized that the political power in that section of the nation was in the hands of the plantation owners. For his immediate purposes he was attempting to ally that power with its counterpart in the North. In the 1820s, Van Buren had come to no definite conclusion regarding slavery. He was neither its foe nor its friend. His papers are remarkably free of any discussion of the question, and while he had great affection for Southerners as a group, he had no strong feeling about their "peculiar institution." His later opposition had not yet developed. What he was doing in this letter was stating an historical fact, as he knew and understood it.

Van Buren's final point to Ritchie was that a nominating

convention would have an enormous effect upon Jackson. If the General won election merely on account of his military service, without reference to party or principle, he said, that would be one thing. "His election as the result of a combined and concerted effort of a political party, holding in the main, to certain tenets & opposed to certain prevailing principles, might be another and a far different thing."

But whether or not a convention ever materialized was unimportant as long as the other objects in the program were achieved—and in particular the formation of a national party united behind Jackson and holding "certain tenets." Van Buren never lost sight of his true goal, and to commence his labors with as strong a "push" as possible he had written to Ritchie "knowing there is not another man in the union can render as much service to the cause in which we are engaged as yourself." [19] Would he consent to the alliance? Van Buren waited for a reply.

The editor of the Richmond *Enquirer,* along with the Junto, controlled many Crawford votes in the South and had been one of the earliest and most vociferous opponents of the Adams administration. Like many another, Ritchie at first was reluctant to support Jackson,[20] but the cogency of Van Buren's arguments, the political necessity of taking sides, and the defeat of John Randolph for reelection to the Senate from Virginia at the hands of John Tyler compelled him to change his mind. Although he hesitated a few months, in April he finally accepted Jackson as his presidential candidate and agreed to the alliance—the union of the "planters of the South and the plain Republicans of the North." [21]

Although the Senator from New York never made his speech on internal improvements to "reprobate" the heresies of Adams and Clay, he seized every opportunity to badger the administration. As the self-appointed watchdog of the Constitution he directed most of his criticism toward particular measures which enhanced Federal powers at the expense of the states. For the next two years he worked hard to force a more precise doctrine into the framework of the Jacksonian party. Even in his letter of acceptance when reelected Senator by the New York state legislature, he promised to use his position to "protect the remaining rights reserved to the states by the federal constitution: [and] to restore those of which they have been divested by construction." [22]

His jovial spirits emanating from his initial success in reorganizing the party and his reelection to office, were shaken on February 13, 1827, when a woolens bill was introduced from the lower house which threatened the very existence of his newborn alliance. Representative Daniel Webster, who had now reversed his earlier position at the insistence of his constituents, was responsible for guiding the bill through the lower house, where it had been passed by the vote of 106 to 95. It was an administration measure loathed in the South, welcomed in the Middle and Western states, and received with mixed sentiments in New England.

The Tariff of 1824 had increased the protective rates on iron, hemp, lead, woolen goods, and glass, and included a specific duty on raw wool. The last provision cut deeply into the profits of manufacturers, because Great Britain, shortly thereafter, reduced her own duty on raw wool and thus permitted the English industrialist to undersell his American rival. The cry of the manufacturers to right this injustice was coupled with, and weakened by, the insistence of the woolgrowers that they too be given additional protection.

When the bill of 1827 reached the Senate, its framers thought it was pleasing to both groups, but Van Buren labeled it a measure "immediately directed to the protection of manufactures. . . ." [23] It amounted, he said, to a "simple and unreasonable increase of duties upon a single article"—woolens— without proportionately improving the condition of farmers.[24] As a woolgrower himself, with $20,000 invested in sheep, he had more than sufficient reason to dislike the bill.[25] But he did not voice his objections on the Senate floor, for there were others who could do that with greater eloquence. As the representative of New York he was morally bound to give the bill his full support; and as a Jacksonian leader depending upon the votes of Pennsylvania, Ohio, Kentucky, Illinois, New Jersey, and Indiana in 1828, he could not give the impression that his party members were freetraders. By the same token he was constrained from openly adopting the principle of protection lest Southerners, in anger, stampede his efforts to drive them into one party with Northerners.

It was a tight dilemma in which Van Buren found himself, and as yet he had no idea how to escape. He took little part in the debates, although he did introduce an amendment on February 19 to raise the duty on raw wool to an amount equal to that on manufactured woolens. His motion was defeated, 24 to 23, but had it passed he would probably have voted for the entire bill out of regard for the wishes of his state.[26] All other efforts to recommit the measure were lost, and on February 28 it came up for final action.

Van Buren was present in the Senate chamber on that day, taking part in a discussion over the regulation of commerce between England and the United States. A short while later, when this debate ended, Senator Robert Y. Hayne of South Carolina rose and moved that the tariff bill be laid on the table. It could be effectively killed this way, since Congress was scheduled to adjourn in three days. As the vote was taken, Van Buren, along with several others, failed to respond when their names were read. A tie resulted, and the Vice-President then repudiated the protective stand he had taken in 1816.   To satisfy the slave-owning minorities of the South, he killed the bill.

It has been erroneously asserted that Van Buren was in his seat when the final vote was taken, but remained silent for expedient reasons.[27] Evidence for this statement is his audible presence a few minutes before. However, during his lifetime he denied the allegation, and in his *Autobiography* he maintained that his absence from the Senate was occasioned by a promise he had given "to accompany a friend on a visit to the Congressional Cemetery. . . ." [28] The excuse is hard to believe, but evidence that he was nowhere near the Senate chamber comes from another source: in July, 1827, he spoke before a meeting of Albany citizens and publicly declared that he missed his vote because the chairman of the committee of manufactures assured him that the measure would not be brought up for final action at that time and he had therefore left the hall. Had he been present, it seems probable that those members of Congress who read his Albany speech, which was widely circulated, would have branded him a liar; yet we have no record of such charges. On the other hand, in his own day, Van Buren was simply charged with purposeful absence and there is no way to prove or disprove it.

There was, of course, an immediate, divided, and violent reaction to the Senate's handling of the tariff. Calhoun's deciding vote, wrote one Rhode Islander, "has killed him everywhere north of the Potomac." [29] The legislature of Virginia referred to tariff laws as "unconstitutional, unwise, unjust, unequal and oppressive." [30] Protectionists, ably abetted by Hezekiah Niles and Mathew Carey, undertook an organized campaign against the principle of free trade. Others spoke of a general convention to support protection, and Henry Clay issued the call. "Let all persons (friends of D.M.I.I.[31] and the Admin) without regard to party denominations heretofore existing, be brought out. . . . Let the meeting publish an address, well drawn, temperate in language, but firm in purpose, and eloquent and animated in composition. This meeting will form a nucleus." [32]

The Albany *Argus*, like other Jacksonian organs, reserved comment.

Van Buren did not allow the session to end without taking one last shot at the administration. When Adams proposed closing American ports to trade with certain British colonial seaport cities in order to extract from the English a fair and reciprocal trade agreement, the New York Senator was on his feet protesting the adverse effect such a policy would have upon the commercial centers of the United States. In a lengthy and comprehensive speech he reviewed the maritime history of the country for the last twenty years to prove that the administration had proposed the most restrictive and prohibitive system ever contemplated by this nation during peace time. [33] Writing with an overtone of self-praise to a friend in Albany, he explained:

The administration have, to say the least of it, been very unfortunate in this affair & will find it very difficult to avoid the imputation of having trifled with a very valuable portion of our commerce.   In the retaliatory measures N York will have to be deprived of her lake trade.   I spoke at some length upon the subject & was gratified by the declarations of very many of the Senators that they had not before understood the merits of the dispute.[34]

A watered-down colonial trade bill finally passed the Senate three days before the close of the session, but the House refused to consent to the amendments and the measure died.[35]

If the opposition party prided itself on obstructing the passage of all bills sponsored by the administration, whether good or bad, then Van Buren, Calhoun, and the other Jackson leaders might well have looked back on the second session of this Nineteenth Congress with great satisfaction. Nothing of importance was accomplished. Adams's great nationalistic program still lay in abeyance. Lacking spectacular and dramatic debates or even interesting measures, with the exception of the tariff, the proceedings of Congress elicited little enthusiasm from the public. Newspapers like the Albany *Argus,* the Richmond *Enquirer,* and Duff Green's *United States Telegraph,* therefore, had ample opportunity to rake over the "corrupt bargain" charge or twit Clay and Adams on any minor incident, either past or present. When the Secretary of State, in accordance with accepted political procedure, removed several Jacksonians as printers of the laws of the United States, the *Argus* cried that it was "the first movement of the same spirit which produced the *alien and sedition laws* and brought in the reign of terror in 1798." Isaac Hill, editor of the *New Hampshire Patriot,* fell victim to Clay's incipient "terror" and Croswell rushed to his defense.[36] Duff Green, who had been diffusing antiadministration propaganda almost singlehandedly for months, welcomed the Regency organ's entrance into the fray. By mid-March the position of the *Argus* was established.   One month later Thomas Ritchie joined the Jackson party and added his bit to the journalistic furor that was beginning to rise.

Van Buren, in the spring of 1827, was anxious to quit Washington and start another one of his celebrated tours.   This time the outlying counties of New York were not on his schedule, for his purpose was not local in nature.   In January he had been invited to journey through the South, and he could ill afford to pass up this splendid opportunity to strengthen the North-South alliance to a greater degree than he had already achieved with Ritchie.[37]   To visit Crawford in Georgia and receive his pledge of loyalty to the new coalition seemed essential to Van Buren.   Coincident with this, he could address gatherings of Republicans along the route, assuring them of Northern affection.   He could demonstrate by his own words and actions that it was "most natural & beneficial to the country" that the "planters of the South and the plain Republicans of the North" ally themselves.   For these reasons he cordially accepted the invitation and urged his friend Colonel James A. Hamilton of New York, son of Alexander Hamilton, to accompany him.   "The jaunt will be a delightful one," he wrote, "& the Major [James Hamilton, Jr. of South Carolina] & Calhoun will shew us all that is good in S.C." [38]   He proposed that they visit all the "intermediate places" between Richmond and Charleston and then return home by way of "the Western States"; but apparently Hamilton begged off.   "You will do yourself great injustice & grievously disappoint me," Van Buren replied, "if you do not go with me."   Perhaps Hamilton did not like the Western portion of the trip, for the Senator said that when they arrived in Richmond "the question can be made whether the western part of the expedition shall be prosecuted or abandoned." [39]   Nevertheless Hamilton persisted in his refusal and Van Buren turned to his crony, Churchill C. Cambreleng, a Southerner by birth, and persuaded him to be his companion on the trip.

The states the two New Yorkers proposed to visit were Virginia, North Carolina, South Carolina, and Georgia. For some reason—perhaps the lack of time—the Western portion of the journey was abandoned. They were accompanied as far as Charleston by William Drayton and Major James Hamilton, Jr., both prominent Southern congressmen. News of the Little Magician's grand tour preceded him; two weeks before his departure Andrew Jackson was given a short account of it by Major Hamilton. "The Buck tail or Republican party," the letter read, "are beginning to move in New York. Van Buren the first man in that State is *zealously cordially* and *entirely* with us. He travels to the South with me after the adjournment to spend his Spring in Carolina and Georgia. . . ." [40]

No sooner had the carriage conveying the four men left Washington when the *National Intelligencer* began a series of editorial attacks on Van Buren. Joseph Gales and William Seaton, the editors of the newspaper, had supported Crawford in the election of 1824 and had found a valuable friend in the Senator from New York. However, with Adams's subsequent elevation to the presidency, the two journalists, who were also the public printers, endorsed the nationalistic program of the new executive and renounced their former adherence to the Radical party.

The break between Van Buren and the editors occurred in 1827 when the New Yorker, on the floor of the upper house, chanced to remark that "the condition of the press might be improved and respect for the Senate and accuracy in publication of its proceedings better secured by a judicious revision of the laws relative to the public printing at large." [41] Gales and Seaton were not men to allow a deliberate slur on their journalistic abilities to pass unnoticed, and they responded promptly and with vigor. They did not limit their rebuttal to a discussion of the particular question Van Buren had raised. Over a period of two months they charged that the Senator was an arch villain who was plotting to subvert the democratic institutions of the country. "There are intrigues on foot," wrote the editors, "to place the election of President and Vice President of the United States within the control of a Central

Junta in Washington, of which Mr. Van Buren's happy genius is the ascendant influence. . . . " He was its spokesman, "the head and representative, if he be not both its parent and guardian. . . ." His projects and "schemes for executing them" were notorious, and it was known that he planned to introduce into the Senate of the United States "his system of party discipline, and to procure the rejection of nominations, not upon the question of honesty or fitness for trust, but upon the test of persons' having voted one way or another at a preceding election." The object of his recent remarks, continued the editors, was plain to all. He intended "to control the press here by means of the printing of the Senate, and elsewhere by other means. . . . " He was a "Master Spirit" by whose agency "machinery has been established to substitute the regular operation of the Government, and to control the popular election by means of organized clubs in the States, and organized presses every where." [42]

The editors closed in on their quarry by broadcasting to the nation the fact that Van Buren was engaged in making the Democratic party. It is "lamentable," they said, that such excellent senators as Dickerson, Macon, Smith, Benton, and Chandlers, "not to speak of others," have joined Van Buren "under the standard of a *new* cabalistic party organization. . . ." [43] In 1824 the Little Magician acted "with firmness and consistency. . . . But when he comes forward with the Shibboleth of a new party in his mouth . . . we must be excused if we treat him as he has treated us, downrightly. . . ." [44]

Gales and Seaton were not the only outsiders who knew of Van Buren's activities. The Virginia *Constitutional Whig* reported that the "combinations for electing Gen. Jackson are nearly complete. *Combinations*—and among whom? The People? No—but the Members of Congress." A month later the editor declared that the "combinations" were of Van Buren's doing.[45]

Unquestionably the Little Magician was engaged in every plan he had been accused of, except one. He was not plotting to subvert the democratic institutions of the country. Rather he believed that the only way to perpetrate a democratic American government—indeed the liberty of the American people—was through a strictly regulated party system. If Jeffersonian idealism were to triumph again, Republicans needed basic training in organization. By ranging them under "the standard" of a revitalized party, their liberties would be safe from attack.

The Albany *Argus,* in Van Buren's name, replied to the tirades of Gales and Seaton and was seconded by the Richmond *Enquirer.* The "Master Spirit" had just passed through Virginia when Ritchie unconditionally went over to Jackson. Henceforth the *Argus* and *Enquirer* exchanged leading articles and the editors began corresponding with one another.[46] The *National Intelligencer,* its eyes peeled for every shift in the political wind, observed this "congeniality of feeling" between the two newspapers and commented that there no doubt existed some hidden "identity of purpose." Croswell cheerfully assented to this last remark but denied that it was secretive: "Professing a common political faith—members of the same great national party—and mutually seeking to promote its welfare, such 'an identity of purpose' was not only natural, but we are free to say for ourselves, desirable." [47]

The planters and plain Republicans, it seemed, were getting along quite well.

Publicly, Van Buren paid no attention to the attack,[48] but Southerners who were fascinated by his charming manner as he passed among them were only too pleased to echo the *Argus* and *Enquirer.* Gales and Seaton "are very angry, too, at Mr. Van Buren," noted the Columbia *Telescope,* "but as this gentleman is not unlikely to *succeed General Jackson* if he keeps steadily to his *present plan of public conduct,* they will be glad by and by to kiss and be friends." [49] At a dinner given to the Hero of New Orleans by the citizens of Gallatin, Sumner County, Tennessee, the celebrants toasted: "Martin Van Buren —A Republican of the Old School." [50]

The first major stop for the two New York travelers was Charleston, South Carolina, where they were most heartily welcomed. Shortly after their arrival both men were invited to a dinner given by the officers of the Seventeenth Regiment in honor of their Colonel, Robert Y. Hayne. There, after the meal had been completed, Van Buren was asked to address the group and propose a toast. The Senator obliged and briefly remarked that he was proud to associate his name "with State Sovereignty." Then he raised his glass and in a firm voice said: "A speedy extinguishment of Sectional and State jealousies—the best and most appropriate sacrifice that can be made upon the altar of State Rights." [51] With words like these he soon had Southerners jostling one another to shake his hand, and it was no wonder that many of them thought he was a presidential candidate himself.[52] The editors of the *National Intelligencer* knew otherwise, and tried to warn their Southern friends. "The 'organization' of a party," they said, "opposed to the present Executive Administration, right or wrong, has been admitted, by the confidential organs of that party. . . . Admitted, did we say? It has been exulted in. . . ." [53]

Having toured the city and spoken with most of its leading citizens about the alliance to promote Jackson's election, Van Buren prepared to leave by ship for Savannah, Georgia, to visit William H. Crawford. But a storm kept him in Charleston for an additional three days. With this extra time on his hands he composed a long communication for his lieutenants in Albany. In one of the most frank and revealing letters he ever wrote— one that he never had the opportunity to destroy—Van Buren enumerated the particular advantages to be gained by his friends in New York as a consequence of his "excursion."

He was convinced, he said, that by extending the number of his acquaintances over the widest possible area he would be much more useful to his Republican friends. "Personally this was important to me but politically considered I regard it as of greater importance to our cause." Unfortunately, in the past, New York politicians confined "their intercourse & views too exclusive to home concerns. The consequence has been that out of the State they were but little known & when their friends at home stood in want of their influence abroad it could not be given." This, he explained, can now be corrected, because "the circumstances of the moment" enabled him to visit "other States under the most favourable auspices. . . ." [54] Watch, he was saying in effect, how the power of New York, under proper direction, will grow.

As soon as the Senator left for Savannah the opposition presses re-sounded their warning cries. "Van Buren has gone to Georgia—*cui bono?* There is some intrigue on foot." They described him as one of "the most dangerous and designing politicians in the United States." And for proof they asked their readers to notice how the "tones" of the Charleston *Mercury* had been "considerably sharpened and elevated" since his visit to that city. [55]

On reaching Georgia, Van Buren went immediately to see Crawford. The old Radical, now totally removed from the national scene, was still recovering from his prolonged illness. He greeted his New York friend while propped up in a large chair, trying to appear like the commanding and imposing politician he once was. But that was now impossible even if Van Buren did keep up the pretense.

The Senator did not mince words with his host but came right to the point. The alliance he had formed had already proved acceptable to Ritchie and other members of the Radical party in the South, he said, and if Crawford would unite with them, his conversion would draw after it the few remaining holdouts. For a moment the Georgian was silent; then in a halting voice he gave his consent to the coalition. But he had a reservation respecting the party's candidates for the presidential election of 1828. Although Jackson met with his unqualified approval, he could not abide the insufferable John Caldwell Calhoun and proposed instead that the office of Vice-President be left vacant on the ballot, allowing the several states to write in the names of their favorite sons. Van Buren expected something of the kind, for he had long known of the political rivalry between the two men. But he refused to countenance such an undisciplined method of conducting a presidential campaign, and stated flatly that Calhoun had to be kept on the ticket.[56] Crawford persisted in his arguments and finally offered old Nathaniel Macon as a possible candidate, but the New Yorker gravely shook his head. The alliance, he maintained, would die prematurely if Calhoun were purged.

Further discussion proved fruitless and Van Buren dropped the matter, satisfied with Crawford's promise of support for Jackson and loyalty to the coalition. For the remainder of his stay in Georgia he visited the most distinguished men of that state,[57] talking to them about the alliance and Jackson's candidacy. To an especially appreciative audience he might launch into a history of the Republican and Federalist parties or discuss states' rights, the Hartford Convention, or the schism of 1824. He spread such good will that his campaign methods were said to have reached new heights.[58]

Not everyone was pleased, however. "Martin Van Buren, *Cabinet maker* and Joiner, No. 1 Albany street, New York," wrote one South Carolinian, "informs his friends and the public that he has with great labour and sagacity succeeded in the composition of a new Panacea. . . ." It treats the "most diffi-cult disorders . . . in the system of political men." It is "sold in bottles each containing printed directions for its use, signed by the proprietor—and may be had of the following persons:" [59]

Boston	The Statesman	Office
New York	The Enquirer	*do.*
Philadelphia	The Palladium	*do.*
Washington City	The Telegraph	*do.*
Richmond	The Enquirer	*do.*
Charleston	The Mercury	*do.*

Having done all that was possible to combine the Jackson, Calhoun, and Crawford factions in the South, Van Buren left Georgia and started back home. He planned to return through Columbia, South Carolina, but was unaware of the fact that Dr. Thomas Cooper was waiting to see him there. This fiercely radical Southerner, who was not above preaching the destruction of the Union whenever Congress spoke of raising the tariff, had watched Van Buren's career with interest, and on occasion had written to him offering advice. As a noted economist and scientist and as a friend of Jefferson he commanded the New Yorker's respect; but sometimes Cooper wanted to dictate policy to the party chieftain. In this spring of 1827 he followed the accounts of Van Buren's tour, and was anxious to speak to him on his return homeward. "Van Buren & Camreling [sic] are parading through our Southern States," he informed Gulian C. Verplanck, "where they will be duly honoured & feted. They have not been here yet, but I expect them in a week. Hamilton shewed them all the Lions of Charleston & Savannah." [60] Very likely he met the Senator the following week, and it is just as likely that he had a long conversation with him about the tariff. For the next year the famed doctor was to continue harassing Van Buren with pleading letters to save the country by advocating the principle of free trade. In July he went further by warning a gathering of townspeople in Columbia that the time was fast approaching when the South would have to "calculate the value" of the Federal Union. [61]

After leaving South Carolina, Van Buren continued his journey northward at a leisurely pace. As the ablest champion of Jackson, as "the absorbing theme of general conversation" (as one Virginian put it [62]), he was invited to attend numerous public dinners, some of which he had to decline. But where he could not appear he sent a letter of regret, which ended usually with a salute to the states' rights doctrine, a call for the passage of resolutions deprecating the policies of the administration, or a plea for the election of Andrew Jackson. [63] He had traversed "the whole Atlantic," remarked one critic, "from New York to Florida, arraying the means which are to relieve the people of the necessity of choosing their rulers, and of governing themselves." [64]

Finally, on May 12, he arrived in Washington after a two-month absence. By now he was a national figure, if he had not already been one, as well as a national politician, perhaps the first of his kind. [65] The administration men gossiped over the purposes of his tour, [66] and watched with undisguised anger and irritation as he calmly paid his respects to Clay and Adams. With the Secretary of State he engaged in "no political conversation," but "very civilly" invited him to visit New York.[67] At the White House, he made a perfunctory call which all the more distressed the dour President. When the New Yorker left, Adams recounted in his *Diary* the movements of Van Buren and Cambreleng since the previous March:

They are generally understood to have been electioneering, and Van Buren is now the great electioneering manager for General Jackson, as he was before the last election for Mr. Crawford. He is now acting over the part in the affairs of the Union which Aaron Burr performed in 1799 and 1800; and there is much resemblance of character, manners, and even person, between the two men. Van Buren, however, has improved as much in the art of electioneering upon Burr as the State of New York has grown in relative strength and importance in the Union. Van Buren has now every prospect of success in his present movements, and he will avoid the rock upon which Burr afterwards split.[68]

The Little Magician, having completed one portion of the work involved in reorganizing the party, left for Albany the following day. As he sat sprawled in his carriage he must have felt very pleased with himself. He had laid a firm basis for the emergence of the Democratic party by bringing about a North-South alliance. He had assisted in reviving the two-party system. He had discredited the Monroe heresy and had pledged himself and the party "anew" to the Jeffersonian faith. More work had to be done, but the start was good. His remaining task was to draw the East and West together. That, however, posed a bit of a problem, since the best means of accomplishing it lay in raising the tariff.

XI: FARMERS, ANTIMASONS, AND LIBERATED CLINTONIANS

A SQUAT, SQUARE-JAWED man sat in his study musing over the last two years of his presidency. Greatness shone in his eyes, but most people saw only the cold, uncompromising stare of an unbending Puritan. If Adams were tactless, irritable, and pessimistic he had more than sufficient cause. Fruitless quarreling had typified his term in office. The Panama congress had ended in a fizzle, and his mighty program was ridiculed as an attempt to build "light-houses in the skies." The Vice-President then started a pointless argument with him that ended with the two highest officers in the country exchanging verbal handgrenades.

The atmosphere in and around Washington itself reflected some of the bitterness that issued from Capitol Hill. The city's social life lacked sparkle, which was partly blamed on the Adamses because of their haughty airs. For recreation all the President ever seemed to do was swim in the Potomac River on summer days. Fortunately, Congress was in session only four or five months a year, and when it adjourned everyone could go home to more pleasant surroundings.[1]

What happened to John Quincy Adams is tragic. He could have been a great President, but like his father before him he was ruined by politics. John Adams had a spy and betrayer for a Secretary of State; John Quincy Adams had a man notoriously "wicked" and charged with corruption and fraud in winning his position. The "vulgar" Clay, who drank Bourbon in "heaping quantities" and swore like a wardheeler, could remember the time when he was much beloved. His swaggering, impudent, and audacious manner had once fascinated, but now seemed only to gall. A great man, he was his own worst enemy; and he too was a victim of fumbling politics.

Some men might have become maudlin over their unhappy fate, but not Clay. He prided himself on being a fighter and was "damned" if he was going to sit idly by watching Van Buren fit together the many Republican factions to form a single party.[2] By the spring of 1827, Clay was trying to start a similar movement among anti-Jacksonians. Finally, an "amalgamation" meeting to form the vanguard for a concerted drive toward shaping a respectable organization to support Adams's reelection in 1828 was held in Boston. It urged the obliteration of the "old political landmarks" (how different from Van Buren's technique) and the fusion of all groups into a new and energetic "American Party."[3] With the President and Secretary of State as standard-bearers, and the American system as the creed of the movement, this was Federalism reasserted on the national level. As such it proved particularly attractive to certain sections in the North and East.

Thus when the Pennsylvania Society for the Promotion of Manufactures and the Mechanic Arts called upon farmers and manufacturers throughout the nation to hold state conventions and appoint at least five delegates to meet at Harrisburg on July 30, 1827, for the purpose of devising some means of improving their conditions, and when the American party showed an excessive interest in the proposed gathering, the Jackson campaign managers logically assumed that the administration was behind it. With protectionist meetings planned in most of the Northern states, the Jacksonians were cautiously hesitant when asked to comment.

In New York a convention was summoned to meet at Albany on July 10, and Hezekiah Niles, the nation's most vocal protectionist, gave it considerable play in his newspaper.[4] Marcy, with his thumb on the popular pulse, advised Van Buren that "political enemies have been insidiously industrious in this part of the state in circulating the report that you defeated the *law for the protection & encouragement of domestic industries."* In light of this he thought the Senator had better do something quickly. The people in the western districts of New York, wrote Marcy, were of the opinion that the Administration favored "protecting & encouraging domestic manufactures etc and that this interest is to be jeopardized if Genl Jackson succeeds." [5]

Van Buren had already anticipated these rumors and planned to give them the lie by taking part in the Albany convention. He instructed Cambreleng to do a bit of research in the "woollen business," and learn the exact duty on woolens prior to the tariff of 1824, along with the approximate increase in capital investment throughout Massachusetts for the last three years. In addition, he asked for a tabulation of the vote by New York representatives on the Pennsylvania amendment for the insertion of iron in the tariff bill of 1827. These figures he wanted by July 10, in time for his address before the Albany manufacturers.[6]

All the while the *Argus,* in highly ambiguous language, was trying to indicate the road that Regency members were expected to follow. "We confess," said Editor Croswell, "that we feel an interest in this question; and that we hope to witness the adoption of such judicious and salutary measures as shall lead to a practical advancement of all the interests dependent upon such encouragement, particularly those of the Wool-grower and Farmer." Lacking the virtues of clarity and directness, the newspaper hoped to appear protariff by upholding the claims of the agrarians, even though, at the same time, it was equivocal regarding the interests of manufacturers. Respecting the Harrisburg convention, Croswell warned that it could only succeed in its object provided "designing politicians" were kept from perverting "these proceedings to party and personal purposes." [7] In short, the convention was suspect until it proved itself free from any connection with Adams and Clay.[8]

In the meantime, Southerners, to neutralize the agitation raised in the North, held meetings of protest. Thomas Cooper reported that in Columbia, Charleston, and elsewhere, "feelings are becoming hourly more exasperated." The time was at hand, he boldly asserted, for the South Carolina legislature to order her representatives to leave the Congress should a new and higher tariff replace the old.[9]

As policy-maker of the party, Van Buren was in a difficult position. He had to placate Southerners on this issue and yet convince Northerners that the Jacksonians were the honest advocates of protection. He was not alone in observing his predicament, for Daniel Webster saw it too. "Mr. Van Buren, I perceive has been too wise to place himself in opposition to the woolens bill. How his Southern & *City* friends will like this, I know not, but think it will cause them some embarrassment." [10]

It was with this bright spotlight of public interest glaring down at him that Van Buren delivered an hour-long speech in Albany on July 10 before a gathering of men intent on securing greater "promotion of the interests of wool growers and manufacturers." His immediate object in attending the meeting, he afterwards reflected, was to deny the imputation that his actions in the Senate the previous February were motivated by a personal distaste for all tariffs.[11] Arriving in the hall after the convention had been organized, and accompanied by his friends Benjamin Knower and Charles E. Dudley, he was invited by the chairman, Stephen Van Rensselaer, to take a seat on the podium. Van Buren refused the offer and instead "chose an eligible position in the crowd," where he waited until everyone had spoken who desired to do so. Then he rose and asked to be recognized.

The crowd was very attentive as he began his address, especially since he opened by giving the reasons for his absence from the Senate the day the tariff bill was voted upon. After explaining away that delicate matter he went on to a consideration of the bill itself, which he said had been "injust" to the woolgrower and unrightfully generous to others. To correct this inequality, he had voted to return the measure to the committee, but to his "surprise and regret" the manufacturers had opposed such a proposal and the motion was killed. Rather cleverly, he then intimated that the bill, taken as a whole, had not gone far enough to suit him, when actually it was merely the raw-wool provision which he felt was inadequate.

At one point in his address Van Buren obligingly stated his opinion on tariffs in general. He resorted to a few high-flown phrases, which could be variously interpreted, but which most of his listeners apparently liked. Some twelve years later he claimed he was trying to tell them that as their representative he felt duty-bound "to carry out their wishes" regarding the needs of manufacturers.[12] What he actually said, however, was not nearly so understandable. He declared ambiguously that he would sponsor any tariff which was "temperate and wise and therefore salutary" in promoting "every branch of domestic production and industry. . . ."

In fairness to Van Buren it should be said that he would have been the first to help the farmer in every possible way. This, he reckoned, was an important Republican doctrine that should be reaffirmed by the Jacksonians. But he would not favor the manufacturers in the same way, partly because this was a Hamiltonian notion but principally because a higher rate of protection would react unfavorably against the great mass of people in the country. Obviously he could not divulge this to his audience, and therefore resorted to such vague words as "temperate," "wise," and "salutary" in describing the type of tariff he favored. In addition, he did not approve of industrialists thrusting their interests into politics—especially the Adams kind of politics. He feared that the Harrisburg convention "proceeded more from the closet of the politician than the workshop of the manufacturer." He concluded his speech by saying that whatever happened at the convention in Pennsylvania, he hoped no one would attempt to disguise its true purpose.[13]

As Van Buren returned to his seat most of the members of the audience were convinced that he was basically in agreement with them on the principle of increased protection. However, Van Buren liked to tell the story about one man, who believed he detected inconsistencies in the speaker's remarks, and turned to Benjamin Knower exclaiming:

"Mr. Knower! that was a very able speech!"

"Yes, very able." was the reply.

"Mr. Knower! on which side of the Tariff question was it?"

"That is the very point I was thinking about when you first spoke to me," answered the puzzled Knower.[14]

Although uncertainty of Van Buren's exact position bothered some, only a few, such as the Albany *Daily Advertiser,* classed him as antitariff. The majority of New Yorkers were otherwise convinced, and letters poured into the *Argus* office congratulating the Senator on his "policy of encouraging domestic manufactures of every kind as well as the agricultural interest. . . ."[15]   Copies of the address were distributed to influential congressmen.[16]   Hezekiah Niles reprinted large portions of it and commented that the Albany convention was of especial significance "because of the attendance and proceedings of Mr Van Buren. . . ."[17]   Thomas Cooper was less favorably impressed by the speech of his friend. "From what I can gather on perusing the imperfect reports of the meeting at Albany, you incline to support the principle of a Tariff of protection. I regret it for it is unworthy [of] your good sense, & political firmness."[18]   Jesse Buel, a stalwart Bucktail, described the address as "a moddle of its kind, its doctrines sound and conclusions irresistible." He believed, however, that with the introduction of another woolens bill in the House of Representatives, the New York delegation would attach hemp and iron riders on it in order to hold Pennsylvania and Kentucky. In that event, he reasoned, "our Yankee brethren will knock the horse in the head, before they will let him carry through such a load."[19]

Disregarding the political jockeying to be essayed in the next Congress, James Wolcott, Jr. said that unless a new woolens bill was passed, factories would close their doors. "It is believed here," he explained to Van Buren, "that . . . the passing or rejecting of the bill, rests much with you." [20]

On Monday, July 30, 1827, 100 delegates (of whom 18 came from New York) representing 13 states arrived in Harrisburg to suggest some means of redressing the grievances of manufacturers and farmers.   Joseph Ritner of Pennsylvania was chosen president of the convention, but the men who took the most active part in the proceedings were Hezekiah Niles, Mathew Carey, and Charles J. Ingersoll.   Only five days were needed for the members to agree to their general object, and in a spirit of perfect accord they drew up a memorial and petition to Congress demanding "early and effectual interposition" to support the woolen interests in the country.   They proposed a duty of 20 cents per pound on raw wool, to be increased $2\frac{1}{2}$ cents annually until it reached 50 cents per pound. Woolens, which sold from 50 cents to $6.00 per square yard in foreign markets, were to receive a 40 percent ad valorem rate, with an annual increase of 5 percent until they stood at 50 percent.   A 1 cent per pound duty on hammered bar iron was suggested, along with protection for flax, hemp, and distilled spirits.   No figures were quoted for the last three items, allowing Congress itself to determine the rates.   On Friday, August 3, the memorial was signed by 97 men, while the task of drafting an address was left in the capable hands of Hezekiah Niles. The members then adjourned, fully satisfied that their suggestions would be enacted into law at the next session of Congress.[21]

The reaction in New York to the Harrisburg convention was generally enthusiastic.   In the main, western farmers and capitalists hoped that the tariff would become a campaign issue in 1828 and would thus permit them to express their feelings through the ballot box.[22] Van Buren and the Regency men, with an eye to the Southern alliance, were reluctant to take such a drastic stand, but they knew that the subject could not be evaded indefinitely.

The commercial groups all over the East stoutly protested the arguments given at Harrisburg, but they were counted part of a fast-diminishing minority. Only in the South was opposition virtually unanimous, and the furor which rose from that section would not be stilled. There, Jackson was pictured as antitariff, which was presumably substantiated by his famous letter of April, 1824, to Littleton H. Coleman. In the letter the General called for a "judicious" tariff, and quite naturally his remark gave rise to various interpretations depending on the particular section of the country in which it was quoted. However, no one had to clarify the position of Adams and Clay. To the Southern mind, they were confirmed protariff men.

During the remaining half year, the *Argus* followed a cautious and somewhat confusing line—or so it seemed to those who did not understand Regency mentality—in respect to the question. The first principle from which the editor proceeded was that no national issue should ever be permitted to disrupt New York politics if it could be avoided. Thus the *Argus* merely reported the many tariff meetings that were held throughout the summer but refrained from commenting upon them.[23] However, in October, when Hezekiah Niles completed and published the address he had been commissioned to write two months before, Croswell pronounced the Harrisburg convention a political device of Adams and Clay, "concocted at Washington . . . to gain northern votes. . . . With the manufacturers and wool growers it was an honest and well intentioned measure—with the authors of the scheme, a political stalking-horse, which the agents of the administration . . . avowed their determination to push to the utmost of political advantage." [24] At the same time that Croswell dismissed the convention as a front organization for Adams, he assured his readers that neither Jackson nor Van Buren was a free trader. He used the Coleman letter extensively, and because of Van Buren's woolens speech calling for higher rates for the farmer, Croswell was able to picture the Senator as a staunch advocate of the protective system.[25] The immediate result of this policy was to minimize the question during the fall state elections and to force it into the background. But such a course could not be long maintained, particularly after the Congress reconvened in December. Then Van Buren, knowing New York's prevailing sentiment and the fact that the tariff might be the one element necessary to cement the East and West together, and faced by his Southern friends, would be hard pressed to find a compromise.

The agitation over the tariff was not the only disturbing factor on the political horizon. Hatred and prejudice, born from a single event which had occurred the previous year, swept through the western counties of New York and threatened to play havoc with the entire political structure of the state. It started when a Mason named William Morgan became involved in a misunderstanding with his fellow lodge members and decided, out of revenge, to publish a book revealing the secrets of the order. His plans were soon discovered by his former friends, who appealed to him to abandon his project. When Morgan turned a deaf ear to their pleas, the master of a lodge in Canandaigua had him arrested on September 11, 1826, for stealing a shirt and a tie. The charge was not sustained and Morgan was freed, only to be rearrested for a debt owed to another Mason. Before his friends could bail him out of prison the unfortunate man was kidnaped and probably taken to Fort Niagara, where—according to Thurlow Weed—he was held for several days before being secretly drowned in the Niagara River.[26]

Curiously enough, the sudden and mysterious disappearance of Morgan set the western counties of New York blazing with an all-consuming hatred for Masons. As the citizenry conjectured the fate of the kidnaped man and discussed the flagrant violation of the law, their passions soared. Town meetings were held and resolutions passed demanding immediate action to apprehend the offenders. Local organizations were created, threatening political annihilation to every office-holder who was a Freemason. As the movement spread it became more and more destructive to long-established political relations and slowly began to appear as the basis of a new, permanent, and distinct party. Proscriptions of all known Masons set the pattern for future activities as the organization reached out toward the state government at Albany. "I have seen many sharp political and social contests in my day," said one contemporary, "but, viewed in some aspects, I think the Anti-masonic feuds excelled them all." [27]

For an entire year the sudden excitement that had whipped the western counties into a near frenzy was paid scant attention by many of the larger cities. The Albany *Argus* hardly mentioned the affair in its columns, whereas other newspapers ventured to guess that Morgan was still alive and did not merit the commotion created by his disappearance. Perhaps one of the first men to understand the full impact of the incident upon the people was Van Buren. As an expert political analyst he was almost immediately aware that Anti-Masonry might foreshadow the abandonment of "Old Party feelings," to the detriment of Jacksonians everywhere. In a letter to Cambreleng he criticized those newspapers who fell

into so great a mistake as to speak lightly of the Morgan affair. Depend upon it that this course may do us much injury. There never was in any part of the world a more deep & general solicitude upon any like subject than now pervades the western counties in relation to the fate of Morgan. You will see by the Argus of today that last week there was a meeting of 3000 persons in one County. The editors are also mistaken as to the fact. There is no rational doubt that Morgan is dead & perished by violence. Speak to them.[28]

In September, 1827, Van Buren made a hurried tour through the "infected" counties to see at first hand what inroads had been made into party organization by the new movement. After conversing with most of the county leaders, he satisfied himself that Republicans were still loyal, except where

Masons were concerned, and that as yet the presidential election had not been affected.[29]   On his return to Albany he wrote a long letter to Andrew Jackson in which he reported his findings:

I have recently been through many of the Counties respecting which I felt the most anxiety, [and] have seen most of the leading men from others. . . .   From the information thus derived I am sure I cannot be mistaken in believing, that we shall be able to give you a very decided majority of the votes of this State, if nothing turns up hereafter to change the present aspect of things. . . .   The politics of this State . . . are yet governed by Old Party feelings.[30]

This was probably one of the earliest letters Van Buren wrote to the General, although their friendship extended back to 1823.[31] The presidential campaign drew them closer together, but Jackson still maintained a certain reserve out of respect for De Witt Clinton, who had supported him long before Van Buren jumped on the bandwagon.[32] The Hero had "old-fashioned" ideas about loyalty.   He never forgot a friend or an enemy.

At this juncture, with the annual state elections approaching, the Senator decided to run his slate of candidates as a Jacksonian ticket.   For the first time in three years he agreed to mingle state politics with those of the nation, mindful that the administration forces were disorganized, leaderless, and "flat down." [33] As the *Argus* listed the names of the Republicans running for office, it specified that each was Jackson's warm supporter and, whenever possible, whether the person was a farmer or manufacturer.[34] "All the machinery," Jabez D. Hammond later noted, "the construction of which had for two years put in requisition the skill and ingenuity of Mr. Van Buren and his friends at Albany, was suddenly put in motion, and it performed to admiration." [35] The friends of Adams watched helplessly, while Clinton, to the consternation of all, rode with the Jacksonian tide.

Only the Anti-Mason movement disturbed Van Buren.

He winced every time a nominating convention was held in the western counties, fearing that a candidate would be proposed who was not a Jacksonian Bucktail. Mordecai M. Noah, in his *Courier and Enquirer*, ridiculed the Anti-Masons, thinking this was the best way to handle them. Van Buren appealed to Cambreleng to use his influence with the editor and "beseech" him to

let the Morgan affair alone. I am sick, heart sick at his reckless indiscretion upon that subject. It is passing strange that a man so capable can commit so great a blunder as unnecessarily & unwisely to run in the face of so irresistable [*sic*] a current of public feeling as exists upon this subject in many of the Western counties. . . . The whole bent of our exertions have been to give the nominations the best practicable directions in this we are constantly counteracted by the Enquirer & Courier. . . . Reflecting masons see that the only relief to be expected must come from the strong feelings now afloat exausting [*sic*] themselves which must be the case if no attempt is made to counteract them. . . . Do see Mr Noah & beg him to save us from more mortification upon this only subject that troubles us in the election field.[36]

Although Van Buren, in another part of this same letter, used the phrase "anti-Mason party," the movement was still too localized and lacking in basic political organization to be worthy of the name. Nevertheless the Senator did not hesitate to employ every precautionary measure to safeguard the election. He made certain that only those men from the western counties were nominated who were strong and loyal Republicans and yet were known to be Anti-Masons. The scheme was a hasty improvisation and at best a stopgap measure.

The November elections, however, afforded a complete triumph for the antiadministration party in New York.[37] It was virtually a complete sweep for the Jacksonians, and as Van Buren had earlier predicted in a letter to the General, only Columbia County failed to respond to the managing skill of the Regency.[38] "It is a sufficient expression of the popular feeling now," the *Argus* proclaimed, "and of what it will be in the great contest of 1828, that, with the exception of Columbia, there is not a county in the state in which the question of the presidency came up distinctly, that the republican friends of gen. Jackson have not prevailed, either wholly or in part, and by great majorities." [39]

The Van Buren political machine, which had done a perfect job in rolling over the administration in New York, did not pause after the election, but was kept moving at a steady pace. Some of the Regency members began preparing for an early caucus of the state legislature to nominate a candidate for President. This was important, commented Silas Wright, who had recently been elected to the House of Representatives, because of the "effect in and out of our own State," and for "fear that Mr Clinton and his friends . . . becoming satisfied that he cannot ride behind Jackson by our help, will . . . rally a people's meeting . . . to nominate Jackson before [us] and himself, as V. P. . . ." But whatever happened, Wright told Flagg, nothing must hazard Bucktail rule of New York. Even "Mr. V. B. would rather jeopardize the Presidential election itself, than to risk a breaking up of our ranks at home, or of destroying our strength and harmony in the present Legislature." On the other hand, if a caucus "can be early held, and Old Hickory nominated without injury to the harmony and strength of the party . . . it will be greatly desirable that it should be done." [40]

What troubled the Regency particularly was the question of the vice-presidency. Calhoun was not very popular, even in the South,[41] and this gave Clinton an excuse, if he needed one, to propose himself for the office. Consequently, rather than stir up more trouble when it could be avoided, Wright thought that an easy solution for the Regency would be to omit nominating a candidate for Vice-President altogether and thereby discharge "us from the responsibility of being the leaders in kicking off Mr. Clinton, or in naming any other man." This was poor party discipline, as Van Buren had told William Crawford a short time before, but Wright's proposal had considerable merit. The Senator would have preferred granting Calhoun a New York nomination for the vice-presidency,[42] but he was forced to agree that the mere *mention* of it might provoke Clinton into nominating himself with Jackson before the Bucktails held their own caucus. Instead, it would be wiser to commit the electors to Calhoun *after* the election—which is what Van Buren finally did—rather than before, in order to avoid "a breaking up of our ranks at home. . . ." This was the line of least resistance, and was certainly the most sensible course.

Nevertheless, some Southerners were not content with vice-presidential matters and set about scheming to have Calhoun expelled from Jackson's camp. Sam Houston and William B. Lewis of Tennessee were the ringleaders. When they came into possession of a letter written by Monroe implying that Calhoun had advised censuring the Hero for his actions in the Seminole campaign of 1818, they showed it to the sensitive General, hoping that it would blast the South Carolinian off the ticket. However, a series of long and wordy explanations from the Vice-President temporarily appeased Jackson and the conspirators were driven to further plottings.[43] They managed to embroil Colonel James A. Hamilton in their schemes and sent him off to Georgia to obtain from Crawford a statement of Calhoun's precise reaction to the Florida expedition. Hamilton was not successful in his mission, but he did get a letter from the state's governor, John Forsyth, which specifically included the Vice-President as one of Jackson's early critics. However, Houston and Lewis judged it inconclusive and for the time being put it aside until corroborating evidence could be produced.[44]

During December of 1827, Hamilton visited Jackson at his home in Nashville and studiously advanced the cause of his friend Van Buren. He had help, at different times, from Houston and Lewis. Just how, when, and why these two Tennesseans were won over to the Little Magician is not clear, but undoubtedly their own special hatred for Calhoun had a

lot to do with it.   Lewis began corresponding with the Senator
shortly after Van Buren declared for Jackson.   Some of his
letters included crude suggestions to improve Jackson's chances
for election; but despite these crudities the New Yorker recognized at once Lewis's superior powers for intrigue and took
pains to draw him to his side.   Other Tennesseans, such as
Houston and John H. Eaton, may have been converted by
Alfred Balch, one of Van Buren's earliest disciples in the
West.[45] With Eaton, the New Yorker himself probably took a
hand.   Both men served in the Senate and Van Buren would
never have wasted the opportunity to befriend a man who was
so close to the General.

By 1827, Van Buren's circle of friends among Jacksonians
was enormous; he was even doing personal and financial favors
for Amos Kendall of Kentucky.[46]

Nevertheless the General had to be convinced of the
Senator's sincerity.   Jackson in his talk with Hamilton, showed
marked interest in the affairs of New York, the moral character
of its leading citizens, and the strange relationship between its
Governor and senior Senator.   The Hero frankly admitted that
his opinion of Clinton was "elevated," but that of Van Buren
he had heard much "that was unfavorable."   Hamilton was
quick to defend his chief, protesting that the Senator was the
continued victim of vicious political gossip.   Van Buren's supposed "cunning" was mentioned, but the Colonel swore it was
illusory.   On the contrary, argued Hamilton, he was "unquestionably sagacious."   His remarkable personal advancement
was due to his industry and skill as a lawyer, to his "proverbi-
ally cautious" approach to all problems, and to "the folly and
want of patriotism of the opposing faction. . . ." [47] Jackson was
impressed by the conviction of his guest and was forced to
admit that Van Buren was indeed one of the ablest senators in
Congress and had immeasurably aided his campaign during the
last two years.   Notwithstanding all this, he was struck by the
problems involved in drawing support from two long-standing
political enemies from the same state.   Should he be elected to

the presidency in 1828, he would have the unpleasant task of
dividing the spoils of victory between them.[48] Such an undertaking would prove far from easy.

The political complexion of Congress was reversed with the
commencement of the new session. Simultaneously, Van
Buren's position also changed. Since both houses contained a
larger number of antiadministration men, he became the majority leader, the spokesman of the Jacksonian Republicans.
Although many congressmen carefully noted the words of
Senator John H. Eaton from Tennessee because of his intimacy
with Old Hickory, they were more prone to acknowledge Van
Buren as the real head of the party. And the New Yorker
played his leading role to the hilt, relying on his powers of
personal persuasion to influence and control the actions of his
colleagues. He was courteous to all, not excepting Clay,
Adams, or the new senator from Massachusetts, Daniel Webster.
With Southerners his friendliness was unrestrained and he
asked Edwin Croswell to "say some civil things" about them in
the *Argus*. "It is gratifying to meet the Republicans of the
South upon the old platform which was laid by Jefferson & supported by Madison," he commented to Croswell. "There they
may always expect to find union & co-operation from the Democrats of the North." [49] He demonstrated the full meaning of
this cooperation by helping to defeat John W. Taylor for reelection as Speaker of the House. By a vote of 104 to 94,
Andrew Stevenson of Virginia was elected to replace Taylor.[50]
This triumph, Wright recorded, "was glorious and we have got
into the bargain . . . a manly dignified and able speaker, and a
very sound democrat and gentlemanly affable man." [51]
Duff Green, with little opposition, was chosen printer for
the Senate. Then, with swift and determined action, both
houses filled all their respective committees with Jacksonians.
"The opposition party," observed John Tyler to a friend, "constitute in fact the *administration*. Upon it rests the entire responsibility of all legislative measures, and you may rest perfectly satisfied that all heat and intemperance will be banished

from our councils. . . ." [52] Henry Storrs, a New York representative and an Adams man, worriedly pondered the future of the session. "You will have seen the arrangement of our committees & the new Speaker," he told a friend. "A difference of opinion existed among the leaders but the course taken was conformable to the advice of Van Buren to them." [53]

And the Senator had very definite ideas about the men he would like to see directing this or any Congress. He could not abide "orators," the pompous kind; he preferred men skilled in reading the "signs of the times," men who would constantly reflect and register the opinions of the people. Their conduct in Congress, he said, to secure the passage of popular legislation and thereby advance the cause of democracy, should be realistic: They should press their measures upon the House "at the proper time, when its members were in the best mood to regard them favorably. . . ." They should quickly "find the weakest point in the position" of their opponents and "overthrow" them at that point. They should avoid debate "whereby time and opportunity" might be afforded the opposition "to recover from mistakes or to take a new position. . . ." They should carefully arrange both the form and the order in which questions were to be proposed "as to force to the surface" and turn to their advantage "latent diversities of feeling and opinion either not at all or only remotely bearing upon the principal subject. . . ." And finally, they should never attempt to attain objects which were beyond their reach.[54]

Van Buren strongly believed that the application of these principles would create a realistic, modern, and democratic Congress. He used them, now that his leadership in Congress was unquestioned, to overpower a "Federalist" administration that had gotten into office through "fraud and corruption."

For the next three months the eyes of the nation were turned toward the proceedings of the House of Representatives, where a new tariff bill was under consideration. The Senate called very little attention to itself, and Van Buren abandoned some of his official duties in the interest of more important matters. As he scurried about the capital he kept one finger in the presidential contest, another in New York politics, a third in the affairs of the lower house of Congress, and a fourth in the over-all management of party discipline. It was no wonder that on two or three occasions he was forced to take to his bed out of sheer physical exhaustion.

The final year of campaigning for the presidential election of 1828 produced some of the most disgraceful examples of American journalism in any election. Honesty had little value; slanderous stories were invented and elaborated upon at will. The report that Jackson had lived with his beloved wife Rachel before she was divorced from her first husband was widely circulated, to which the antiadministration presses countered by accusing Adams of procuring an American girl for the lustful czar of Russia when the President was minister to that country.

Jackson's military career was besmirched by the printing of the "coffin handbill." This leaflet depicted a series of black wooden coffins, representing six militiamen who were supposedly murdered in cold blood by the Hero in 1815 because they wanted to return to their homes after their enlistments expired. Actually these men had been shot when a regularly constituted court-martial found them guilty of desertion. The General's connection with Burr's conspiracy commanded attention until it was learned that Henry Clay had also been involved as an attorney for the accused.

On the other hand, Adams was charged with the wildest sort of extravagance in using public funds to purchase a billiard table and other "gambling furniture" for the White House. The "corrupt bargain" of 1825 was raked over relentlessly, and variations on the same theme were manufactured, depending on the imagination of the Jacksonian editors.

The Albany *Argus* followed the lead of other newspapers, but with less rancor. Many of its featured articles were borrowed from other journals, and Croswell satisfied his readers by principally defending Jackson's reputation and playing up the "corrupt-bargain" theme.

The other members of the Regency left the formulation of the *Argus's* policies to the editor and temporarily suspended their regular contributions to the paper. Continually hounded by Van Buren to "play a little deeper" into politics and to use "inducements which are not acceptable to arguments" to bring about a state nomination of the Hero, they were busy trying to plan their strategy. This, despite the fact, said Marcy, that there were difficulties "over [the] diversity of views relative to a caucus, the tariff and the anti-masonic" feuds. Silas Wright reduced their problems to one. The "greatest obstacle with our best men in taking the side of Genl Jackson," he noted, "was the fear that his success might win the elevation of Mr. Clinton and that but for that apprehension they would long since have espoused the Jackson cause openly." Van Buren was impatient with this sort of reasoning, pointing out that a Congressional caucus and a national convention would not be held and that it was imperative for the legislature to give "an expression of opinion. . . ." They had no alternative, and the Regency brethren set to work satisfying their chief."[55]

Henry Clay, who kept himself informed on all New York political developments, hoped that a clash between the Clintonians and the Bucktails would arise from these "diversity of views" and would prevent a presidential nomination.[56] Others, who were unacquainted with the skills of the Regency, foolishly thought that Van Buren's absence from the state suffered the wrangling to go unchecked and wondered if local politicians might not seize the opportunity to throw off "their leading strings." "But it must not be forgotten," cautioned one experienced observer, "that such is the perfection of Mr. Van Buren's party discipline, that, present or absent, he wields a tremendous power." The Regency, during his absence from Albany, was managed "by a most faithful corps educated in his school, and mostly under his open eye," and its influence and power extended "to every county and principal village in the State." [57]

Inasmuch as the plan for a national nominating convention appeared abandoned and the report was substantiated that a

Congressional caucus would not be convened, the Regency had
no recourse but to call a legislative caucus as Van Buren had
directed.   On January 31, 1828, one was duly held.   Drilled
to follow orders, the Bucktails placed Andrew Jackson in nomination for the presidency but said nothing as to the second
place.   In the states of Virginia, Pennsylvania, New Jersey,
Ohio, and Kentucky, similar caucuses were held, but only New
York refused Calhoun his rightful position on the ticket.   It
can now be seen, wrote one Adams partisan, that "the decisions
of King Caucus who hitherto muzzled by the policy of V.B. is
now made ready to Hazza for Old Hickory." [58]

When the news of the Regency's achievement reached Washington, Van Buren sent his lieutenants a warm letter of con-
gratulations.   "Our friends at Albany have done themselves
the highest honor and carried dismay into the administration
camp." [59]

But dismay was also carried into the Jackson camp.   Calhoun was highly incensed by the slight dealt him in New York
and suspected Van Buren of "secretly playing a deep game
against him and for himself. . . ." [60]   There was no mistaking
the Vice-President's temper, noted Wright, and it made him
"a very jealous *friend*" of the Little Magician.[61]   Calhoun
should have known that the present state of New York politics
prevented the naming of a vice-presidential candidate.   Governor Clinton had not lost hope of succeeding to the place and
the Regency men were "disinclined" to "kick" him off, for fear
that it would react unfavorably against Jackson.   Besides, the
South Carolinian would get New York's vote as soon as the
Electoral College met.   Nevertheless, it became increasingly
clear that the towering Calhoun watched his little "friend"
with growing distrust.   He was afraid of Van Buren—and was
jealous too.   A feud between them was inevitable because of
their intense ambition.   Each schemed to be President.   Their
future actions were keyed to its fulfillment, and each recognized the other as a dangerous rival.

Heretofore it has been customary to sympathize with the
"innocent" Vice-President as the unfortunate victim of the

"unprincipled" New York Senator. A good many abusive words have been heaped on Van Buren for denying Calhoun his "rightful" place as President of the United States. Perhaps this it not the time to go into the famous Calhoun-Van Buren quarrel, but it is passing strange that the New Yorker should go to a great deal of trouble after 1828 to plot Calhoun's downfall when at the height of Jackson's presidential campaign before 1828 he was doing absolutely nothing about De Witt Clinton. Certainly Clinton was an obstacle to his presidential ambitions. Van Buren was quite aware that Jackson's election would force the President-elect to choose between the two New Yorkers, and yet there is not a shred of evidence to indicate that he was attempting to discredit Clinton in Jackson's eyes. Was Van Buren so clairvoyant as to know that Clinton would die prematurely in 1828? Hardly. Why then would he plot against the one and not against the other; surely the circumstances were not so completely different. The answer, it would appear, is that Van Buren plotted against neither. There was never any need; he recognized that both, sooner or later, would destroy themselves politically. He recognized that Clay would do the same, and said so in his *Autobiography*.

As events subsequently proved, the Vice-President had been stacking the cards against himself since 1818. He was quite capable of ruining himself with Jackson without any outside assistance. Except, of course, the assistance his wife Floride kindly provided. To place the blame solely on Van Buren is an unwarranted dismissal of Calhoun's own foolish mistakes.

One of the causes of the bitter feuds, the embarrassment, and the confusion that had long disrupted New York was abruptly removed on February 11, 1828. De Witt Clinton, while sitting in the midst of his family, suddenly fell forward in his chair and died of a heart attack. His passing was quiet and peaceful, in sharp contrast to his brilliant and ebullient career. Almost as quickly as the report of his death was communicated outside Albany, there was a wild reshuffling of party affiliations. The Regency disrespectfully sighed with relief.

Many Clintonians—probably a substantial majority of them—now freed from the personal and unpredictable whims of their leader, rushed to join the followers of Adams.[62]   "All accounts concur," exclaimed the enthusiastic Clay, "that the political effect of Mr. Clinton's death will be favorable to the administration; and intelligence generally from that State, especially from the western portion of it, is very cheering." [63]   Flagg, Marcy, Butler, Knower, and Croswell made every effort to welcome the Clintonians into the Bucktail fold—excluding merely those they termed "the apostate federalists"—but for the most part they were greeted with flat rejections.[64]

Jackson, like Van Buren, Adams, and Clay, was also saved from a predicament by Clinton's untimely death.   For him there was no longer a complication respecting New York in the awarding of cabinet posts, should he be elected President.   As the sole leader of the antiadministration forces in his state, as the guiding hand in the present Congress, as the principal architect of what would become the reconstituted Republican party, and as the man most of Jackson's Tennessee friends kept pushing—for all these reasons Van Buren was virtually the only possible choice for the post of Secretary of State.

In Washington, on February 19, the New York delegation in Congress held a meeting to express their "deep and sincere sorrow for a dispensation of Providence which has, in the midst of active usefulness, cut off from the service of [his] State . . . a great man"—De Witt Clinton.[65]   As senior Senator, Van Buren was the principal speaker and delivered what one contemporary termed an "appropriate and elegant address, the concluding part of which [was] so beautiful, both in style and sentiment, and so just to the deceased, as well as creditable to the orator," as to wipe away the bitter memories of the past fifteen years. Van Buren, with genuine sincerity and charity, said:

I can say nothing of the deceased that is not familiar to you all. To all he was personally known, and to many of us intimately and familiarly, from our earliest infancy.   The high order of his talents, the untiring zeal and great success with which those talents have, through a series of years, been devoted to the prosecution of plans of great public utility, are also known to you all; and by all I am satisfied duly appreciated. The subject can derive no additional interest or importance from any eulogy of mine. All other considerations out of view, the single fact that the greatest public improvement of the age in which we live was commenced under the guidance of his counsels, and splendidly accomplished under his immediate auspices, is of itself sufficient to fill the ambition of any man, and to give glory to any name. . . . We cannot indeed but remember that in our own public career, collisions of opinion and action, at once extensive, earnest and enduring, have arisen between the deceased and many of us. For myself, sir, it gives me a deep-felt, though melancholy, satisfaction, to know . . . that our political differences have been wholly free from that most venomous and corroding of all poisons—personal hatred. But in other respects it is now immaterial what was the character of those collisions. They have been turned to nothing, and less than nothing, by the event we deplore, and I doubt not that we will, with one voice and one heart, yield to his memory the well deserved tribute of our respect of his name and our warmest gratitude for his great and signal service. For myself, sir, so strong, so sincere and so engrossing is that feeling, that I, who whilst living never no never envied him anything; now that he has fallen, am greatly tempted to envy him his grave with its honours.[66]

There was no hypocrisy in this splendid eulogy. Because the Senator was unfamiliar with "corroding" personal hatred, which normally attended political battles, he could speak in this manner without fear of criticism. Nor need he ever have blushed with embarrassment at the thought of others reading his comments. New Yorkers studied them and were moved by their eloquence. It was fitting, they agreed, that he should have uttered them.

XII: TO DRAW THE EAST AND
WEST TOGETHER

THE HISTORY of the Van Buren's activities in Congress during
the months in which he guided the Tariff of Abominations
through Congress has been recorded many times. The generally accepted theory is quite false, however, because it contra-
dicts the testimony of the authors of the tariff and because it
is illogical.

The standard interpretation regarding this Tariff of Abominations is that the Little Magician deliberately introduced it
into Congress to kill it, as the best means of holding the South
and West under the Jackson banner. By raising rates on raw
materials out of all proportion to manufactured goods, he
could compel New England to join the South to crush the bill.
In the West and Northwest credit for the defeat would be
attributed to the New England Adams men; and in the South
credit for defeat would go to the Jacksonians. But when this
plot failed by the "unexpected" passage of the law, the interpretation continues, Van Buren quickly revamped his strategy
and paraded the Jackson party before Westerners as their bene-
factor, and before Southerners as their undaunted champion,
betrayed the wickedness of the administration party.[1]

This theory, however else it may sound, is completely illogical. To begin with, Van Buren was much too clever to
propose a scheme which had so many variables in it, and which
might go astray—as it did. In addition, he would have to be
out of his mind to shape a tariff with the expectation that New
England would join the South to kill it. In the past New Eng-

land had been divided over the issue, and there was no certain way of telling how its representatives would vote. Conceivably New England *might* accept the bill, and Van Buren did not maneuver on the basis of such an uncertainty. Finally, in connection with the presidential election, he had no reason to conspire against the tariff. With the Jacksonians in control of Congress they would be held responsible for the success or failure of every measure.[2] And if they did not pass a bill to increase protection, how could anyone, least of all Van Buren, attempt to explain away their remissness by lying and telling conflicting stories in different sections of the country? The administration would never permit them such propaganda, and the effect on Jackson's campaign could have unfortunate consequences.

It has been stated that the tariff of 1828 was written and passed to "manufacture" a President. This is quite true. But the framers of the bill were not so shortsighted as to believe that this might be accomplished by defeating the measure; rather they were convinced that only in its *passage* would it help Jackson in the coming presidential contest. The problem facing them was not holding the South but capturing the West and Northwest, where Clay had won Ohio, Missouri, and Kentucky in 1824. Furthermore, a protective tariff would attract a considerable number of votes from the East, particularly from the Middle states.

Whether right or wrong, for good or ill, many Western farmers—especially the producers of hemp and raw wool— embraced the principle of protection as necessary to their economic well-being. And only by assuring them of Jacksonian adherence to this doctrine was there a reasonable guarantee of coaxing them away from Clay and his presidential candidate, John Q. Adams.[3] No other issue could produce the same effect.

To engineer a higher tariff through Congress, however, was certain to antagonize the Southerners who were sworn to the free-trade position. To challenge their stand might goad them into some form of defiance.[4] Nevertheless, Van Buren knew that whatever the Southerners did, their defiance would not take the form of bolting the party now that the presidential election was confined to a race between two candidates. No matter which way the tariff question went they could not vote for Adams, because in their minds he was "the acknowledged leader" of the manufacturing interests, and they wanted no part of him.[5]

The final, and most convincing, proof that Van Buren never intended to defeat this tariff is the existence of a relatively large number of documents written at the time by the men who were actually responsible for its passage. An examination of these documents proves that the Little Magician steadily moved toward enacting the measure into law.

America had recovered rapidly after the panic of 1819–21 and entered an era of economic development characterized by an intense vitality. The frontier was pushed further westward, thanks to improved transportation and communication. The spectacular success of the Erie Canal not only brought untold wealth to New York but encouraged a tremendous amount of canal building throughout the nation. The fabulous history of railroading began on July 2, 1828, when Charles Carroll of Carrollton, the sole surving signer of the Declaration of Independence, officiated at the ceremonies that marked the commencement of the building of the Baltimore and Ohio. Turnpikes were stretched across the Allegheny Mountains into the lush and fertile Ohio valley region, and the Cumberland Road moved steadily inland.

Manufacturing also increased in some districts, but not at the anticipated rate. Although woolen mills had multiplied, competition from abroad threatened their existence. Many new mills opened and shortly thereafter shut down—the tariff of 1824 notwithstanding. Owners publicly aired their difficulties and demanded of Congress a revision of the schedules of rates. Not only the manufacturers, but the producers of raw materials, such as hemp, raw wool, and flax, insisted on higher protection and would not tolerate halfway measures.

Thus when the first session of the Twentieth Congress convened in December, 1827, there was little doubt that a new tariff law would be attempted. The House committee on manufactures was chosen by the Speaker, Andrew Stevenson, with particular care to satisfy the swelling demands. Although the majority of members were Jacksonians and protariff, the committee continued under the chairmanship of Rollin C. Mallary of Vermont, an Adams supporter and a strong protectionist, whom the Speaker felt he could not honorably remove.[6] "We pushed to have Mallory [sic] displaced," confessed Silas Wright, "and a true man put in his place. Perhaps the part of prudence has been pursued. . . . We however suppose the committee is perfectly safe, and certain it is that there is but one anti-tariff man upon it." [7] The remaining members comprised a majority of five Jacksonians, all of whom were judged to be "of the most plastic materials in the hands of the leaders." [8] The dominant figure of the committee, and the man who later acknowledged his authorship of this tariff,[9] was the New Yorker and Regency lieutenant, Silas Wright, Jr. He was Van Buren's most trusted follower in the House of Representatives. He was Van Buren's liaison with the committee.

On December 31 Mallary asked the House to give his committee power to subpoena reports and hear testimony both for and against the contemplated measure. Certain testy Congressmen objected to the proposal as a crude device to waste time, but they were quickly overruled.[10] The committee then proceeded to examine the petitions and memorials coming from all parts of the country, listen to the arguments of various witnesses, and study the documents submitted by the different governmental agencies.[11] The object of this highly modern practice was to weigh both sides, declared Wright, and try to "extract an honest and fair rule or rate of protection to the woolen manufacturers." But they would not stop there, he said emphatically. They did not intend, in their "sympathy for manufactures, to overlook or forget the farmers." [12]

There were few interruptions while the members gathered their information, but when they completed their self-imposed assignment and began the arduous task of writing a bill, the smiling and cordial Van Buren was repeatedly seen "lurking" outside the committee room. He was in the habit, observed the Boston *Massachusetts Journal*, "of calling out the Jackson members of the committee daily, and many times a day, to hold talks with them; and it is presumed that nothing important was done or has been reported, without his knowledge and consent." [13] The Washington *National Journal* confirmed the report and sarcastically added: "We believe that every thing has been arranged under the superintendence of Mr. Van Buren, who, from managing the Albany legislature, has kindly taken upon himself the management of congress, so far as relates to the the tariff, &c. &c." [14] Duff Green, editor of the *United States Telegraph*, attempted to refute these claims by assuring his readers that the Senator from New York "did once . . . call at the committee room, and that was done upon the request of his friend, Mr. McLane of Delaware." [15] Green's protest notwithstanding, Van Buren was responsible for the tariff bill as eventually reported.

Although the New York Senator favored a bill which would please Westerners so that they would vote for Jackson in 1828, this was not his only consideration. Indeed, it subsequently became a lesser consideration. Repeatedly hounded by his constituents to help their industries now that he and his Jackson cohorts controlled the new Congress, he suddenly took sharp notice of their demands when his lieutenants at home warned him that unless he did something to satisfy the clamor, "infinite mischief to the cause of General Jackson in this State would result, and we should have a difficult and doubtful conflict at the next elections." In addition, Marcy reminded Van Buren of the Anti-Masonic furor which was certain to "be turned in favor of Adams because he is not a Mason." The Senator and his friends, the letter concluded, must do "all that mortal men can do for the success" of the tariff, otherwise the Regency was in serious trouble." [16]

Van Buren was not spared the possible consequences of a tariff badly managed by Congress. The problem was put squarely before him: either sponsor a new and improved law, or risk a difficult contest in the next election. And as he himself said many times, he would rather "jeopardize the Presidential election itself" than lose control of his own state.[17]

The recommendations of the Mallary committee were laid before the House of Representatives early in 1828. They were accompanied by sustained jeers from all corners of the hall. The sincere friends of protection gasped at what they read, and pointed with critical finger at section after section. Some were worse than others. A duty of 10 cents per gallon was levied on molasses, and that on distilled spirits was raised 10 cents. The duty on sail duck was established at 9 cents per square yard, and those on hemp and flax were fixed at $45.00 per ton, to be increased $5.00 each year until a maximum of $60.00 was reached. Startling was the protection given raw wool. A charge of 7 cents per pound was suggested, plus a 40 per cent ad valorum rate which would be increased 5 per cent annually until it amounted to 50 per cent. On *manufactured* wool, however, the story was completely different. An involved schedule was set up, depending on the price range, which did not begin to meet the bare minimum demanded by producers.[18] The bill was thus generous to a fault, except to the industry which possibly stood in greater need of protection than any other. Many farmers, because of the preference given to raw materials, were pleased at the prospect of the measure; but manufacturers, especially woolen manufacturers, distillers, ropemakers, and shipbuilders, condemned it as worse than no tariff at all.

Did Wright and Van Buren purposely frame this bill to force the representatives of the industrial areas to kill it? Not when such tactics would excite New Yorkers and threaten the existence of the Albany Regency! Why then did they refuse the wool manufacturer sufficient protection? And how could they place heavy duties on hemp, molasses, sail duck, and iron when they were fully aware that distillers, merchants, shipowners, and shipbuilders would raise a howl that would be heard from the Kennebec River to the Mississippi?

The answer was very simple, according to Silas Wright; no fact was omitted from the committee's deliberations. They started, he wrote, by raising the rates upon "all kinds of woolen cloths," as "high as *our own friends* in Pennsylvania, Kentucky & Ohio would vote them." [19]   After that, he continued, they jumped the molasses rates in order to induce Westerners "to go for the woolens" provision. The hemp, lead, and flax rates were fixed for the identical reason of meeting the conditions imposed by particular states as the price of their support, and the duty on iron was "the Sine qua non with Pennsylvania. . . ." [20]

Thus, in order to raise the rate as far as they dared on woolen cloths, the committee had to increase the schedule of rates on one commodity after another until the measure was so rigged that it could be eased through Congress with a minimum of pressure and exertion. But there was more involved. Although fundamentally Jeffersonian in concept—or so the framers believed—with the farmer given special consideration, the bill was also meant to bribe the Middle and Western states into declaring for Jackson. For this reason raw materials and certain manufactured goods such as iron were favored. New England, on the other hand, with its large number of distillers, shipowners, shipbuilders, and merchants—and its preference for Adams—was to be discriminated against.

When the partisans of the administration in Congress read this lopsided bill they could hardly believe their eyes, and subsequently suspected the Jacksonians of plotting its destruction. "They do not really desire the passage of their own measure," wrote Henry Clay, "and it may happen in the sequel that what is desired by *neither party* commands the support of both." [21] Hezekiah Niles, who despaired when he examined the recommendations of the committee, did not agree with Clay's conclusion. "I will not say this bill was reported to be defeated, but it will be, unless materially altered." [22]

Southerners, too, were appalled, and incorrectly inferred that their Jacksonian colleagues meant the bill as a ruse to fool constituents back home.[23]   They further reasoned that by simply beating off all efforts to amend and improve the bill, which would make it more palatable to manufacturers, Northerners would join them on the final vote to kill it.[24]   No knowledge of a "plot" was necessary to tell them this.   No "assurances" from Van Buren or anyone else were needed to show them what they must do.   They had no choice.

But had Clay, Southerners, and other skeptics looked to the activities of Van Buren's machine in New York, they would have had a more exact knowledge of the intentions of those managing the tariff's progress through Congress.   Early in the year the Regency-controlled New York legislature called on all Congressmen from that state "to make every proper exertion to effect such a revision of the tariff, as will afford a sufficient protection to the growers of wool, hemp and flax, and the manufacturers of iron and woollens." [25]   Obviously this resolution would not have been passed without specific instructions from Van Buren.   It was too important a question.   When Wright's bill was reported out of committee the *Argus* praised it as "a liberal and sufficient increase of the protection of the domestic industry of the country" and deserving the "cordial support" of every Republican representative.[26]   A circular letter, endorsing the reported bill, was written in March and sent to every Bucktail editor in the state.   The old political war horse of New York, Ambrose Spencer, watched the campaign and informed John W. Taylor that the "Jackson presses in this state are already extremely abusive towards those members of congress who have exposed the injurious consequences of the bill as reported. . . ." [27]   These "tories," Azariah Flagg told Wright, will be blown "sky high. . . . [Our] ranks are firm.   My notion is, that you should press the bill, as you are doing, with such modifications as are obviously just, and if the *political spinners* of the East go against it, it will require many *long years* to extricate them from the odium.   I think you have them on the hip." [28]

Debate on Wright's bill opened in the House of Representatives on March 3, 1828, when Mallary disclaimed all connection with the report of his committee.   He denounced what the members had done, and then proposed a series of constructive amendments. His attack centered mainly on the woolens provisions, which had to be righted, he argued, if the American industrialist were to secure adequate protection. Mallary was answered by Silas Wright in a lengthy speech that took two days to deliver. Quoting largely from the testimony of witnesses heard by the committee, he insisted that the benefits "to manufacturers should be given with express reference to the effect upon agriculture. . . ." Enough wool, he contended, was grown in this country to satisfy the needs of the mills, and it should never be the policy of this government to hand over the industrial capital of the United States to the foreign exporters of raw materials. "The American Manufacturer, has, by the bill as reported, all the protection which he swears he needs." [29]

There was nothing noncommittal about Wright's remarks and they showed the whole agricultural bent of the Regency mind. Here was a long recitation of Jefferson's agrarian philosophy which was being reaffirmed as a cardinal doctrine of the Democratic party.

When Van Buren received a copy of his friend's speech, he promptly sent it off to the Regency with specific instructions. "I send you the whole of Mr Wrights speech. I hope our friends will immediately have it struck off & extensively circulated. This is the accepted time. Let the catastrophe follow instead of precede its appearance." [30] At once the *Argus* began printing copies. Its editorials became wondrously solicitous of the farmer, condemned the Mallary amendments in unqualified terms, and authoritatively pronounced the administration men to be the disguised opponents of protection. Only the Jacksonians, trumpeted the newspaper, were the "real friends of a national tariff. . . ." [31]

Although the Southerners in the House formed a solid corps to oppose all corrective amendments to the bill, including Mallary's, they were loath to play a purely defensive role. Impatient with the views of every congressman who differed with them, they at length seized the initiative and went to Wright with what they thought was an ultimatum. They would have no misunderstanding their position, and they warned him, or so Wright reported to Flagg, that any contemplated increase of their "burdens by a still further increase upon the woollens" would force them to join "the Eastern" Representatives of the manufacturing and commercial New England states. Together the Southerners and Easterners would move to strike out the molasses, iron, hemp, and flax provisions. If they were successful, Wright went on to state, the Jacksonians from Pennsylvania, Ohio, and Kentucky would go the rest of the way and kill what remained.[32]

The threat intimidated no one, however, least of all Van Buren. He had no intention of increasing the rate on woolen manufactures, and consequently on April 9, 1828, the Mallary amendments were defeated *in toto*.

Despite this initial victory, the overanxious Wright was still perturbed about a possible East-South alliance against the tariff and discussed his fears with Flagg. "It is in the power of the Eastern and Southern men to destroy the bill," he wrote, "and the Eastern men will do it if the Southern will help them." [33] These fears, possibly shared by Van Buren, may account for the sudden introduction of an amendment to reduce the duty on raw wool by three cents. Perhaps it was felt that the reduction would attract a few "Eastern" votes. Perhaps it was intended as added guarantee against a possible East-South alliance. In any event the amendment passed, but by the closest possible margin. A single vote separated it from defeat.

By now a few New England representatives began wondering whether they could accept the tariff in its present form. "Can we *go* the *hemp,* iron, spirit and molasses," asked Daniel Webster, "for the sake of any woolen bill?" [34] A good many other men asked themselves the same question, and on April 22 gave their collective answer. By the vote of 105 to 94 the bill carried through the House. Almost the entire delegations from the Western and Middle states supported the measure. New England was split. All the Southern representatives, with the exception of three, remained obdurate to the end.

In high spirits Wright notified the Regency of their victory. "May it live through the Senate, but I fear and tremble. We have made a few of the Yankees swallow, though most of them have voted against the bill. If our friends wish to do any thing further on this subject, they should recommend to the Senate the passage of the bill in its present shape." [35]

Wright had reason to "fear and tremble." It was the considered opinion of most Congressmen that the tariff could never meet the acid test of Senate approval.[36] There the Southerners were proportionately in greater numbers and much more confident of themselves. A few of them excelled in parliamentary debate and were gifted with speaking talents of the highest order. With Vice-President John C. Calhoun as presiding officer, to dispose of all ties, the balance was weighted in their favor.

The bill first went to the Senate committee on manufactures, and on May 5 was reported out. Accompanying it were 17 amendments to bring the tariff closer to the hopes and wishes of the commercial and manufacturing classes of the country. Southern Senators, never deviating from their original position, assured themselves that its "fate" rested on their "ability to preserve the bill in its present shape. If we can do so, it will be rejected." [37]

The task of protecting the tariff and ensuring its swift passage in the Senate fell squarely on Van Buren. Almost immediately upon hearing the committee's report and examining the proposed amendments he was at work devising some sort of strategy. Early in May he questioned Silas Wright about the number of people in New York engaged in the iron, wool-growing, and wool-manufacturing industries. He was told that some "20,000 operation hands" were making iron, while approximately "40 persons," with a capital averaging $40,000 each, operated woolen factories. As to "wool raisers," Wright did not know the precise number but estimated that there were at least 6½ million sheep in New York.[38] Van Buren did not state in writing what he planned to do with these figures, but

it appears likely that they were to justify his strategic move of
accepting the recommendations of the committee on manufactures where they applied to woolens. He could not lower the
rates on raw materials without offending his political friends
in the West. Since wool constituted the greatest point of controversy, and since the rate on raw wool had already been
lowered in the House, the obvious move was to raise the rate
on woolen manufactures. Although he stated emphatically
that he would have "preferred to pass that Bill in the shape in
which it came to us," and although he had no desire to grant
any favor to New Englanders, he had to make some change in
order to counter the strong opposition which was prepared to
crush the entire measure.[39] When Wright was informed of the
move, he undoubtedly experienced a sense of disappointment,
since he had expressed the hope that his bill would survive
the Senate unamended. He was enough of a realist, however,
to recognize with Van Buren that the change was essential if
they were going to accomplish their primary purpose of enacting a tariff during that session of Congress.

Once he conceived the idea of adjusting the woolens schedule, Van Buren was faced with the problem of dealing with
his colleagues from Pennsylvania, Missouri, Kentucky, and
Ohio. They had long since declared that the woolens duties
were as high as they would vote them. He spoke with them,
or so it can be presumed from the remark of one senator.[40]
No record exists of what Van Buren said or what reaction he
received, but in all probability he presented them with the
choice of greater protection for the woolens industry or no bill
at all. Whatever arguments he employed they were convincing. When the vote was taken on May 6 to raise the duty on
manufactured wool to a 40 per cent ad valorem rate with a 5
per cent increase each year until it reached 50 per cent, the
amendment passed, 24 to 22.[41]

This was the decisive vote! A few Southerners let out a
fearsome howl, and their bitter recriminations did not abate
with time. What had happened was all too apparent. The
strategy for defeating the bill had been based on keeping it

unamended. Now the measure had been sufficiently improved to give many New Englanders a plausible excuse for accepting it.[42] One Massachusetts manufacturer informed Representative John Bailey that he was "perfectly satisfied with the Bill as amended in the Senate." [43]

There followed, just as the Southerners had threatened, the inevitable attacks on molasses, hemp, and other indispensable provisions of the measure, but they were beaten down.[44] During the voting on these important amendments Van Buren switched sides, and the switch was most significant. He voted *for* the woolens amendment, but *against* all the others. Had he really wished to kill the bill, as has been claimed, he could easily have done so by opposing the woolens revision.[45] The resulting tie would have been broken by Calhoun and the amendment defeated.[46] Without the improved woolens schedule, Webster and other New England senators would have joined Southerners on the final vote and rejected the entire tariff.[47]

Because Van Buren switched sides and was seemingly inconsistent in his voting on the amendments he was accused of deception. Senator Tazewell of Virginia supposedly cornered him one day and said: "Sir, you have deceived me once; that was your fault; but if you deceive me again the fault will be mine." [48] Actually Van Buren's voting was quite consistent with his desire to see the tariff safely through Congress. There was never any deception; some Southerners simply chose to believe that there was.

On May 13, after a vain attempt by Robert Y. Hayne to postpone action indefinitely, the entire measure came up for a final vote and passed by the count of 26 to 21.[49] The voting by senators from the different sections of the nation followed a pattern that had been established at the beginning of the decade, but the hostility of the South and the indecision of New England had at last been overcome.

The House of Representatives took exception to two minor Senate amendments. George McDuffie of South Carolina, one of Calhoun's trusted henchmen, moved that the House insist on disagreement with the third and fifth amendments (woolens was the fourth). Silas Wright immediately objected, "not upon the ground of any principle contained in the bill, but from the risk of its failing entirely." [50]   In the final compromise the fifth amendment was adhered to but the third was slightly revised.

With respect to the woolens, Representative Richard Wilde of Georgia moved a change from the Senate's 40 per cent ad valorem to a 30 per cent ad valorem in order to "test the principle, and allow him time to discuss the merits of the bill." But his proposal was rejected, 44 to 83, and the Senate's amendment sustained, 85 to 44.   Wright voted with the majority in both instances.[51]

Many genuine friends of the protective system were disgusted with the tariff of 1828 and they called it "abominable." Few newspaper editors dared to defend it, although Croswell was an exception. The Albany *Argus* ascribed to the Jacksonian Congress "the merit of having given to the country a national tariff, which protects, with a just and natural equality, all the great interests of the nation." [52]

Van Buren's studied course of action is fairly discernible during these bitter months of conflict.   Because of conditions in New York he was obliged to raise the tariff; but simultaneously he used the issue to promote Andrew Jackson's election to the presidency in 1828.   Quite certain of the South's loyalty to his candidate—since the only alternative for them was John Q. Adams—he framed a bill to win votes in those sections where he believed the General needed them most. New England was discounted as unalterably attached to Adams. The Western, Northwestern, and Middle states therefore became the object of his schemes.   Beginning with what he imagined to be a genuine Jeffersonian dislike of higher protection for manufacturers, and strengthened by his convictions about the Harrisburg Convention, which he tagged pro-administration, he was not prone to be overgenerous toward industrialists.   With the farmers he was magnanimous, which was in keeping with his agrarian ideas and his own $20,000 investment. Then he raised the duties on the principal commodities of Kentucky, Missouri, Illinois, Pennsylvania, Ohio, New York, and Indiana in the hope that these states would reciprocate by voting the Jackson ticket. After that, it was a matter of jockeying a few rates up and down to win passage of the bill through Congress. Thus with the South and Southwest lacking any choice but to support the Hero of New Orleans, and the West and Middle states completely won over —leaving New England to Adams—Jackson would easily triumph over his rival in the presidential election.

At no time did Van Buren intend to defeat this tariff. His own words and actions at the time, and those of his closest friends, amply document this fact.[53] Unfortunately, the bill proved to be intensely sectional in character, and later, when he was spoken of as a candidate for the presidency, he tried to lie his way out of an embarrassing situation. Some Southerners had long memories and did not forget what they regarded as their "betrayal." John C. Calhoun never ceased grinding his teeth over this "Northern perfidy," but his opinions were certainly not typical of Southern feeling toward Van Buren personally. His charges were repeated almost verbatim by future historians even though Calhoun admitted that they were not based on his "own personal knowledge." [54] As a matter of fact, many Southerners were so well disposed toward Van Buren in 1828 that his cooperation was asked "in soothing over Southern friends under their fears & sufferings by the . . . Tariff." [55]

Unquestionably Van Buren said some very equivocal things to the Southerners. He certainly would not be so reckless as to take complete advantage of their "captured" position and possibly rupture the union of the "planters of the South and the plain Republicans of the North." After all, the tariff, among other things, was meant to unify the sections within the Democratic party, not divide them. And Van Buren had too much genuine affection for Southerners to want to hurt them more than was absolutely necessary. Years later he swore that he had been forced to support the measure on orders from the New York legislature.[56]   But when the New York *American* made this same charge in 1828, the *Argus* denounced the editor as a "falsifier." [57] The following year Croswell said that Van Buren had "authorized a public and direct denial" that he either opposed the tariff or voted for it solely in compliance with the wishes of his state.[58]   In March, 1829, when the Congress contemplated a new tariff, Cambreleng told the Little Magician that there was "no necessity for any departure from the position assumed last winter—make a *national* tariff—act up to the principle you then assumed—give equal protection to all branches of industry. . . ." [59]

By and large, in 1828, Van Buren was eminently satisfied with his work. He had presumably avoided party conflict on the issue in New York and had removed its usefulness to the administration in the campaign. Whether or not it drew the East and West together, in the manner he planned, cannot be positively stated, despite some evidence that it did. During the past decade New England had undergone an economic transformation and subsequently became a confirmed advocate of the protective system. To Edward Everett this had unfortunate political consequences because everyone knew that "Van B is of course stronger in all the tariff States." [60] In Congress there was "much good feeling in all the *NE* delegation for *Mr V. B.,*" wrote another representative. "On the subject of the Tariff and internal improvements, the feelings of the western states the middle & N England states are *in almost perfect* consonance." [61]

Although Jackson did win the West and Northwest in the election of 1828, his own personal popularity had probably more to do with it than the Tariff of Abominations. What is important, however, is that Van Buren thought the tariff would play a more decisive role than it actually did. As a political measure it was one of his most successful accomplishments. It was also one of the most potentially dangerous issues he ever tampered with in his life.

XIII: REVOLUTION

PEACE in New York, which Van Buren had worked feverishly in Washington to achieve, faded away as the Anti-masonic violence rolled over the state from the western counties. Unchecked and gaining momentum, this movement continued to spill forth its hate against Masons. Its unbridled fanaticism mesmerized large segments of the population and held them in its sway. Many Jacksonians were caught in the tempest and suddenly found themselves joining in the general outcry.[1] As with other popular outbursts of feeling in New York, this one gave birth to a new political party.

The Regency, horrified by the distraction from the basic Adams—Jackson controversy, tried to reduce the "fever," but when they learned in the spring of 1828 that Old Hickory was a practicing and outstanding Mason they knew their efforts were wasted. Adams, to their chagrin, was reported free "from all imputed criminality of that sort," and within weeks these facts were common knowledge.[2] The opportunist Thurlow Weed, now editor of the Rochester *Anti-Masonic Enquirer*, grasped the full meaning of this new information, and immediately essayed the task of combining the Anti-Masons and Adams men into one party.[3] But from the beginning he encountered repeated obstructions to his project, because many administration men were Masons themselves.

Before returning to the turbulent New York scene, Van Buren delivered one last important speech on the Senate floor. His remarks could quite properly be entitled "A History of the Political Parties of the United States, Their Origin and Their Principles." The subject was one that fascinated him and to which he repeatedly returned. He spent considerable time gathering materials to support his ideas and he was later to write a book—or, as his sons called it, "a digression" from his memoirs—expounding his views in full.[4] Few intellectual exercises gave him as much pleasure as analyzing the basic causes for the division between the Republican and Federalist parties. More important, his remarks on this particular occasion served to strengthen his belief in Jeffersonian concepts as well as to clarify them in his own mind.

Although his speech in the Senate presumably dealt with the constitutional powers of the Vice-President, he purposely digressed to expatiate upon the creed of the Jacksonian party. The fundamental doctrines of the Jeffersonian school were enumerated, and the dogma of states' rights was the central theme of the whole. The essential conflict between Hamilton and Jefferson, he maintained, was the same conflict that divided the Whigs and Tories during the Revolutionary period. It was, moreover, identical with the struggle between the friends of Jackson and those of Adams. The members of the Democratic party—the true descendants of the Patriots of 1776—were mindful, he said, of history and of the causes of this long-standing dispute. They were therefore averse to a national government that sought to enlarge its area of activity beyond the fixed boundaries set by the Constitution. Only through the continued existence of powerful states, he averred, could the liberties of the people be protected. He amplified this idea in a letter to a friend when he observed:

The only chance for the perpetuity of existing institutions depends upon the preserved vigor and constant watchfulness of the State Governments; that from the proneness on the part of agents so far removed from the people to corruption and other causes, there is not at this moment sufficient honesty in the administration of this Government to keep decent men in countenance; and that we are indebted for the little that remains to constant apprehension of rebuke and resistance from the States.[5]

Van Buren had nothing original to offer in his speech.
What he said was as old as the nation itself. He simply wanted
the political principles of the Democratic party to be understood by all.

Because of the publicity given to the trials begun in the
western counties of persons suspected of involvement in
Morgan's disappearance, public curiosity and interest would
not diminish. With each new report of witnesses who were
spirited away or who suddenly vanished, Anti-Masonry increased in strength.[6] Although pages of testimony piled higher
and higher, no one could state with accuracy what had become
of the hapless Morgan. It was the mystery of the decade and
the public was overcome by an insatiable desire to know his
fate.

Returning to Albany after Congress adjourned on May 22,
Van Buren was set upon by the Bucktails. They fretted over
present conditions and implored him to produce a scheme
which would scotch the Anti-Masonic snake and restore harmony throughout the west. As usual he was optimistic; he
promised to take charge of the campaign and visit the infected
areas again during the summer.

The visible relief among Bucktails after their leader's return to New York not only indicated how much they needed
him but also served to harass, confuse, and frustrate the administration men. "Van Buren is a host in himself," one
sighed, "the *idol and pride* of his party. . . ."[7] Although the
supporters of Adams had set up a central committee to conduct
the campaign—which gave some semblance of a bustling political organization—their efforts were amateurish in the extreme.
Compared to the well-oiled Jacksonian machine supervised by
the Little Magician, theirs was remarkably ineffective. Yet with
all the advantages the Regency men possessed by their knowledge of the science of winning elections, they were not foolish
enough to suppose they could get by their present difficulties
on the strength of the organization alone. A weak candidate

for governor, they concurred, would be as disastrous to Jackson
as to the party itself. If nothing else, wrote one local politician,
our troubles "ought to teach us to nominate our strongest men.
With any other I fear we shall be beaten. Mr. Van Buren
ought to be our Candidate for Gov." [8]

As early as the spring of 1828, the Bucktails would consider
no other man than their *"idol and pride"* to head their ticket.
They repeatedly urged him to announce his candidacy, but
Van Buren, who had been told to reserve himself "for another
Destiny under the General Govt" as Secretary of State if Jackson were elected, was not inclined to accept, since if he joined
the cabinet his term as Governor would be less than two
months.[9] However, when he returned to Albany in May and
surveyed the disruption and, to some extent, revolt against the
party caused by the Anti-Masonic furor, all his misgivings disappeared. For the good of both the state and national elections, and on the strong advice of his friends—which was ever a
guide to his conduct—he consented to run. No other Jacksonian could unite the Republicans so readily against the opposition. He alone could win New York's large electoral vote for
the General.[10]

It was probably in July that Van Buren signaled his willingness to stand as the Bucktail nominee, but he did so with
the understanding that if Jackson became President and called
him to the cabinet, he was free to resign.[11] When his friends
agreed to the condition, he allowed them to nominate him.

Jacksonians in other parts of the country were also girding
themselves for the final stages of the campaign. In some places
their task was difficult, in others as easy as comparing the personalities of the two candidates. The newspaper war continued
its furious pace, accountable no doubt to the pleasure and satisfaction which the people derived from reading the scurrilous
editorials.

Old Hickory, who claimed he wanted only one term in
office, respected the advice of his counselors and said nothing
about party affairs. Instead he looked after his plantation, met

the many people who visited him at the Hermitage, and accepted an invitation to go to New Orleans for the anniversary of his great military victory against the British in 1815. His companions Houston and Lewis persisted in their schemes to alter the ticket without having much luck. And in South Carolina, the imprudent Calhoun was writing the *Exposition and Protest* to expound his pernicious doctrine of nullification.

If Jackson took little part in the national campaign, Adams took even less. Henry Clay was busy writing to his henchmen in the several states, but the odds against his candidate kept getting worse. With the "common" people prepared to decide between Old Hickory and John of Braintree, there really was little choice. The element of personality entered this election and gave Jackson a distinct advantage. Even though he might not fit the part, in the minds of some he was a romantic hero, who killed Indians, saved the country from the hated British, and defended the honor of his wife against the best shots in the Southwest. How much imagination did it take to see him sitting astride his horse, commanding armies and annihilating his country's foes? All things considered, a voter in 1828 could huzza for "General Andy," but what could he do for "King John?"

Late in July Van Buren started on what was now his annual peregrination through the several counties, and invited Churchill C. Cambreleng and one or two other lieutenants to accompany him. With leisurely progress he stopped at all the important cities along the way. He cut quite a figure among westerners, dressed as he was in an outfit which displayed all the colors of the rainbow. Every Sunday, in a different city, churchgoers could get a glimpse of him, in white duck trousers, snuff-colored broadcloth coat, a tie of brilliant orange, a vest of pearl hue, and yellow kid gloves, sitting in the pew of a leading Clintonian and singing the hymns with rare devotion.[12] But who could laugh at this personable, pious, sagacious and hardworking Senator? He typified many of New York's best qualities—its sureness of future success, its acquisitiveness, enthusiasm, vigor, and resourcefulness.

By the last week in August, Van Buren was back from his "excursion" and immediately reported his findings to James A. Hamilton, who was with Jackson. He said that his trip had

been very pleasant, and I hope, politically speaking, has been equally profitable. We shall beat them greatly. The anti-masonic affair is the only thing that requires looking to. Beg Noah and Coleman [the editor of the New York *Evening Post*] to treat the matter cautiously. I have written to the former upon the point. The excitement has been vastly greater than I supposed, but has assumed a much milder aspect. . . . Let me entreat you to give your undivided attention to the subject of funds. You must absolutely do more in New York than you promised. . . . Don't forget to bet all you can.[13]

Whatever thoughts the Regency chief may have had about directing the national campaign were abandoned when he declared his candidacy for governor. To win as many of New York's electoral votes for Jackson as possible was a sizable job requiring all his energies. The administration forces were fighting hard, and had Smith Thompson, an associate justice of the Supreme Court, as their gubernatorial candidate. The Anti-Masons, refusing an alliance with the Adams men,[14] made the great mistake of choosing the farcical, half-mad Solomon Southwick to be their standard-bearer.[15] A more ridiculous nomination was impossible, since Southwick was a suspected thief. "I presume," laughed one Bucktail, ". . . Mr. Van Buren's long fingers will be found in it by the sage editors of the Intelligencer. As time rolls on, and the period of active engagement approaches, the cause of Jackson improves. Jackson & reform —is [sic] the watchwords."[16]

With all his concern for the New York election, Van Buren kept in touch with the General and regularly reported his progress in dealing with Anti-Masonry.[17] But during the summer, the Hero's aides became so nervous over a possible opposition alliance in New York that they inquired of the Senator whether the members of the legislature could not take upon themselves the responsibility of changing the electoral law "so as to give the whole 36 votes to the Gen."[18] Van Buren was amazed by the crudity of the question and replied that it could not be done. Such a move, he retorted, would provoke more excitement than the entire Morgan affair.[19]

Unfortunately, the opposition journals got wind of the suggestion and accused Van Buren of sponsoring it. The editors of the *National Intelligencer,* who never stopped calling attention to his alliances, used the story to preface a series of articles denouncing him as "dangerous" to the welfare of the nation. Referring to him as the "Master Spirit," Gales and Seaton accused him of forming a "combination" with Thomas Ritchie for purposes both "personal and sinister." The nation was about to witness, they abusively exclaimed, the restoration of "State rights" conceived by the "Master Spirit" and dedicated to the caucus, the junta, and the prostration of all manufactures.[20]

The stalwarts Croswell and Ritchie wrote long and fervent refutations—after all it was disrespectful to call the Democratic party a sinister combination—but Van Buren knew the extent to which the mischief might go, especially over the electoral question, unless he personally intervened. In a strongly worded letter to the editor of the Albany *Daily Advertiser* he branded the story that he intended to change the electoral law an insidious lie and disclaimed all association with the revisionists.[21] His denial was so emphatic that while the report continued to be circulated for the next few weeks, most of its bite was gone.

Van Buren's handling of the campaign during the last remaining months before the election was little short of brilliant. Old techniques of vote-getting were "modernized" by the use of parades, buttons, and other paraphernalia. He so dazzled the opposition with the splendor of his political ingenuity that he drove them to "apathy" and a desire for "Matyrdom [sic]." [22] He coaxed public addresses from the pens of New York's most illustrious writers. Others who mistakenly thought they possessed the literary gifts of a Hamilton, Madison, or Jefferson, he discouraged with humor and courtesy. In collecting funds for the campaign treasury he was adroit, pleasantly persistent, and thorough. His home became a "mad house" of crowds looking for advice and instruction or precious information from among his many papers. And with it all he could always find a spare moment to counsel Jackson. For the most part he urged the General to maintain a discreet silence regarding the "Calumnies" and "crimes" leveled against him. The leaders of the new Democratic party—such as James Buchanan of Pennsylvania, Caleb Atwater of Ohio, Francis P. Blair and Amos Kendall of Kentucky, Isaac Hill of New Hampshire, Edward Livingston of Louisiana, John H. Eaton and William B. Lewis of Tennessee, and himself, to mention a few—could handle the problem of defense.[23] Within their respective bailiwicks they could find the necessary palliatives to soothe the public mind.

In short, the age of the professional politician had arrived. This phenomenon resulted from a general revision of electoral laws in the states giving the people—the common people—the vote. To win those votes and organize them into solid blocs became the special task of the trained politician. He stood complete with the accouterments of his trade: parades, campaign songs and speeches, newspapers, wide grin and open hand, a memory for names and faces, and specially designed articles of clothing—including hats, buttons, and vests with his candidate's name or features plainly stamped upon them. The list could be made longer, for it included everything that would appeal to the masses, even the worst forms of demagoguery.

From the beginning, the American people loved the performance put on for them. For some the party was the only stable element in their lives, providing them with companionship and a sense of belonging. The organization was virtually a society in itself, with a formal code of laws and the coercive power of rewards and punishments to enforce them.

The New York campaign swung into high gear during October and November, with the state and national elections

mixed together in the right proportion. Endeavoring to wash
away some of the muck associated with the Hero's name by
many administration sheets, the *Argus,* in bold capital letters,
proudly presented the General as the "Soldier Boy of the First
War of Independence. The Veteran Hero of the Second. He
Saved the Country. Let the cry be Jackson, Van Buren &
Liberty." [24] To set the tone and pace of the campaign, em-
phasis was placed on the words "People" and "Reform." Because the electors were chosen by districts and the contests
might be close, a concerted drive was made to educate the
masses to use their vote with the idea of stamping out the last
vestige of the old "1798 brand of aristocrats."

The precise direction all this "reform" was to take was not
explained. There was no need to. The people were simply
banding together to take the national government out of the
hands of the favored few. They were claiming what belonged
to them. They were dispossessing the "wise, the good and the
well born."

When the Regency campaigners in New York reached their
stride, Van Buren and Jackson moved ahead to hold a slight
edge over their opponents.[25] It was "frightful," wrote Edward
Everett, congressman, editor of the *North American Review,*
and former professor of rhetoric at Harvard, to think that the
result of the election was narrowed down to a few districts
"directly under the wand of the great magician." [26] Those who
were frank enough to admit the truth conceded that Bucktail
superiority was owing in part to the division and disunity
among anti-Jacksonians as well as the superb supervision given
every phase of the campaign by Van Buren.[27] No local election was too insignificant to engage his attention, and when
"difficulties" arose he acted quickly and decisively. At the last
possible moment, William H. Crawford made another bid to
defeat Calhoun's reelection to the vice-presidency by urging
Van Buren to substitute Nathaniel Macon on the New York
electoral ballot. To this proposal the Senator replied sharply.
"Our electors," he said with finality, "are committed for Mr
Calhoun." [28]

The November contests in New York were savagely fought, and the Jacksonians lost many districts because of "the disgraceful direction given to the excitement growing out of the Morgan affair." [29] Throughout the entire state, Van Buren polled 136,763 votes as against 106,444 for Thompson and 33,345 for Southwick. He had three thousand less than the combined tallies of his opponents. Jackson fared little better. He received 140,763 votes to 135,413 for Adams. Since the electors were chosen by districts, New York gave the Hero 20 of its 36 votes. Had the general ticket system been in use, as it was throughout the nation with the exception of Massachusetts, Maine, Tennessee, and Maryland, the General would have taken them all.

From the vantage point of the Electoral College, after the results from the whole country had been turned in, the contest looked overwhelmingly one-sided. Jackson captured the South, West, and Northwest, for a total of 178 electoral votes. Kentucky, Ohio, and Missouri, which Clay had won in 1824, all voted for Jackson. Adams was a poor second with 83 votes, most of which came from New England. However, the final returns of the popular vote brought Adams within twelve percent of his rival—647,276 to 508,064—largely because of heavy Eastern majorities from the merchant, commercial, landed, and some workingmen's groups.

In New York, Adams won the old Federalist strongholds bordering the upper Hudson River, the western counties given over to Anti-Masonry and a group of five counties running down the center of the state. The remainder went to Jackson. Van Buren offered one explanation for Adams's remarkable showing in New York. "It seemed as if old '98 Federalists had risen from the dead," he said. "Men of that school who have not been seen at the polls for years & several whom we supposed dead for years were in the hottest of the fight." [30] The Hamiltonians, according to Van Buren, had responded to the challenge of the people but had failed to meet it.

William B. Lewis regarded the results in a different light, and scored Jackson's "injury" to the Anti-Masons as well as the fact that the presidential contest was "mixed up with your state elections." [31]   But there was no reason to complain. Considering the disadvantage against which they were forced to campaign, the Jacksonians had done a splendid job. The state was in their hands and the majority of its electoral votes, which had been given to Adams in 1824, were now awarded to Jackson. Only the greedy complained. The Hero never did.

The election of 1828 brought about the triumph of what is commonly referred to as Jacksonian Democracy. This phenomenon defies definition because, fundamentally, it was a faith. It glorified such words as "people," "their will," and "reform," but had not yet given them precise meaning. Perhaps, for some men, this new democracy had no precise meaning; nevertheless, it was something which they knew existed and was important, something they could be loyal to and cherish.

Jackson was elected because the majority of people throughout the entire United States closed ranks in his favor. Party organization, marvelously revitalized by Van Buren and others, was one of the important factors that helped them do this. Channeling their will through the machinery of the party, they obtained the necessary power to elect a government truly representative of their wishes. Perhaps the procedure was not wholly democratic considering the role politicians had played and were to continue to play in the future; but the fact remained that the system could always be improved if the people so desired and if they remained faithful to the organization.

Van Buren's part in this "revolution" of 1828 is of paramount importance. His remodeling of Jefferson's party constituted a major step in transferring the government from the control of the "few" to the "many." As great a President as he was, Jackson could never have assisted the fundamental democratic changes taking place in the country without the people's support and the means for them to express their support effectively.

More remained to be done before the Democratic party fully emerged, but these were details. Further discipline was necessary to tighten the organization, to give it greater internal strength and force. With the Federal patronage now happily at hand, and with Van Buren's vast knowledge to explain how such things were manipulated, the discipline would shortly be forthcoming. A caucus would never be held again to nominate presidential candidates, but as the Little Magician had earlier indicated, a national convention could easily replace it. Just as long as "we have either," he had said. A Washington newspaper would also have to be founded to spell out in clear terms the party line on all issues. There might be a struggle with Calhoun about this, but the Little Magician knew how to handle the Vice-President. Finally, party doctrines would have to be constantly reiterated to leave no doubt about the creed of Jacksonians, and Van Buren notified the President-elect, through Colonel Hamilton, that he hoped the General in his inaugural address would not express any constitutional opinion at war with the doctrines of Thomas Jefferson.[32] Beyond that, beyond a doctrinal position, Van Buren had no suggestions about issues. He said nothing regarding internal improvements, the tariff, or banks.

The Little Magician had no conception of the long-range results his work would have upon the nation. He had acted instinctively, master politician that he was. He probably supposed that his constant appeals to the electorate to protect states' rights and the Republican creed, the time he spent in reawakening "old party feelings," and even his tampering with the tariff were remedies to deal with a present situation—the defeat of the Federalist, Adams, and the election of the Republican, Jackson. He never fully realized that from these simple beginnings a great party of the people emerged, cutting across all sections and classes of the country and holding the Union together.

After surveying what had happened in 1828, one contemporary said that Jackson's election "was notoriously the work of Martin Van Buren. . . ."[33] This is only partly true. Old Hickory won because the people voted for him; and they voted for him because he appealed to them and fired their imagination. Organization, although important, is not enough; it needs leaders, personalities, strong-willed men.

But the system works both ways. The party is indispensable to every candidate, no matter who he is. Without it the presidency is unobtainable under our present form of government. Even if a prospective candidate possesses a greatness to match Lincoln's, it does him and the people absolutely no good unless he is ready to accept the one support that can lift him to the position where his greatness can be applied. Because of the party system, the "common" man can run this nation and raise anyone to the highest office in the land.

Martin Van Buren, along with a number of other men in the 1820's, can claim a measure of credit for this. Between them they put together a splendid organization, and then gave it to the people.

NOTES

Notes to I: *THE LITTLE MAGICIAN*

1. The man having his head examined was Aaron Burr. Parton, *The Life and Times of Aaron Burr,* II, 320.

2. Crockett, *Autobiography,* pp. 297–98.

3. Raymond, *Biographical Sketches of the Distinguished Men of Columbia County,* p. 50.

4. Foote, *Casket of Reminiscences,* p. 59; James A. Hamilton, *Reminiscences,* p. 124; Hosack, *Memoir of De Witt Clinton,* p. 453.

5. Sargent, *Public Men and Events,* II, 24; John Q. Adams, *Memoirs,* IX, 425.

6. Foote, *Reminiscences,* p. 59.

7. Butler, *A Retrospect of Forty Years,* p. 46.

8. Van Buren to Rufus King, September 21, 1822, in King, *Life and Correspondence,* VI, 478.

9. Foote, *Reminiscences,* pp. 59–60. See also Scott, *Memoirs,* II, 301.

10. Sargent, *Public Men and Events,* I, 204.

11. "Mr. Van Buren," *The United States Magazine and Democratic Review,* XV (1844), 5.

12. Van Buren to Gorham A. Worth, March 15, 1822, Van Buren Papers, Library of Congress.

13. Brockway, *Fifty Years in Journalism,* p. 40.

14. *Ibid.,* p. 41; Hamilton, *Reminiscences,* p. 124.

15. Foote, *Reminiscences,* p. 59; Poore, *Perley's Reminiscences of Sixty Years in the National Metropolis,* I, 65.

16. Jenkins, *Lives of the Governors of the State of New York,* p. 258. For a well-written pen portrait of Clinton, see Fox, *The Decline of Aristocracy in the Politics of New York,* p. 200.

17. "A cold & haughty selfishness seems to have pervaded all his feelings," exclaimed one contemporary. Nathan Williams to Van

Buren, December 19, 1819, Van Buren Papers, Library of Congress. "The charge of a cold repulsive manner," Clinton was told to his face, "is not the most trifling charge, that your political enemies have brought against you. . . ." John Brennan to Clinton, postmarked September 23, 1823, De Witt Clinton Papers, Columbia University Library.

An anecdote often told, which if not true is typical of others that are, involves the personalities of Clinton and Daniel D. Tompkins, another governor of New York. It seems a farmer asked Tompkins to free his son, who had been convicted of a felony, and was repeatedly refused. Later on, Governor Clinton pardoned the son, believing the father to be an influential man in his county. The farmer afterwards reported that "although I have seen Gov. Tompkins but twice, and although at each time he positively refused to grant me the favor I desired, and Gov. Clinton has granted me that very favor upon the first time of asking, I like Gov. Tompkins better than I like or can like Gov. Clinton—I can not tell the reason why." Hammond, *The History of Political Parties in the State of New York,* II, 271–72.

18. William Plumer, Jr. to William Plumer, November 27, 1820, in Brown ed., *Missouri Compromises and Presidential Politics,* p. 61.

19. Fox, *Decline of Aristocracy,* p. 200.

20. Brockway, *Fifty Years in Journalism,* pp. 27–28.

21. Hale, *William H. Seward,* p. 35.

22. Brockway, *Fifty Years in Journalism,* pp. 27–28.

23. Van Buren to Jesse Hoyt, January 31, 1823, in Mackenzie, *The Lives and Opinions of Benjamin Franklin Butler and Jesse Hoyt,* p. 190.

24. Donovan, *The Barnburners,* p. 7.

25. William L. Marcy to Azariah C. Flagg, November 26, 1823, Flagg Papers, New York Public Library.

26. Silas Wright, Jr. to Flagg, January 28, 1826, Flagg Papers, New York Public Library. For a more complete account of the Regency, see Robert V. Remini, "The Albany Regency," *New York History,* XXXIX (October, 1958), 341–55.

27. Van Buren, *Autobiography,* p. 401.

Notes to II: "THE MONROE HERESY"

1. Bryan, *A History of the National Capital,* II, 32–66.

2. *Ibid.,* II, 47–55.

3. Rufus King to John A. King, January 19, 1822, in King, *Life and Correspondence,* VI, 453.

4. Poore, *Perley's Reminiscences,* pp. 64–65.

5. Towers Manuscript Diary, entry dated April, 1831, Columbia University Library.

6. Adams, *Memoirs,* V, 428.

7. "Pray what course will the bucktail members from this State take on the subject of Speaker," Taylor was asked. "I know that some of them have been drilled to opposition and Van Buren no doubt will be on the ground to lead or rather to drive them to the charge." Albert Tracy to Taylor, September 21, 1821, John W. Taylor Papers, New York Historical Society.

8. Van Buren to John Van Ness Yates, November 6, 1821, Miscellaneous Papers, New York State Library.

9. Adams, *Memoirs,* V, 431; Taylor to W. D. Ford, January 18, 1822, Taylor Papers, New York Historical Society.

10. William Plumer, Jr. to William Plumer, December 3, 1821, in Brown, ed., *Missouri Compromises and Presidential Politics,* p. 65.

11. William Plumer, Jr. to William Plumer, December 4, 1821, *ibid.,* p. 67; Adams, *Memoirs,* V, 436, 474.

12. Adams, *Memoirs,* V, 451, 474; Brown, ed., *Missouri Compromises,* p. 67; Taylor to Ford, January 18, 1822, Taylor Papers, New York Historical Society.

13. Marcy was the one who actually called Taylor a "trimmer." Marcy to John Bailey, November 24, 1821, John Bailey Papers, Massachusetts Historical Society.

14. William Plumer, Jr. to William Plumer, December 28, 1821, in Brown, ed., *Missouri Compromises,* p. 69.

15. Van Buren, *Autobiography,* p. 513.

16. *Ibid.*   17. *Ibid.*

18. *Ibid.,* p. 574; John D. Dickinson to Solomon Van Rensselaer, January 29, 1822, Stephen Van Rensselaer to Solomon Van Rensselaer, April 9, 1822, in Bonney, *A Legacy of Historical Gleanings,* I, 397, 402.

19. Michael Ulshoeffer to Van Buren, February 17, 1822, Van Buren Papers, Library of Congress.

20. Van Buren may have had something to do with Southwick's appointment in 1815. See Smith Thompson to Van Buren, November 24, 1815, Van Buren Papers, Library of Congress.

21. Solomon Van Rensselaer to Stephen Van Rensselaer, December 26, 1821, in Bonney, *Historical Gleanings,* p. 370.

22. James McKown to Solomon Van Rensselaer, December 26, 1821, *ibid.,* p. 371.

23. Van Buren to Knower, Dudley, Skinner, *et al.,* January 5, 1822, *ibid.,* pp. 374–76.

24. Stephen Van Rensselaer to Solomon Van Rensselaer, January 2, 1822, *ibid.,* p. 373.

25. Van Buren and King to Meigs, January 3, 1822, Van Buren Papers, Library of Congress.

26. "Whip me such republicans," snorted Daniel D. Tompkins when he saw a copy of the petition. Tompkins to J. Thompson, January 4, 1822, in Bonney, *Historical Gleanings,* p. 373.

27. Tompkins, King, and Van Buren to Meigs, January 4, 1822, Meigs to King and Van Buren, January 4, 1822, Van Buren Papers, Library of Congress; Adams, *Memoirs,* V, 479.

28. Tompkins to J. Thompson, January 4, 1822, in Bonney, *Historical Gleanings,* p. 373.

29. Van Buren to Monroe, January 5, 1822, Van Buren Papers, Library of Congress.

30. Van Buren to Knower, Cantine, Dudley, *et al.,* January 6, 1822, in Bonney, *Historical Gleanings,* p. 377.

31. *Ibid.,* p. 377; Solomon Van Rensselaer to Dr. William Bay, January 7, 1822, p. 378.

32. Van Buren to Knower, Dudley, Skinner, Duer, *et al.,* January 5, 1822; William B. Rochester to Solomon Van Rensselaer, January 7, 1822; Adelaide Van Rensselaer to Solomon Van Rensselaer, January 8, 1822, *ibid.,* pp. 374–76, 378, 381.

33. Adams, *Memoirs,* V, 480–82.

34. Monroe to Van Buren, January 7, 1822, Monroe Papers, New York Public Library.

35. Tompkins and Van Buren to Meigs, January 7, 1822, in Bonney, *Historical Gleanings,* pp. 391–92. See also a statement on the personalities of Van Rensselaer and Lansing in the Van Buren Papers, Library of Congress.

36. Both Van Buren and King believed Monroe would have appointed Lansing had it been up to the President. Rufus King to

Charles King, January 8 and 14, 1822, in King, *Life and Corre-spondence,* VI, 438, 449.

It should be stated clearly that in the beginning Van Buren exonerated Monroe from all blame connected with the appointment. "I have no reason to complain of Mr. Monroe," he wrote on January 10, 1822. "On the receipt of my letter he called a cabinet council, and the course he took was in pursuance of their opinion on the abstract question of his right to interfere. He has throughout shown great anxiety on the subject, and would, I am convinced, if the question had laid with him, have done us justice." Van Buren to Charles Dudley, January 10, 1822, in Bonney, *Historical Gleanings,* p. 383. However, Van Buren changed his mind about Monroe shortly thereafter, perhaps when the President appointed a Federalist marshal to office in Pennsylvania. "On the other hand," he wrote, "Mr. Monroe, at the commencement of his second term, took the ground openly, and maintained it against all remonstrances, that no difference should be made by the Government in the distribution of its patronage and confidence on account of the political opinions and course of applicants. The question was distinctly brought before him for decision by the Republican representatives from the states of Pennsylvania and New York, in cases that had deeply excited the feelings of their constituents and in which those constituents had very formally and decidedly expressed their opinions." Van Buren, *Autobiography,* p. 124.

37. Italics mine.

38. Van Buren to Dudley, January 10, 1822, in Bonney, *Historical Gleanings,* pp. 382–84.

39. Van Buren, *Autobiography,* p. 125.

40. *Ibid.,* pp. 125–27. See Van Buren's comments regarding Monroe's conduct with respect to the 1824 caucus in his *Inquiry into the Origin and Course of Political Parties in the United States,* pp. 4–5.

41. However, Eugene H. Roseboom, in his study of presidential elections, states categorically that Monroe wished to eliminate party differences. *A History of Presidential Elections,* p. 76.

42. Dudley to Van Buren, January 14, 1822, in Bonney, *Historical Gleanings,* p. 385; Ulshoeffer to Van Buren, January 13, 1822, Van Buren Papers, Library of Congress.

43. Memorial dated January 22, 1822; Ulshoeffer to Van Buren, January 27, 1822, Van Buren Papers, Library of Congress.

44. Clinton to Jabez D. Hammond, January 12, 1822, Miscellaneous Papers, New York State Library.

45. Marcy to John Bailey, January 31, 1822, Bailey Papers, Massachusetts Historical Society.

46. It was said that Van Buren was determined to have Meigs removed but did not have the power to do it. Walter Patterson to Solomon Van Rensselaer, January 29, 1822, in Bonney, *Historical Gleanings,* p. 397; Rufus King to John A. King, January 19, 1822, in King, *Life and Correspondence,* VI, 452; Ulshoeffer to Van Buren, January 27, 1822, Van Buren Papers.

47. Resolutions of a meeting held on January 25, 1822, in Bonney, *Historical Gleanings,* p. 396.

48. Van Buren to Rufus King, February 18, 1822, King Papers, New York Historical Society.

49. Monroe to ?, June 10, 1823, Monroe Papers, New York Public Library.

50. Talcott to Van Buren, February 7, 1822, Van Buren Papers, Library of Congress.

51. Van Buren to Benjamin F. Butler, February 12, 1822, in Harriett C. Peckman, *History of Cornelis Maessen Van Buren,* p. 122; Van Buren, *Autobiography,* pp. 128–29.

52. Stephen Van Rensselaer to Solomon Van Rensselaer, April 9, 1822, in Bonney, *Historical Gleanings,* p. 402; Peter B. Porter to Clay, January 29, 1822, in Clay, *Private Correspondence,* pp. 62–63.

53. William Plumer, Jr. to William Plumer, December 30, 1821, January 3, 1822, in Brown, ed., *Missouri Compromises and Presidential Politics,* pp. 70, 74; Bemis, *John Quincy Adams and the Foundations of American Foreign Policy,* pp. 417–23.

54. Van Buren to Gulian C. Verplanck, December 22, 1822, Van Buren Papers, Library of Congress.

55. Porter to Clay, January 29, 1822, in Clay, *Private Correspondence,* p. 63; Rufus King to Van Buren, September 24, 1822, Van Buren Papers, Library of Congress.

56. William Plumer, Jr. to William Plumer, January 3, 1822, in Brown, ed., *Missouri Compromises and Presidential Politics,* p. 74; Rufus King to John A. King, January 1, 1822, Van Buren to John A. King, February 4, 1822, in King, *Life and Correspondence,* VI, 434, 458.

57. Van Buren, *Autobiography,* p. 126.

58. Ulshoeffer to Van Buren, April 2, 1822, Van Buren Papers, Library of Congress. Ambrose Spencer, who wrote to Van Buren thanking him for a favor, said he heard the Senator was getting married. March 28, 1822, Van Buren Papers, Library of Congress.

59. Van Buren to Gorham A. Worth, March 15, 1822, Van Buren Papers, Library of Congress.

Notes to III: OLD-FASHIONED JEFFERSONIAN REPUBLICANISM

1. *Annals of Congress,* 17th Congress, 2nd Session, p. 443.

2. Cresson, *James Monroe,* pp. 392–93.

3. *Annals of Congress,* 17th Congress, 2nd Session, p. 92.

4. Van Buren, *Autobiography,* p. 117.

5. Memorandum of Rufus King, dated February 2, 1823, in King, *Life and Correspondence,* VI, 509–11; Smith Thompson to Van Buren, March 17, 1823, Van Buren Papers, Library of Congress.

6. Thompson to Van Buren, March 25, 1823, Van Buren Papers, Library of Congress.

7. Van Buren to Thompson, March 30, 1823, Van Buren Papers, Library of Congress.

8. The obvious ease with which the Bucktails would install the governor in the 1822 election gave some Republicans the idea that Van Buren should have the office. But he replied: "I have seen enough of State politics for many years. *I have made my debut here* [Washington] *and am abundantly satisfied.*" Van Buren to Gorham A. Worth, February 18, 1822, Van Buren to Erastus Root, January 16, 1822, Van Buren Papers, Library of Congress.

9. George Brancroft to Mrs. S. D. Bancroft, December 27, 1831, in Howe, *Life and Letters of George Bancroft,* I, 195.

10. Rufus King to Monroe, April 2, 1823, in King, *Life and Correspondence,* VI, 513.

11. King to Adams, April 1, 1823, *ibid.,* 512.

12. Adams to King, April 7, 1823, *ibid.,* 514; George Bancroft to Mrs. S. D. Bancroft, December 27, 1831, in Howe, *Life and Letters of George Bancroft,* I, 195. Adams later claimed that he also helped Van Buren seek the appointment, but there is doubt whether this amounted to much.

13. Monroe to ?, March 31, 1823, April 6, 14, 1823, Monroe Papers, New York Public Library.

14. Thompson to Van Buren, April 6, 1823, Van Buren Papers, Library of Congress.

15. Van Buren to King, April 14, 1823, in King, *Life and Correspondence,* VI, 516.

16. Van Buren to Thompson, April 15, Thompson to Van Buren, April 25, 1823, *ibid.,* VI, 516–17.

17. Monroe to ?, May 1, June 5, William Wirt to Monroe, May 5, 1823, Monroe Papers, New York Public Library; Crawford to Van Buren, May 9, 1823, Van Buren Papers, Library of Congress; Monroe to James Barbour, June 14, 1823, James Barbour Papers, New York Public Library.

18. Van Buren to Thompson, June 4, 1823, Van Buren Papers, Library of Congress. Van Buren wrote that he heard it rumored that Monroe was opposed to his appointment. "That the President would sooner appoint an alligator than me. That he would not appoint me as long as their [*sic*] was an other man to be found in the State & such like sayings." Van Buren indicates that he believed the rumors.

19. Crawford to Van Buren, August 1, 1823, Van Buren Papers, Library of Congress.

20. Thompson to Van Buren, July 11, 1823, Van Buren Papers, Library of Congress.

21. King wrote the letter that Van Buren finally sent to Thompson, but before it reached Washington the Secretary notified the President he would accept the appointment. S. L. Southard from New Jersey replaced Thompson as Secretary of the Navy. Hamilton, *Reminiscences,* p. 62; Van Buren to King, July 18, July 25, 1823, King to Van Buren, July 22, 1823, King Papers, New York Historical Society; Monroe to ?, July 20, 1823, Monroe Papers, New York Public Library; Adams, *Memoirs,* VI, 173.

22. King to Van Buren, July 22, 1823, King Papers, New York Historical Society.

23. King to Christopher Gore, March 13, 1817, in King, *Life and Correspondence,* VI, 66.

24. Robert V. Remini, "New York and the Presidential Election of 1816," *New York History,* XXXI (July, 1950), 320.

25. Van Buren, *Inquiry into the Origin and Course of Political Parties in the United States,* pp. 3–4.

26. James, *The Life of Andrew Jackson,* p. 354.

27. Van Buren, *Autobiography,* p. 131.

28. John A. Dix to Dr. George C. Shattuck, December 19, 1822, "John A. Dix Letters, 1812–1848," *Massachusetts Historical Society Proceedings,* L (January, 1917), 143.

29. Van Buren to Thomas Ritchie, January 13, 1827, Van Buren Papers, Library of Congress.

30. It should be remembered that Van Buren wrote this many years later, and he unquestionably projected his thoughts in 1854 back to 1823.

31. Van Buren, *Autobiography,* p. 513.

32. Van Buren to Johnston Verplanck, December 22, 1822, Van Buren Papers, Library of Congress.

33. De Witt Clinton Manuscript Diary, entry dated October 24, 1823, New York Historical Society.

34. Clay to Peter B. Porter, February, 1823, Porter Papers, Buffalo Historical Society.

35. King to Charles King, February 26, 1823, King to Christopher Gore, February 9, 1823, in King, *Life and Correspondence,* VI, 500, 504.

36. King to Charles King, February 26, 1823, *ibid.,* VI, 504.

37. *Ibid.;* John A. King to Van Buren, February 23, 1823, Van Buren Papers, Library of Congress; New York *American,* March 15, 1823.

38. Root to Van Buren, January 3, 1823, Van Buren Papers, Library of Congress.

39. Memorandum of Rufus King, in King, *Life and Correspondence,* VI, 521; Clinton to G. G. Haines, December 9, 1823, Clinton Papers, Columbia University Library; Clinton to Henry Post, August 6, 1823, in John Bigelow, ed., "De Witt Clinton as a Politician," *Harper's New Monthly Magazine,* L (December, 1874 to May, 1875), 568.

40. Van Buren, *Autobiography,* p. 514; Van Buren to Smith Thompson, May 23, 1823, Van Buren Papers, Library of Congress.

41. John Ellicott to General Blackshear, September 4, 1822, in J. E. D. Shipp, *Giant Days, or the Life and Times of W. H. Crawford,* p. 171.

42. Calhoun to Samuel Gouverneur, April 28, 9, 1823, Gouverneur Papers, New York Public Library; Calhoun to General J. G. Swift, April 29, May 10, 1823, in Thomas R. Hay, "John Calhoun and the Presidential Election of 1824; Some Unpublished Calhoun Letters," *American Historical Review,* XL (October, 1934), 84–86.

43. Calhoun to Gouverneur, April 28, May 25, June 6, October 4, 1823, Winfield Scott to Gouverneur, April 8, 1823, Gouverneur Papers, New York Public Library.

44. One of the specific purposes for founding *The Patriot* was to offset the propaganda of M. M. Noah's *National Advocate.* Thomas R. Hay, "John C. Calhoun and the Presidential Election of 1824," *The North Carolina Historical Review,* XII (April, 1935), 32; Joseph Gardner Swift, *Memoirs,* p. 192.

45. Hammond, *The History of Political Parties in the State of New York,* II, 130. A general meeting was held in Albany on April 22, and the members of the legislature dutifully resolved that a Congressional caucus should select the Republican candidate. This, Van Buren boasted in sending a copy of the memorial to John Taylor of Caroline, is "evidence of the patriotism of New York...." Printed circular dated April 23, 1823, to John Taylor, with the note in Van Buren's handwriting, Everett Papers, Massachusetts Historical Society.

46. King to Christopher Gore, February 9, 1823, in King, *Life and Correspondence,* VI, 499.

47. Nathaniel Macon to Van Buren, May 9, 1823, Van Buren Papers, Library of Congress.

48. Van Buren to Smith Thompson, May 23, 1823, Van Buren Papers, Library of Congress.

49. Van Buren to Smith Thompson, June 4, 1823, Van Buren Papers, Library of Congress.

50. Ritchie to Van Buren, July 2, 1838, in Charles H. Ambler, "Unpublished Letters of Thomas Ritchie," *John P. Branch Historical Papers,* III (June, 1911), 229.

51. Ambler, *Thomas Ritchie, a Study in Virginia Politics,* pp. 89–90.

52. *Ibid.,* pp. 90–91.

53. Calhoun to Gouverneur, November 9, 1823, Gouverneur Papers, New York Public Library.

54. Clinton to Oliver Forward, October 12, 1823, Clinton Papers, Columbia University Library; Flagg to Van Buren, November 12, 1823, Van Buren Papers, Library of Congress; Silas Wright to Flagg, November 12, 1823, Flagg Papers, New York Public Library; Henry Wheaton to John Bailey, November 9, 1823, Bailey Papers, Massachusetts Historical Society.

55. John A. Dix to John W. Taylor, July 25, 1823, Taylor Papers, New York Historical Society.

56. Barker to Butler, October 2, 1823, Miscellaneous Papers, Library of Congress.

57. C. H. Rammelkamp, "The Campaign of 1824 in New York," in American Historical Association, *Annual Report for the Year 1904* (1905), p. 185.

58. Hammond, *Political Parties in the State of New York,* p. 131.

59. Van Buren, *Autobiography,* p. 142.

Notes to IV: THE SCHISM OF 1824

1. Shipp, *Giant Days, or The Life and Times of W. H. Crawford,* p. 174, footnote.

2. Rufus King to Charles King, December 21, 1823, in King, *Life and Correspondence,* VI, 541.

3. Adams, *Memoirs,* VI, 235; Wiltse, *John C. Calhoun, Nationalist,* p. 281.

4. Rufus King to Charles King, December 19, 1823, in King, *Life and Correspondence,* VI, 540; William Plumer, Jr. to William Plumer, December 31, 1823, in Brown, ed., *Missouri Compromises and Presidential Politics,* p. 93; Clay to Peter B. Porter, 1823, Porter Papers, Buffalo Historical Society.

5. Van Buren, *Inquiry into the Origin and Course of Political Parties in the United States, pp.* 4–5.

6. William Plumer, Jr. to William Plumer, December 10, 12, 22, 1823, in Brown, ed., *Missouri Compromises and Presidential Politics, pp.* 88–90.

7. *Annals of Congress,* 18th Congress, 1st Session, p. 74.

8. Flagg to Van Buren, November 12, 1823, Van Buren Papers, Library of Congress; Butler to Jesse Hoyt, January 29, 1824, in Mackenzie, *The Lives and Opinions of Benjamin Franklin Butler and Jesse Hoyt,* p. 168–69.

9. Draft of a reply written by Van Buren in January, 1824, to a resolution against a Congressional nomination adopted by the Tennessee legislature, Van Buren Papers, Library of Congress.

10. Flagg to Wright, October 28, 1823, Flagg Papers, New York Public Library; Flagg to Van Buren, November 12, 1823, Van Buren Papers, Library of Congress.

11. William Marcy spoke to several senators of the legislature and reported that they were apprised of the dangers involved in changing the system because "it is certain our opponents will act against us in union & with vigour. . . ." Marcy to Van Buren, December 14, 1823, Van Buren Papers, Library of Congress. Edwin Croswell thought "the change w'd threaten the prostration of the rep. party." Worse, De Witt Clinton himself might try to run for the presidency. Croswell to Flagg, December 9, 1823, Flagg Papers, New York Public Library; Croswell to Jesse Hoyt, January 31, 1824, in Mackenzie, *Butler and Hoyt,* p. 194.

12. Stephen Van Rensselaer to Solomon Van Rensselaer, December 27, 1823, in Bonney, *Historical Gleanings,* p. 409; John A. King to Rufus King, January 9, 1824, in King, *Life and Correspondence,* VI, 546; Adams, *Memoirs,* VI, 216.

13. Lincoln, ed., *Messages from the Governors,* III, 30.

14. Butler to Jesse Hoyt, January 29, 1824, in Mackenzie, *Butler and Hoyt,* pp. 168–69; Jacob Sutherland to Van Buren, January 24, 1824, Van Buren Papers, Library of Congress.

15. James, *Andrew Jackson,* pp. 389.

16. McDuffie to Charles Fischer, December 14, 1823, in A. R. Newsome, "Correspondence to John C. Calhoun, George McDuffie and Charles Fisher, Relative to the Presidential Campaign of 1824," *The North Carolina Historical Review,* VII (October, 1930), 491.

17. Mower to Solomon Van Rensselaer, January 5, 1824, in Bonney, *Historical Gleanings,* p. 409.

18. Rufus King to Charles King, February 13, 1824, in King, *Life and Correspondence,* VI, 551.

19. Van Buren to Jesse Hoyt, March 6, 1824, in Mackenzie, *Butler and Hoyt,* p. 198.

20. The anti-Radical canvass is mentioned by William Plumer, Jr. to William Plumer, February 5, 9, 1824, in Brown, ed., *Missouri Compromises and Presidential Politics,* pp. 96, 98.

21. Stephen Van Rensselaer to Solomon Van Rensselaer, February 15, 1824, in Bonney, *Historical Gleaning,* p. 410.

22. Van Buren, *Autobiography,* pp. 665–66.

23. Rufus King to Charles King, March 11, 1824, in King, *Life and Correspondence,* VI, 564.

24. William Plumer, Jr. to William Plumer, May 3, 1824, in Brown, ed., *Missouri Compromises and Presidential Politics,* p. 117.

25. James Gallatin, *A Great Peace Maker; the Diary of James*

Gallatin, pp. 195, 249. (Raymond Walter, Jr. in his article, "James Gallatin Diary: A Fraud?," *American Historical Review,* LXII (July, 1957), 878–85, suggests that James Francis Gallatin, the grandson of James Gallatin, is the true author of this *Diary*). A. Stewart to Gallatin, February 6, 1824, Walter Lowrie to Gallatin, February 10, 1824, Gallatin Papers, New York Historical Society.

26. Clay to Francis Brooke, February 23, 1824, in Clay, *Private Correspondence,* pp. 86–87; William Plumer, Jr. to William Plumer, February 16, 1824, in Brown, ed., *Missouri Compromises and Presidential Politics,* p. 100; Daniel Webster to Ezekiel Webster, February 15, 1824, in Daniel Webster, *Letters,* p. 102.

27. *Niles' Weekly Register,* March 13, 1824. For the unpopularity of the caucus, see Charles S. Sydnor, "The One Party Period of American History," *American Historical Review,* LI (April, 1946), 443.

28. William Plumer, Jr. to William Plumer, February 29, 1824, William Plumer, Jr. to Selma Hale, March 3, 1824, in Brown, ed., *Missouri Compromises and Presidential Politics,* pp. 103–4; Rufus King to Charles King, March 10, 1824, in King, *Life and Correspondence,* VI, 555.

29. Van Buren to Benjamin F. Butler, February 17, 1824, Van Buren Papers, Library of Congress.

30. Clay to Francis Brooke, February 23, 1824, in Clay, *Correspondence,* pp. 86–87.

31. Van Buren to Butler, February 17, 1824, Van Buren Papers, Library of Congress.

32. Thomas R. Hay, "John C. Calhoun and the Presidential Election of 1824," *The North Carolina Historical Review,* XII (April, 1935), 39.

33. Wiltse, *John C. Calhoun, Nationalist,* p. 283.

34. It seems fairly clear that if Van Buren had consented to the latter course he would have been closer to the general wishes of his own state. At the same time he would have discharged a slight obligation he owed Adams for his help in trying to get Van Buren the ministerial post in Mexico. Adams, *Memoirs,* VI, 366; Clinton to Stephen Van Rensselaer, January 21, 1823, Miscellaneous Papers, New York State Library.

35. Adams, *Memoirs,* VI, 316.

36. *Annals of Congress,* 18th Congress, 1st Session, pp. 134–36.

37. *Ibid.,* p. 336.

38. Adams, *Memoirs*, VI, 328.

39. Van Buren to Edwin Croswell, May 26, 1824, Van Buren Papers, Library of Congress.

40. Rufus King to Charles King, May 22, 23, 1824, in King, *Life and Correspondence*, VI, 571; Adams, *Memoirs*, VI, 345.

41. Jackson to L. H. Coleman, April 16, 1824, in Andrew Jackson, *Correspondence*, III, 249.   Adams was just as "cautious" as Jackson.   See Bemis, *John Quincy Adams and the Union*, p. 89.

42. Van Buren, *Autobiography*, p. 240.

43. *Ibid.*   44. *Ibid.*, p. 241.   45. *Ibid.*, p. 242.

46. *Annals of Congress*, 18th Congress, 1st Session, p. 708, 733.

47. It is true that Rufus King and a minority of the New York delegation in the House voted against the tariff, but they reflected the views of the commercial and navigating interests from such places as New York City, not the farming and manufacturing interests of the entire state.

48. *Annals of Congress*, 18th Congress, 1st Session, p. 744.

49. Butler, *Martin Van Buren*, pp. 24–25.

50. Marcy to Van Buren, January 11, 1824, Van Buren Papers, Library of Congress.

51. Hammond, *Political Parties in the State of New York*, II, 165.

52. Thurlow Weed, *Autobiography*, p. 109.

53. *Ibid.*, p. 109–10.

54. Hammond, *Political Parties in the State of New York*, II, 163.   Another shock had occurred just two weeks before when the state Senate by the vote of 17 to 14 agreed to postpone any action on an electoral law until the first Monday in November.   This action hit the state with a shattering impact.   It stirred old hostilities, and the number "17" took on special meaning.   The senators who voted with the majority were denounced as "infamous," and their names were printed in the newspapers in broad, black letters. Some were hanged and burned in effigy.   Handbills were circulated describing the Senate's affrontery and threatening dire retribution in the next election.   To the Albany Regency, the action of the seventeen was one of the greatest demonstrations of party loyalty and discipline ever witnessed in New York.   That a small group of men were willing to hazard their own personal careers for the good of the organization at large was never to be forgotten. In the future party men would recall with wistful sentiment the

days that nurtured such "heroes."   Albany *Daily Advertiser,* April 8, 1824; New York *Statesman,* April 13, 1824; Gillet, *The Life and Times of Silas Wright,* I, 59.

55. Jenkins, *History of Political Parties in the State of New York,* p. 292.

56. New York *Evening Post,* April 20, 1824.

57. *Niles' Weekly Register,* April 24, 1824.

58. April 15, 1824.

Notes to V: THE RESCUER OF HIS COUNTRY

1. The "A. B." papers were published from January 20 to April 9, 1823, and comprised nineteen letters in all.

2. Rufus King to John A. King, April 21, 1824, in King, *Life and Correspondence,* VI, 566; Adams, *Memoirs,* VI, 296.

3. Adams, *Memoirs,* VI, 299.

4. Van Buren to Benjamin F. Butler, April 22, 1824, Van Buren Papers, Library of Congress.

5. Adams, *Memoirs,* VI, 312.   The belief that politics was the sole basis for exonerating Crawford is still held by some modern writers.   See Wiltse, *John C. Calhoun, Nationalist,* p. 292.

6. Adams, *Memoirs,* VI, 365.

7. Clay to Francis Brooke, May 28, 1824, in Clay, *Correspondence,* p. 93.

8. Colonel Charles P. Tutt to Jackson, June 12, 1824, in Jackson, *Correspondence,* III, 255.

9. Van Buren, *Autobiography,* p. 182.

10. *Ibid.,* p. 183.

11. Adams, *Memoirs,* IX, 276, 369.

12. Van Buren, *Autobiography,* p. 183.

13. Van Buren to John C. Hamilton, October 28, 1851, Van Buren Papers, Library of Congress; Van Buren, *Autobiography,* p. 183.

14. Van Buren, *Autobiography,* pp. 183–84.

15. *Ibid.,* p. 183.   16. *Ibid.,* p. 184.   17. *Ibid.,* p. 188.

18. The work was Timothy Pickering's *A Review of the Correspondence between the Hon. John Adams, Late President of the United States and the Late Wm. Cunningham, esq. . . .*

19. Van Buren to Jefferson, June 8, 1824, Van Buren Papers, Library of Congress.

20. Jefferson to Van Buren, June 29, 1824, Jefferson, *Writings,* XVI, 52–68.

21. Van Buren to Jefferson, July 13, 1824, Van Buren Papers, Library of Congress. The Senator had an appreciative word for Monroe regarding his conduct during the "A.B." affair but watered it down by saying, "I had no reason to expect so much from him." On rewriting this letter, before mailing it, Van Buren struck out this final sentence.

22. William Plumer, Jr. to William Plumer, May 3, 1824, in Brown, ed., *Missouri Compromises and Presidential Politics,* pp. 116–17.

23. Wheaton to S. Gouverneur, February 3, 1824, Gouverneur Papers, New York Public Library.

24. William B. Rochester to Clay, May 29, 1824, Clay Papers, Library of Congress. Thurlow Weed takes credit for having goaded Yates into calling the session. He claimed he told the Governor that Samuel Talcott had said that he doubted whether Yates had enough courage to take such action. When the Governor heard this, Weed reported, he sprang up and exclaimed:

"Tallcott [sic] said dat it will require decision and nerve to write a proclamation, did he?"

"That is my information," Weed replied.

"Well, I'll show dat I possess decision and nerve enough to do right." Weed, *Autobiography,* p. 115.

25. "What can I do or say to the strange or ridiculous notions of Gov Yates?" Van Buren asked a friend. "If he is determined to make himself the laughing stock of the nation so let it be. . . . If he does the deed which will forever sink him with all parties I think it cannot be doubted that the Legislature would meet him with indignation and spirit." Van Buren to James Campbell, May 14, 1824, Van Buren Papers, Library of Congress. See also Clinton to John Eaton, July 1, 1824, Clinton Papers, Columbia University Library.

It was reported that Yates having made up his mind to act refused to listen to reason. "If you attempt to expostulate with him on the subject," said James Campbell, "he immediately falls into a violent passion & then you hear nothing but oaths and foul language." Campbell to Van Buren, May 19, 1824, Van Buren Papers, Library of Congress.

26. Clinton to John Eaton, July 1, 1824, Clinton to Jacob Barker, July 1, 1824, Clinton to J. B. Moses [?], July 23, 1824, Clinton Papers, Columbia University Library. Van Buren informed Jefferson that the New York legislature "will do nothing that they ought not to do," Van Buren to Jefferson, July 13, 1824, Van Buren Papers, Library of Congress.

27. After the Governor's message was read (Lincoln, ed., *Messages from the Governors*, III, 41–43), Azariah C. Flagg took the floor in the Assembly and asserted that nothing had changed since last spring to require an extra session. He condemned the Governor's proclamation as unwarranted and then offered a resolution to adjourn. Tallmadge and Wheaton fought the motion but they were overruled after the Regency-dominated Senate notified the Assembly that it considered Yates's action unconstitutional and that it intended to adjourn immediately. On August 6, the Legislature disbanded. Albany *Argus,* August 5, 6, 1824.

28. Benjamin Ruggles, the chairman of the last Congressional caucus, advised Van Buren that a majority of people in Ohio preferred Clay and that their second choice was Crawford. Ruggles to Van Buren, July 31, 1824, Van Buren Papers, Library of Congress. Peter B. Porter, on the other hand, assured Clay that he and Adams led all others in New York. Porter to Clay, April 5, 1824, Clay Papers, Library of Congress; Clay to Francis Brooke, February 26, 1824, in Clay, *Correspondence,* p. 88.

29. P. N. Nicholas to Van Buren, October 31, 1824, Van Buren Papers, Library of Congress.

30. Van Buren to Ruggles, August 26, 1824, Van Buren Papers, Library of Congress.

31. J. B. Stuart to Clay, September 6, 1824, Clay Papers, Library of Congress.

32. Henry R. Storrs to Clay, September 23, 1824, Clay Papers, Library of Congress.

33. Claiborne Gooch to Van Buren, September 14, 1824, Van Buren Papers, Library of Congress.

34. Walter Lowrie to Van Buren, September 14, 1824, Van Buren Papers, Library of Congress.

35. William Smith to Samuel Smith, October 17, 1824, Van Buren Papers, Library of Congress.

36. McLane to Van Buren, October 21, 1824, Van Buren Papers, Library of Congress.

37. Clay to Johnston, September 3, 1824, in Clay, *Correspondence*, pp. 100–1.

38. Johnston to Clay, September 4, 1824, *ibid.*, pp. 102–3.

39. Clay to Johnston, September 10, Johnston to Clay, September 26, 1824, *ibid.*, p. 103.

40. McLane to Van Buren, October 21, 1824, Van Buren Papers, Library of Congress.

41. Gales and Seaton to Van Buren, September 15, 1824, John Forsyth to Van Buren, September 20, 1824, Van Buren Papers, Library of Congress.

42. Lowrie to Van Buren, September 24, 1824, Van Buren Papers, Library of Congress.

43. Lowrie to Gallatin, September 25, 1824, Gallatin Papers, New York Historical Society.

44. Gallatin to Van Buren, October 2, 1824, Van Buren Papers, Library of Congress. See also Gallatin to Lowrie, October 2, 1824, Gallatin Papers, New York Historical Society.

45. Gales and Seaton to Van Buren, October 14, 1824, Van Buren Papers, Library of Congress; Henry Storrs to Clay, September 23, 1824, Clay Papers, Library of Congress; Van Buren to N. S. Benton, October 30, 1824, Miscellaneous Papers, New York State Library; Smith Thompson to Calhoun, October 24, 1824, Miscellaneous Papers, New York State Library.

46. Ralph Lockwood to Clay, October 9, 1824, Clay Papers, Library of Congress.

47. Storrs to Clay, September 23, 1824, Clay Papers, Library of Congress.

48. Gales to Van Buren, October 17, 1824, Van Buren Papers, Library of Congress.

49. Gales to Van Buren, October 26, 1824, Van Buren Papers, Library of Congress.

50. Van Buren, *Autobiography*, pp. 665–66.

51. Gales to Van Buren, October 26, 1824, Van Buren Papers, Library of Congress.

52. Albany *Daily Advertiser*, September 27, 1824. See also Henry Storrs to Clay, September 23, 1824, Clay Papers, Library of Congress.

53. Weed, *Autobiography*, p. 107; *Niles' Weekly Register*, March 13, 1824.

54. Clinton to George P. Maccullogh, March 14, 18, 1824, Clin-

ton Papers, Columbia University Library; John Bigelow, ed., "De Witt Clinton as a Politician," *Harpers New Monthly Magazine,* L (1874–75), 417, 563; Clinton to Henry Post, December 2, 1820, *ibid.,* p. 415.

55. Van Buren to N. S. Benton, October 30, 1824, Miscellaneous Papers, New York State Library.

56. James A. Hamilton to Van Buren, October 7, 1824, Van Buren Papers, Library of Congress.

57. Storrs to Clay, September 23, 1824, Clay Papers, Library of Congress.

Notes to VI: "TREASON BY G——"

1. Van Buren, *Autobiography,* p. 144. This was the second time that his vote was challenged. The first vote he ever cast in his life was challenged by Peter Van Ness and Peter Van Schaack, both supporters of Aaron Burr. *Ibid.,* p. 15.

2. *Ibid.,* p. 144.

3. Hammond, *Political Parties in the State of New York,* II, 175.

4. Butler to Jesse Hoyt, November 6, 1824, Miscellaneous Papers, New York Public Library.

5. Jacob Barker to Van Buren, November 7, 1824, Van Buren Papers, Library of Congress.

6. Van Buren, *Autobiography,* p. 144.

7. Weed, *Autobiography,* p. 123; Hammond, *Political Parties in the State of New York,* II, 177.

8. Ralph Lockwood to Francis Brooke, November 17, 1824, Clay Papers, Library of Congress.

9. It is not certain how many electoral votes they asked for. Butler claims they wanted the entire ticket. Van Buren says they merely wished to "divide the ticket," but does not specify whether it was an even division. Butler to Jesse Hoyt, November 6, 1824, Miscellaneous Papers, New York Public Library; Van Buren to William H. Crawford, November 17, 1824, Van Buren Papers, Library of Congress.

10. Butler to Hoyt, November 6, 1824, Miscellaneous Papers, New York Public Library.

11. Ralph Lockwood to Francis Brooke, November 17, 1824, Clay Papers, Library of Congress.

12. Van Buren to Crawford, November 17, 1824, Van Buren Papers, Library of Congress; Butler to Hoyt, November 9, 1824, Miscellaneous Papers, New York Public Library.

13. Van Buren to Crawford, November 17, 1824, Van Buren Papers, Library of Congress.

14. Weed, *Autobiography,* p. 123.

15. Writing fifty-seven years later, Oran Follett, a member of the legislature of 1824, asserted that the Regency held a series of evening meetings presided over by Roger Skinner, who was "Mr Van Buren's *locum tenens* while he was absent," and agreed that their first object was to come to a joint ballot.   It was not material whether the Clay or Adams ticket was nominated, just as long as the deadlock in the Assembly was broken.   Follett claimed that he was responsible in forcing them to decide in favor of Adams.   Oran Follett to the editor of the New York *Tribune,* February 10, 1881; Weed, *Autobiography,* p. 134.

16. Butler to Jesse Hoyt, November 13, 1824, Miscellaneous Papers, New York Public Library.

17. The following morning, Peter B. Porter called on Flagg, and to indicate that the two groups could resolve their differences, promised to move for a postponement in the Assembly that very day.   Flagg agreed to support the motion and the two men parted. However, when the Assembly convened, Clay's friends refused to offer the motion and Flagg himself was forced to do it.   By the vote of 79 to 38, the proposal was killed, proving that the Clay men had rejected Van Buren's scheme.   Van Buren to Crawford, November 17, 1824, Van Buren Papers, Library of Congress; *Journal of the New York Assembly,* 47th Session, p. 1241.

18. Van Buren to Crawford, November 17, 1824, Van Buren Papers, Library of Congress.

19. *Ibid.*

20. Lockwood to Francis Brooke, November 17, 1824, Clay Papers, Library of Congress.

21. A. Conkling to John W. Taylor, December 24, 1824, Taylor Papers, New York Historical Society; Roger Skinner to Van Buren, December 1, 1824, Van Buren Papers, Library of Congress.

22. Weed, *Autobiography,* pp. 123–24.

23. *Ibid.,* pp. 124–26.

24. *Journal of the New York Senate,* 47th Session, p. 459.

25. Weed, *Autobiography,* p. 127.

26. *Journal of the New York Senate,* 47th Session, p. 459; *Journal of the New York Assembly,* 47th Session, p. 1242.

27. T. S. Smith to S. L. Gouverneur, November 15, 1824, Gouverneur Papers, New York Public Library; *Niles' Weekly Register,* November 20, 1824.

28. Ralph Lockwood to Francis Brooke, November 17, 1824, Clay Papers, Library of Congress; *Niles' Weekly Register,* November 20, 1824.

29. Albany *Daily Advertiser,* November 16, 1824, *et seq.*

30. T. S. Smith to S. L. Gouverneur, November 15, 1824, Gouverneur Papers, New York Public Library.

31. Henry Wheaton to Gouverneur, November 21, 1824, Gouverneur Papers, New York Public Library.

32. Calhoun to General J. G. Swift, November 20, 1824, Thomas R. Hay, "Some Unpublished Calhoun Letters," *American Historical Review,* XL (October, 1934), 294.

33. Van Buren to Crawford, November 17, 1824, Van Buren Papers, Library of Congress.

34. Henry Wheaton to Samuel L. Gouverneur, November 21, 1824, Gouverneur Papers, New York Public Library.

35. Weed, *Autobiography,* p. 130; Roger Skinner to Van Buren, December 1, 1824, Van Buren Papers, Library of Congres.

36. Weed, *Autobiography,* p. 128.

37. John Q. Adams, *Memoirs,* VI, 446; *Niles' Weekly Register,* December 25, 1824, is the first time Louisiana's vote is recorded in that newspaper. "The news from Louisiana make it now certain that Crawford, & not Clay, will come in to the House," wrote William Plumer, Jr. to his father on December 16, 1824, Brown, ed., *Missouri Compromises,* p. 123. John W. Taylor received a letter from A. Conkling dated December 8, 1824, which stated that no one had heard from Louisiana, upon whose vote so much depended, Taylor Papers, New York Historical Society.

38. The popular vote: Jackson 153,544, Adams 108,740, Clay 47,136, Crawford 46,618.

39. Stephen Van Rensselaer to G. W. Featherstonehaugh, December 13, 1824, Miscellaneous Papers, New York State Library; Stephen Van Rensselaer to Clinton, December 7, 1824, Clinton Papers, Columbia University Library; Plumer, Jr. to Plumer, December 16, 1824, Brown, *Missouri Compromises,* p. 123.

40. The final count was Calhoun 182; Sanford 30; Nathaniel Macon 24; Jackson 13; Van Buren 9; and Clay 2.

41. Gales to Van Buren, November 22, 1824, Van Buren Papers, Library of Congres.

42. Van Buren, *Inquiry into the Origin and Course of Political Parties in the United States,* pp. 4–5.

Notes to VII: A FEDERALIST-REPUBLICAN

1. Van Buren, *Autobiography,* p. 149.

2. Van Buren to Butler, December 27, 1824, Van Buren Papers, Library of Congress.

3. Bassett, *The Life of Andrew Jackson,* I, 364; Wiltse, *John C. Calhoun, Nationalist,* p. 307; Denis T. Lynch, *An Epoch and a Man,* p. 279.

4. The word is Plumer's. William Plumer, Jr. to William Plumer, December 24, 1824, Brown, ed., *Missouri Compromises,* p. 125.

5. Williams to Van Buren, November 25, 1824, Van Buren Papers, Library of Congress.

6. This seemed to be common knowledge. See James Strong to Clinton, December 22, 1824, Clinton Papers, Columbia University Library.

Stephen Van Rensselaer predicted that Jackson would be elected by the House but would not continue in office for more than four years because "by that time the effects of the Tariff will be developed & Clay will be very strong. Penn Jersey & Maryland will be added to his party." Van Rensselaer to G. W. Featherstonehaugh, December 13, 1824, Miscellaneous Papers, New York State Library.

7. Webster to Henry R. Warfield, February 5, 1825, Webster, *Private Correspondence,* I, 379. Adams recorded in his Diary: "My great object will be to break up the remnant of old party distinctions and bring the whole people together in sentiment as much as possible." *Memoirs,* VI, 474.

8. Said Willie P. Mangum of North Carolina: "Crawford is a long way behind, but I should not be greatly surprised, if Jackson and Adams friends ultimately compromise to a certain extent by meeting on Crawford." Mangum to John Robertson, January 3, 1825, Mangum, *Papers* I, 169.

9. William Plumer, Jr. to William Plumer, December 24, 1824, Brown, ed., *Missouri Compromises,* p. 125; James Strong to Clinton, December 22, 1824, Clinton Papers, Columbia University Library.

10. H. R. Warfield to Daniel Webster, February 3, 1825, Webster, *Correspondence,* I, 377.

11. Clay to Francis Blair, January 8, 1824, Clay Papers, Library of Congress.

12. Clay to Francis Brooke, January 28, Clay to Blair, January 8, 29, 1825, Clay, *Correspondence,* pp. 109–12. Bemis, *John Q. Adams and the Union,* pp. 32–47, gives an excellent account of the movement into Adams's camp.

13. Van Buren, *Autobiography,* p. 150.

14. January 28, 1825.

15. Van Deusen, *The Life of Henry Clay,* pp. 188–90.

16. William Plumer, Jr. to William Plumer, January 24, 1825, Brown, ed., *Missouri Compromises,* p. 134; Rufus King's "Notes" dated January 29, 1825, King, *Life and Correspondence,* VI, 583; Adams, *Memoirs,* VI, 501.

17. Adams, *Memoirs,* VI, 458, 462, 493.

18. Van Buren to James A. Hamilton, January 26, 1825, Hamilton, *Reminiscences,* p. 62. One Bucktail believed Adams had ten states as against Crawford's five. Lot Clark to Roger Skinner, February 28, 1825, Van Buren Papers, Library of Congress.

19. James, *Andrew Jackson,* p. 436.

20. Van Buren, *Autobiography,* p. 152.

21. Van Buren to James A. Hamilton, January 26, 1825, Hamilton, *Reminiscences,* pp. 62–63.

22. There is some doubt as to whether Van Buren actually had seventeen votes under control. Two delegates eventually voted for Jackson. It must be presumed from his actions, however, that Van Buren counted these votes as part of his seventeen.

23. Mrs. Samuel H. Smith, *The First Forty Years of Washington Society,* pp.175–76; Stephen Van Rensselaer to Solomon Van Rensselaer, January 22, 1825, Bonney, *Historical Gleanings,* p. 415; Rufus King, "Memorandum," King, *Life and Correspondence,* VI, 585.

24. Mrs. Smith quotes Van Rensselaer as saying to a friend, " . . . Here is my hand, I give you my word of honor I will not vote for Adams." *Washington Society,* p. 176; Van Buren, *Autobiography,* p. 151; King, "Memorandum," King, *Life and Correspondence,*

VI, 585. James, *Andrew Jackson,* p. 850, note 100, says that Van Buren only requested Van Rensselaer *not* to vote for Adams. He is mistaken in this. See Van Buren, *Autobiography,* p. 151.

The long established and generally accepted opinion of Van Buren's intentions during this election has been that he contrived to keep New York deadlocked for at least the first ballot and then throw his support to Adams later on with the expectation of receiving "the credit, and, of course, the reward from Mr. Adams, in appointments and influence." Nathan Sargent in his *Public Men and Events,* I, 76–77, is the authority for this story, and he cites the testimony of Dudley Marvia, a Representative from New York, and Colonel John Taliaferro, a Radical from Virginia, as proof. Bassett, *Andrew Jackson,* I, 364, Wiltse, *Calhoun,* p. 307, and Denis T. Lynch, *An Epoch and a Man,* p. 279, accept this view. Marquis James, *Andrew Jackson,* p. 849, note 98, tends to doubt it. The evidence Sargent offers is indirect and was gathered twenty to thirty years after the event. Contemporary testimony proves its falsity. In the first place if Van Buren had schemed to abandon Crawford he would never have gone over to Adams. Between the New Englander and the Tennessean, he preferred the latter. Van Buren to James A. Hamilton, January 26, 1825, Hamilton, *Reminiscences,* pp. 62–63.

In his correspondence both in 1825 and later, Van Buren insisted he would stand by Crawford to the bitter end. When Jabez D. Hammond published the first edition of his *History of Political Parties in the State of New York,* he too accused Van Buren of conspiring to support Adams on the second ballot. Van Buren immediately picked Hammond up on the error and corrected him. Hammond apologized, stating his evidence came from some of the Senator's friends, and in the fourth edition of his book (1852) changed the text. Jabaz D. Hammond to Van Buren, August 21, 1842, Van Buren Papers, Library of Congress.

But the most convincing proof of Van Buren's loyalty to Crawford is his own words written at the time. On December 27, 1824, he declared: "His [Crawford's] friends here are determined to stand by him & should no where waver." (Van Buren to Butler, Van Buren Papers, Library of Congress.) On January 26, 1825, just two weeks before the House election, he wrote: "Clay and his friends have settled down for Adams. . . . The push on the part of Mr. Adams' supporters will be to succeed on the first ballot. . . . *I do not believe they will so succeed,* but their chance is far from desperate. . . . [Crawford's] friends adhere to their determination to abide by him. . . . It is certain that there would be greater probability of success if Jackson's friends were to support Crawford. To that we look. . . . As long as Eddy [Croswell?] holds out, there is a moral certainty that Adams cannot be elected; but you know how he will stand if Adams got the twelve States." (Van Buren to James A. Hamilton, Hamilton, *Reminiscences,* pp. 62–63.) A month before, on December 12, Hamilton had written to Van Buren and said: "Our friends agree with you that if Crawford goes into the House to continue to vote for him, giving assurances we have no second place." (Van Buren Papers, Library of Congress.) Walter Lowrie of Pennsylvania, a few weeks after the election, commented: "If we had been able to have prevented the election of Mr Adams on the first ballot, we had great hopes that we could have elected Mr Crawford." (Lowrie to Albert Gallatin, February 28, 1825, Gallatin Papers, New York Historical Society.) In December, 1824, De Witt Clinton received the following report from Stephen Van Rensselaer: "Crawford's friends are determined to remain firm trusting that the Yankees will prefer him to Jackson." (December 18, 1824, Clinton Papers, Columbia University Library.) Representative James Strong said: "Mr. Van Buren, I am told, is endeavouring to secure the vote of N. Y. for Mr. Crawford. . . . There is little hope of his succeeding in this. He will effect it if he can. . . ." (Strong to Clinton, December 22, 1824, Clinton Papers, Columbia University Library.)

In his *Autobiography* (p. 150), written thirty years later, Van Buren denied, once again, all intention of plotting to elect Adams on the second ballot. All this evidence, written by Van Buren and others in 1824, 1825, and later, certainly outweighs the meager testimony of Marvia, Taliaferro, and Sargent.

25. Van Buren's *Autobiography,* p. 151, is the only source for this account. However, it is substantiated in part by Lot Clark in his letter to Roger Skinner, February 28, 1825, Van Buren Papers, Library of Congress. In 1828, J. D. Westcott said that a Federalist friend of his told him that Daniel Webster had spoken to Van Rensselaer (Westcott to Thomas Ritchie, January 18, 1828, Van Buren Papers, Library of Congress). In fact, it appears that Webster spoke to a good many congressmen. Armed with a letter "founded upon previous conversations with Mr Adams" to the effect that Adams would be just toward Federalists if elected Presi-

dent, Webster went to Louis McLane, a former Federalist who was voting for Crawford, and "remarked that if Mr Adams should not be elected on the first ballot" he wanted McLane to see his letter before they went into a second ballot (McLane to Van Buren, June 18, 1827, Van Buren Papers, Library of Congress). This letter was also shown to Henry R. Warfield of Maryland and Stephen Van Rensselaer, Webster to Warfield, February 5, 1825, Webster, *Correspondence*, I, 379; J. D. Westcott to Ritchie, January 18, 1828, Van Buren Papers, Library of Congress.

26. Van Buren, *Autobiography*, p. 151.

27. *Ibid.;* Mrs. Smith, *Washington Society*, p. 176.

28. Van Buren, *Autobiography*, p. 152.

29. Once again Van Buren's *Autobiography* (p. 152) is the only source explaining how Van Rensselaer came to vote for Adams. Nathan Sargent (p. 77) claims that the Patroon was out to defeat Van Buren's scheme of deciding the election because he disliked the little Senator. But this account is necessarily false because the two men were on friendly terms with each other and had messed together for the past several years. Sargent's interpretation of the entire election is questionable, while many parts of Van Buren's story can be corroborated by other witnesses. The Senator had no motive to invent an outlandish tale thirty years after the election took place.

Other sources tend to discredit Sargent as well. Walter Lowrie, in a letter to Albert Gallatin dated February 28, 1825, claimed that Van Rensselaer finally changed his vote because of the "fears with which it was attempted to alarm him." (Gallatin Papers, New York Historical Society.) Mrs. Smith assigns his motive to "sheer weakness." (*Washington Society,* p. 192.) Nothing is said in either of these contemporary accounts about the Patroon's actions being prompted because of a dislike for Van Buren. Van Rensselaer himself said that the Clay combination could not be resisted and "to allay the excitement we agreed to vote for Adams." (Van Rensselaer to Clinton, March 10, 1825, Clinton Papers, Columbia University Library.)

30. New York's vote was: Adams 18, Jackson 2, and Crawford 14.

31. Adams won Maine, New Hampshire, Massachusetts, Rhode Island, Connecticut, Vermont, New York, Maryland, Kentucky, Ohio, Louisiana, Illinois, and Missouri. Jackson, New Jersey,

Pennsylvania, South Carolina, Tennessee, Indiana, Alabama, and Mississippi. Crawford, Delaware, Virginia, North Carolina, and Georgia. *Niles' Weekly Register,* February 12, 1825.

32. Mrs. Smith, *Washington Society,* p. 191.

33. *Ibid.,* p. 192.

34. Wheaton to Gouverneur, February 15, 1825, Gouverneur Papers, New York Public Library.

35. Lowrie to Gallatin, February 28, 1825, Gallatin Papers, New York Historical Society.

36. John A. Dix to Gouverneur, February 13, 1825, Gouverneur Papers, New York Public Library.

37. Jackson to William B. Lewis, February 14, 1825, Bassett, ed., *Correspondence of Andrew Jackson,* III, 276.

38. Clay to Crawford, February 18, 1828, Clay, *Correspondence,* p. 193.

39. James A. Hamilton to Van Buren, February 21, 1825, Van Buren Papers, Library of Congress. The Senator claimed later that Adams originally invited Clinton to become Secretary of State but was refused. *Autobiography,* p. 162.

40. Van Buren told Rufus King that Clay's nomination would be opposed but he would not join in it. The vote was 27 to 14 in favor of confirmation. John Q. Adams, *Memoirs,* VI, 524–25.

41. Clay to Francis Brooke, April 29, 1825, Clay, *Correspondence,* p. 126.

42. Aware, however, that Van Buren was walking the streets of Washington with an air of aloofness, Clark wrote: "I know that there are some who possess great sagacity & great integrity that believe we ought to wait a while speak favorably of Mr Adams & see whether he will not ultimately lean toward us. I see the Argus speaks that language virtually & we have a very few Crawford men who don't 12 out of the 14 of our caucus men from NY however speak a different language. The voice of nine tenths of the party is 'still for war.' Our holding back at this time will loose [sic] us the confidence of our Southern brethren." Clark to Roger Skinner, February 28, 1825, Van Buren Papers, Library of Congress.

Despite the hue and cry from such men as Clark, Van Buren's attitude was soon adopted by the Regency. It was much wiser to delay action until Adams' policies were clearly outlined. As Silas Wright said: "All things here, and all parties I may say here too, are waiting to determine whether they are to support or oppose the national administration." Silas Wright to Minet Jenison, March 3, 1825, R. H. Gillet, *The Life and Times of Silas Wright,* I, 88.

43. Van Buren, *Autobiography,* p. 153.

Notes to VIII: SHIFTING LOYALTIES

1. Rufus King, "Memorandum" dated February 11, 1825, King, *Life and Correspondence,* VI, 589.

2. Van Buren was slated to argue the Eden cases in New York but had to withdraw because he was so busy. Van Buren to Aaron Burr, January 14, 1825, "Pages from an Autograph Collection," *University of California Chronicles,* XXVII (1925), p. 342.

3. Charles Z. Lincoln, *Messages from the Governors,* III, 52.

4. *Argus,* October 4, 1825.

5. Silas Wright to Minet Jenison, December 9, 1824, Gillet, *The Life and Times of Silas Wright,* I, 84.

6. James Strong to Clinton, December 22, 1824, Clinton Papers, Columbia University Library.

7. William A. Duer to Rufus King, February 17, 1825, King, *Life and Correspondence,* VI, 592–3; James A. Hamilton to Van Buren, February 21, 1825, Van Buren Papers, Library of Congress.

8. Plumer, Jr. to Plumer, February 21, 1825, Brown, ed., *Missouri Compromises and Presidential Politics,* p. 143; Clay to Porter, November 29, 1825, Porter Papers, Buffalo Historical Society.

9. Lot Clark to Roger Skinner, February 28, 1825, Van Buren Papers, Library of Congress.

10. Wright to Minet Jenison, March 3, 1825, Gillett, *Silas Wright,* I, 88.

11. Marcy to John Bailey, March 7, 1825, Washburn Papers, Massachusetts Historical Society.

12. Earlier King had been refused renomination to the United States Senate by the Bucktail and Clintonian parties. His career, wrote Van Buren, "failed to fulfill the expectations which were justified by its early promise. . . . In politics he was from first to last a federalist of the Hamiltonian school." No doubt King's hostile actions during the past election also prejudiced Van Buren against him. Van Buren, *Autobiography,* pp. 155, 149.

13. Van Buren to King, April 19, 1825, Charles King to John A. King, July 22, 1825, King, *Life and Correspondence,* VI, 610–11.

14. "The People's men in N. York are not satisfied with our great Father at Washington, they think him rather too *kingly* & he will not commune with, or take the advice of . . . any of his warmest friends." James Mallory to A. C. Flagg, July 19, 1825, Flagg Papers, New York Public Library.

15. Clay to Porter, November 29, 1825, Porter Papers, Buffalo Historical Society; Weed, *Autobiography,* pp. 177–81; John Q. Adams, *Memoirs,* VI, 531.

16. Hammond, *Political Parties in the State of New York,* II, 206.

17. *Argus,* November 5, 1825.

18. As state senator, Van Buren had investigated, whenever possible, the men who applied for bank charters. On one occasion he remarked: "I fear that some of our friends would establish a Bank to fill their pockets. . . ." And such men he was out to stop. Van Buren to John W. Taylor, March 11, 1814, Taylor Papers, New York Historical Society.

19. Michael Hoffman to Flagg, January 8, 22, 1827, Flagg Papers, New York Public Library.

20. Fox, *Decline of Aristocracy in New York,* p. 285.

21. Lincoln, *Messages,* III, 235.

22. Krout and Fox, *The Completion of Independence,* p. 226.

23. Van Buren to Butler, December 25, 1825, Van Buren Papers, Library of Congress.

24. J. D. Richardson, ed., *Compilation of the Messages and Papers of the Presidents,* II, 311–16.

25. *Argus,* December 9, 1825.

26. Willie P. Mangum to Bartlett Yancey, January 15, 1826, Mangum, *Papers,* Henry T. Shanks, ed., I, 231. Mangum was not speaking specifically about the message, but he undoubtedly had it in mind when he wrote this letter.

27. Benton, *Thirty Years View,* I, 54.

28. Wiltse, *John C. Calhoun, Nationalist,* p. 321; William E. Smith, *The Francis Preston Blair Family in Politics,* I, 38.

29. *Argus,* December 9, 1825.

30. Marcy to Van Buren, December 17, 1825, Van Buren Papers, Library of Congress.

31. Van Buren's correspondence during these years indicates how conscious he was of the threat of an increasingly powerful Federal government. As one example, in February, 1825, Littleton D. Teakle proposed some undisclosed "scheme" which Van Buren condemned because it was "not warranted by the Constitution of the U. States." Van Buren to Teakle, February 5, 1825, Miscellaneous Papers, New York State Library.

32. Van Buren, *Autobiography,* p. 195.

33. *Register of Debates,* 19th Congress, 1st Session, p. 20.

34. *Ibid.,* p. 21.

35. Van Buren to Butler, December 25, 1825, Van Buren Papers, Library of Congress.

36. Tallmadge to Taylor, February 2, 1826, Taylor Papers, New York Historical Society.

37. Van Buren to Gales and Seaton, February 5, 1826, Miscellaneous Papers, New York State Library.

38. James Tallmadge to John W. Taylor, February 2, 1826, Taylor Papers, New York Historical Society.

39. Van Buren, *Autobiography,* p. 197.

40. *Ibid.,* p. 196.

41. Van Buren to Butler, March 22, 1826, Van Buren Papers, Library of Congress.

42. Benton, *Thirty Years View,* I, 65; Bassett, *Life of Andrew Jackson,* I, 384.

43. Adams, *Memoirs,* VI, 531.

44. *Ibid.,* VII, 112.

45. *Register of Debates,* 19th Congress, 1st Session, pp. 142–43.

46. *Ibid.,* pp. 149–51.

47. Porter to Clay, February 17, 1826, Clay Papers, Library of Congress.

48. Clay to Porter, February 22, 1826, Porter Papers, Buffalo Historical Society.

49. Van Buren to Butler, March 22, 1826, Van Buren Papers, Library of Congress.

50. *Register of Debates,* 19th Congress, 1st Session, pp. 154–74.

51. *Ibid.,* pp. 234–37.   52. *Ibid.,* pp. 237–62.

53. Kent to Van Buren, April 15, 1826, Van Buren Papers, Library of Congress.

54. Butler to Van Buren, April 24, 1826, Van Buren Papers, Library of Congress.

55. Spencer to Van Buren, May 2, 1826, Van Buren Papers, Library of Congress.

56. *Argus,* April 17, 1826.

57. *Ibid.,* April 3, 1826. See also the issue for February 24, 1826.

58. Croswell to Van Buren, April 3, 1826, Van Buren Papers, Library of Congress.

59. Van Buren's endorsement to Croswell's letter of April 3, 1826; Van Buren, *Autobiography,* pp. 197–98.

60. *Register of Debates,* 19th Congress, 1st Session, p. 401.

61. Benton, *Thirty Years View,* p. 77.

62. Willie P. Mangum to Charity A. Mangum, April 16, 1826, Mangum, *Papers,* I, pp. 274–75.

63. Mangum to Charity A. Mangum, April 8, 1826, *ibid.,* I, 268.

Notes to IX: THE MASTER OF NEW YORK

1. The intent of the administration was to ease McLean out of office without invoking his wrath or that of his friends in the West. Van Buren to Butler, May 14, 1826, Van Buren Papers, Library of Congress.

2. *Register of Debates,* 19th Congress, 1st Session, pp. 422, 566–57.

3. Sargent, *Public Men and Events,* I, 117. The author quotes, as the source of his information, a letter of Seaton to Colonel Johnson dated April 18, 1827. But it was Sargent and not Seaton who *guessed,* after fifty odd years, that Van Buren was the author of the statement, although he had no proof for the assertion.

4. *Register of Debates,* 19th Congress, 1st Session, p. 717.

5. Mangum to Charity A. Mangum, April 8, 1826, in Willie P. Mangum, *Papers,* I, 268.

6. Calhoun to Van Buren, July 7, 1826, in Van Buren, *Autobiography,* pp. 514–15.

7. Madison to Van Buren, September 20, 1826, Van Buren to Madison, September 28, 1826, Van Buren Papers, Library of Congress; James Madison, *Letters and Other Writings,* III, 528.

8. Van Buren to P. N. Nicholas, November, 1826, Van Buren Papers, Library of Congress.

9. Van Buren, *Autobiography,* pp. 161–63. The Regency brethren were disposed to nominate William Paulding but Van Buren

talked them out of it. He reminded them that Paulding had opposed the building of the Erie Canal and, what was worse, had "a singular monomania in regard to his physical condition. . . ." Knowing Clinton's "proclivity to that species of assault, and having on several occasions witnessed his ability to make it effectual," Van Buren feared Paulding would be laughed out of the campaign. *Ibid.*

On the other side of the political fence, Clinton reported that a number of People's men, because of their pro-Adams sympathies, "wished to amalgamate our State Elections with the politics of the general govt." Clinton—who called them "fiery spirits"—ridiculed the idea as "wrong in principle & mischievous in practice." Clinton to Jacob Brown, September 24, 1826, Clinton Papers, Columbia University Library.

10. Rochester, said the Regency chief, was honest and in his debt for an appointment he once received from the government. In addition, should Rochester succeed in his election, there would be a sufficient number of reliable men in other departments "to prevent him from doing much injury to our cause." Van Buren, *Autobiography,* p. 163.

Some of the Regency men were skeptical regarding Rochester's ability to win the election. Wright to Flagg, November 15, 1826, Flagg Papers, New York Public Library. Probably Van Buren knew his candidate would be defeated, but this in no way lessened the effectiveness of his plan. The foolish Clinton, win or lose, would hurl his verbal thunderbolts at Adams for favoring Rochester, and thereby split the pro-administration, pro-Clinton faction in New York.

11. *Argus,* November 10, 1826.

12. Van Buren, *Autobiography,* p. 165.

13. Clinton to Hector Gray, November 15, 1826, Clinton Papers, Columbia University Library.

14. Spencer to Jacob Brown, February 14, 1826, Jacob Brown Papers, Massachusetts Historical Society.

15. *Argus,* December 8, 1826.

16. Adams, *Memoirs,* VII, 179.

Notes to X: THE MAKING OF THE DEMOCRATIC PARTY

1. Michael Hoffman to Flagg, January 22, 1827, Flagg Papers, New York Public Library.

2. Clay to Porter, December, 1826, Porter Papers, Buffalo Historical Society.

3. Assurances from Jacksonians, not the General himself. See Van Buren to Flagg, December 22, 1826, Flagg Papers, Columbia University Library.

4. Not until 1830 did the terms gain popular currency.

5. For example, see Willie P. Mangum's correspondence during 1826. Mangum, *Papers,* pp. 219–301.

6. A list of all their names would include every antiadministration man in Congress almost without exception, and of course every politician who helped Jackson in the election of 1828. Thomas Hart Benton listed Senators Macon of North Carolina, Tazewell of Virginia, Samuel Smith of Maryland, Dickerson of New York, Rowan of Kentucky, and Findlay of Pennsylvania as especially hostile to Adams and his administration. Benton, *Thirty Years View,* p. 55. Gales and Seaton added Benton and Chandlers to the list. *National Intelligencer,* March, 1827. In addition to those already mentioned, such politicians and editors as Caleb Atwater, Duff Green, Edward Livingston, and Edwin Croswell must be included.

7. The slight role Jackson played in formulating party policy is shown by Thomas P. Abernathy in his article, "Andrew Jackson and the Rise of Southwestern Democracy," *American Historical Review,* XXXIII (October, 1927), 71–76.

8. Sellers, *James K. Polk, Jacksonian,* p. 104.

9. Ambler, *Thomas Ritchie,* p. 107; *National Intelligencer,* September 23, October 4, 1828.

10. Van Buren conveyed his message through James Hamilton, who was with Jackson at the time. Van Buren to Hamilton, February 21, 1829, in Hamilton, *Reminiscences,* p. 94. See also Van Buren to Jackson, September 14, 1827, Van Buren Papers, Library of Congress.

11. Van Buren to Flagg, December 22, 1826, Flagg Papers, Columbia University Library. See also Van Buren to Jesse Hoyt, December 30, 1826, in Mackenzie, *Butler and Hoyt,* p. 200; Van Buren to Hamilton, December 20, 1826, in Hamilton, *Reminiscences,* p. 63.

12. Van Buren to Butler, December 12, 1826, Van Buren Papers. Charles M. Wiltse in his *John C. Calhoun, Nationalist* errs when he says Van Buren sought to eliminate Calhoun from the party. He misquotes the above letter by substituting the Vice-President's name for Adams's, p. 347.

13. After making "the friends of Calhoun and of Crawford believe that they had each been badly treated by the alliance between Adams and Clay, he [Van Buren] united them in the support of General Jackson." Poore, *Perley's Reminiscences,* I, 64.

14. Houston to Jackson, January 13, 1827, in Jackson, *Correspondence,* VI, 490.

15. Van Buren, *Autobiography,* p. 514.

16. Italics mine. Van Buren's first concern was creating the Democratic party, not the calling of a convention. The convention was only a means to an end.

17. Italics mine.

18. Here is proof that the convention was not his main concern in writing the letter, inasmuch as he was ready to accept another caucus.

19. Van Buren to Thomas Ritchie, January 13, 1827, Van Buren Papers, Library of Congress.

20. Weston, *The Presidential Election of 1828,* p. 88.

21. Richmond *Enquirer,* April 27, 1827; Ambler, *Thomas Ritchie,* pp. 107–10; Weston, *The Presidential Election of 1828,* p. 88; Wiltse, *Calhoun, Nationalist,* pp. 348–49.

22. Hammond, *Political Parties in the State of New York,* II, 247; Van Buren to Nathaniel Pitcher, February 13, 1827, Van Buren Papers, Library of Congress.

23. *Register of Debates,* 19th Congress, 2nd Session, p. 337.

24. Van Buren's "Notes," dated August 4, 1840, Van Buren Papers, Library of Congress.

25. Speech delivered by Van Buren in Albany on July 10, 1827, *Albany Argus,* July 24, 1827.

26. *Register of Debates,* 19th Congress, 2nd Session, pp. 389–90.

27. Stanwood, *American Tariff Controversies in the Nineteenth Century,* I, 258.

28. Van Buren, *Autobiography,* p. 169.

29. William E. Richmond to John Bailey, April 16, 1827, Bailey Papers, New York Historical Society.

30. *Niles' Weekly Register,* March, 1827.

31. Domestic Manufactures, Internal Improvements.

32. Clay to Benjamin W. Crowinshield, March 18, 1827, *The Quarterly Journal of Economics,* II (1888), 491.

33. *Register of Debates,* 19th Congress, 2nd Session, pp. 469–80.

34. Van Buren to Harmanus Bleecker, February 25, 1827, Miscellaneous Papers, New York State Library.

35. *Register of Debates,* 19th Congress, 2nd Session, pp. 495, 505–6.

36. *Argus,* February 9, 23, March 20, 23, 27, 1827.

37. Weston, *The Presidential Election of 1828,* p. 88.

38. Van Buren to Hamilton, January 28, 1827, Miscellaneous Van Buren Papers, New York Public Library.

39. Van Buren to Hamilton, February 15, 1827, Miscellaneous Van Buren Papers, New York Public Library.

40. James Hamilton, Jr. to Jackson, February 16, 1827, in Jackson, *Correspondence,* III, 344.

41. *Register of Debates,* 19th Congress, 2nd Session, pp. 498–99.

42. *National Intelligencer,* March 10, 13, 20, 22, April 7, 19, 1827. There were approximately a dozen such articles, most of which appeared under the title, "Signs of the Times."

43. Italics mine.

44. Reprinted in the *Constitutional Whig,* March 14, 1827.

45. At first the *Whig* was referring to a letter by Dr. Floyd, then the newspaper tied in Van Buren. See the issues for February 16 and March 16, 1827.

46. Van Buren to Jackson, November 4, 1827, in Jackson, *Correspondence,* III, 384.

47. Albany *Argus,* April 24, 1827.

48. Although Van Buren did refer to it in a letter to Flagg. "They [Gales and Seaton] are very guilty upon that point [the subject of the improvement of the press] & for public considerations should not be suffered to escape. You see Ritchie has silenced them in regard to it. Their jeramiads about party too . . . could be used with great effect in NYork." Van Buren to Flagg, April 2, 1827, Flagg Papers, Columbia University Library.

49. Columbia, South Carolina, *Telescope,* March 22, 1827.

50. *National Intelligencer,* April 7, 1827.

51. Charleston *Southern Patriot,* March 30, 1827.

52. Weston, *The Presidential Election of 1828*, p. 158; Van Buren to Jesse Hoyt, April 23, 1827, in Mackenzie, *Butler and Hoyt*, p. 200.

53. *National Intelligencer*, March 29, 1827. The editors also remarked that since the visitation of Van Buren to Charleston the city's newspaper, the *Mercury*, had been "fired with fresh zeal. . . ." That this remark could be applied to other newspapers can be seen in the editorial of the *Constitutional Whig* for April 20, 1827.

54. Van Buren to Flagg, April 2, 1827, Flagg Papers, Columbia University Library.

55. *Constitutional Whig*, March 20, April 3, 7, 1827; *National Intelligencer*, March 29, April 7, 1827.

56. It is commonly believed that Van Buren coveted Calhoun's position and plotted to remove him from the ticket. Wiltse, *Calhoun, Nationalist*, p. 347, argues the point on the basis of a letter which he misquoted (Van Buren to Butler, December 12, 1826, Van Buren Papers). Van Buren wrote that he wished to "reprobate" the heresies of Messrs. Adams and Clay but his handwriting is so bad that the name "Adams" looks very much like "Calhoun." Only it isn't.

Actually the Senator was quite explicit on the question of the vice-presidency. In a letter to Andrew Jackson, dated September 14, 1827, he wrote: "Attempts will doubtless be made to entangle your friends in the Vice-Presidential and other questions but they will I am persuaded have good sense enough not to meddle in them. I have no other feelings in the relation to the Vice Presidency than as it may operate on the main question." Jackson, *Correspondence*, III, 382. See also Crawford to Van Buren, December 21, 1827, Van Buren Papers, Library of Congress.

57. Crawford to Van Buren, December 21, 1827, Van Buren Papers, Library of Congress; Van Buren, *Autobiography*, p. 368.

58. Adams compared him to Aaron Burr, but decided that Van Buren had greatly improved electioneering methods since they were first used in 1800. *Memoirs*, VII, 272.

59. *Constitutional Whig*, April 20, 1827.

60. Cooper to Verplanck, April 13, 1827, Verplanck Papers, New York Historical Society.

61. Malone, *The Public Life of Thomas Cooper*, pp. 307–11.

62. *Constitutional Whig*, May 3, 1827.

63. Raleigh, North Carolina, *Register*, May 4, 1827.

64. *Constitutional Whig,* April 24, 1827.

65. "I am very happy," wrote Louis McLane to Van Buren at this time, "to find that, you'r about to devote yourself in earnest to the active duties of the campaign. . . ." June 18, 1827, Van Buren Papers, Library of Congress.

66. John W. Taylor to Edward Everett, May 18, 1827, Everett Papers, Massachusetts Historical Society.

67. Clay to Porter, May 13, 1827, Porter Papers, Buffalo Historical Society.

68. Adams, *Memoirs,* VII, 272.

Notes to XI: FARMERS, ANTIMASONS, AND LIBERATED CLINTONIANS

1. Bryan, *A History of the National Capital,* II, 178–83.

2. Clay to John W. Taylor, May 14, 1827, Jabez D. Hammond to Taylor, June 24, 1827, Taylor Papers, New York Historical Society.

3. Albany *Argus,* May 4, 29, 1827.

4. *Niles' Weekly Register,* June 21, July 21, 28, 1827.

5. Marcy to Van Buren, June 25, 1827, Van Buren Papers, Library of Congress.

6. Van Buren to Cambreleng, June 22, July 4, 1827, Van Buren Papers, Library of Congress.

7. Albany *Argus,* July 3, 10, 13, 1827.

8. *Ibid.*

9. Cooper to Van Buren, July 5, 1827, Van Buren Papers, Library of Congress.

10. Webster to John W. Taylor, July 15, 1827, Taylor Papers, New York Historical Society.

11. Van Buren to John Van Buren, 1836, Van Buren Papers, Library of Congress; Van Buren, *Autobiography,* p. 169.

12. Van Buren's "Notes," dated August 4, 1840, on his woolen's speech of 1827, Van Buren Papers, Library of Congress.

13. Albany *Argus,* July 24, 1827.

14. Van Buren, *Autobiography,* p. 171.

15. *Argus,* July 13, 21, August 17, 1827.

16. Edward Everett to Van Buren, August 9, 1827, Van Buren Papers, Library of Congress.

17. *Niles' Weekly Register,* July 21, 1827.

18. Cooper to Van Buren, July 31, 1827, Van Buren Papers, Library of Congress.

19. Jesse Buel to Flagg, August 3, 1827, Flagg Papers, New York Public Library.

20. James Wolcott, Jr. to Van Buren, November 10, 1827, Van Buren Papers, Library of Congress.

21. The entire account of the proceedings can be found in *Niles' Weekly Register*, August 11, 1827.

22. Fox, *Decline of Aristocracy in New York*, p. 331.

23. *Argus*, June 23, 30, July 4, 21, 1827.

24. *Ibid.*, October 9, 1827.

25. *Ibid.*, July 24, August 17, 21, September 18, December 21, 28, 1827.

26. Weed, *Autobiography*, p. 297. Weed did not witness the murder but is the only authority for the events that transpired after Morgan was kidnaped from prison, and his testimony is open to question. The actual fate of Morgan will probably never be known with certainty.

27. Stanton, *Random Recollection*, p. 25. For an account of the movement, see Charles McCarthy, "The Antimasonic Party: A Study of Political Antimasonry in the United States, 1827–1840," in American Historical Association, *Annual Report for the Year 1902*, I, 371–85, and Hammond, *Political Parties in the State of New York*, II, 381 ff.

28. Van Buren to Cambreleng, July 4, 1827, Van Buren Papers, Library of Congress.

29. General harmony among Republicans seemed universal throughout New York, said W. F. Haile to Flagg, September 3, 1827, Flagg Papers, New York Public Library.

30. Van Buren to Jackson, September 14, 1827, Van Buren Papers, Library of Congress.

31. They first met one another, however, in Washington in the winter of 1815–16. Van Buren, *Autobiography*, p. 232.

32. Jackson to W. B. Lewis, November 25, 1827, photostat copy in the Miscellaneous Papers, New York Public Library; Hamilton, *Reminiscences*, p. 68; Duff Green to Ninian Edwards, May 6, 1827, in Ninian Edwards, "The Edwards Papers," *Chicago Historical Society's Collections* (1884), III, 281–82.

33. Rudolph Bunner to Gulian C. Verplanck, October 27, 1827, Verplanck Papers, New York Historical Society.

34. *Argus,* October 16, 20, November 2, 1827.

35. Hammond, *Political Parties in the State of New York,* II, 259.

36. Van Buren to Cambreleng, October 23, 1827, Van Buren Papers, Library of Congress.

37. Commented Henry Clay: "As to politics, every thing appeared to be doing well of late, until recent developments in N. York." Clay to Edward Everett, November 7, 1827, Everett Papers, Massachusetts Historical Society. See also Adams, *Memoirs,* VII, 341; James Tallmadge to Stephen Van Rensselaer, December 26, 1827, Miscellaneous Papers, New York State Library.

38. Van Buren to Jackson, November 4, 1827, Van Buren Papers, Library of Congress.

39. *Argus,* November 13, 23, 1827.

40. Wright to Flagg, December 20, 1827, Hoffman to Flagg, December 21, 1827, John Morgan to Flagg, December 4, 1827, Flagg Papers, New York Public Library.

41. Crawford to Van Buren, December 21, 1827, Van Buren Papers, Library of Congress; James, *Andrew Jackson,* p. 470.

42. Van Buren to Jackson, September 14, November 4, 1827, in Jackson, *Correspondence,* III, 382–84.

43. Jackson to H. L. White, March 28, 1828, Jackson Papers, Library of Congress; Calhoun to Jackson, April 30, May 25, July 10, 1828, in Jackson, *Correspondence,* III, 400, 404, 413–15.

44. James, *Andrew Jackson,* p. 417.

45. For a fascinating account of the maneuvering in Tennessee to advance Van Buren's position, see Sellers, *James K. Polk, Jacksonian,* pp. 135–41.

46. Kendall to Van Buren, November 10, 1827, Van Buren Papers, Library of Congress.

47. Hamilton, *Reminiscences,* p. 68.

48. John Tyler to Dr. Henry Curtis, December 16, 1827, in Tyler, *The Letters and Times of the Tylers,* I, 379.

49. Van Buren to Croswell, December 25, 1827, Van Buren Papers, Library of Congress.

50. Stevenson was Ritchie's personal choice for the post. Van Buren had lodged with the new Speaker and both men were on very cordial terms. Ambler, *Thomas Ritchie,* p. 113; Rufus King to John A. King, April 20, 1823, in King, *Life and Correspondence,* VI, 518; Wayland, *Andrew Stevenson,* p. 75.

51. Wright to Flagg, December 13, 1827, Flagg Papers, New York Public Library. Clay said that John W. Taylor was too "heavy to carry" and was therefore defeated. Clay to Francis Brooke, December 6, 1827, in Clay, *Private Correspondence,* p. 185.

52. John Tyler to J. Rutherford, December 8, 1827, in Tyler, *Letters and Times of the Tylers,* 377; Charles Butler to Flagg, December 15, 1827, Flagg Papers, New York Public Library.

53. Storrs to ?, December 11, 1827, Henry R. Storrs Papers, New York Historical Society.

54. These ideas were not explicitly stated until years later. In context they refer to Lord Palmerston's career. Van Buren, *Autobiography,* pp. 466–72.

55. Van Buren to Butler, January 13, 1828, Marcy to Van Buren, January 29, 1828, Van Buren Papers, Library of Congress; Wright to Marcy, February 18, 1828, Flagg Papers, New York Public Library.

56. Clay to F. Brooke, February 2, 1828, in Clay, *Correspondence,* p. 191.

57. William Stone to John Bailey, January 1, 1828, John Bailey Papers, New York Historical Society.

58. R. M. Livingston to John W. Taylor, January 31, 1828, Taylor Papers, New York Historical Society.

59. Van Buren to Flagg, February 5, 1828, Flagg Papers, Columbia University Library.

60. Adams, *Memoirs,* VII, 428.

61. Wright to Marcy, February 18, 1828, Flagg Papers, New York Public Library.

62. Hammond, *Political Parties in the State of New York,* II, 268.

63. Clay to Francis Brooke, February 22, 1828, in Clay, *Correspondence,* p. 195.

64. Wright to Marcy, February 18, 1828, Flagg Papers, New York Public Library.

65. Van Buren, *Autobiography,* pp. 166–67.

66. *Ibid.;* Washington *National Journal,* February 22, 1828. See also Thomas J. Oakley to Van Buren, February 18, 1828, Van Buren Papers, Library of Congress.

Notes to XII: TO DRAW THE EAST AND WEST TOGETHER

1. This interpretation may be found in most standard texts.

2. Clay to Francis Brooke, December 6, 1827, in Clay, *Private Correspondence,* p. 185. After the Jacksonians had taken over all the committees Clay advised his friend that "they assume all the responsibilities of public measures."

3. In a letter to Benjamin Knower, Van Buren stated that the South would give him no trouble with respect to the tariff. See Knower to Van Buren, January 27, 1828, Van Buren Papers, Library of Congress.

4. Eventually South Carolina replied with the "Exposition and Protest." It was the best that could be done under the circumstances since secession or abandoning Jackson were impossible at this time.

5. Calhoun, *Works,* III, 48–9.

6. Stevenson had received many votes from the protariff men in his election as Speaker in return for a promise to appoint a committee in favor of a protective measure. Adams, *Memoirs,* VII, 369; Henry Storrs to ?, December 15, 1827, Storrs Papers, New York Historical Society.

7. Wright to Flagg, December 13, 1827, Flagg Papers, New York Public Library.

8. Storrs to ?, December 15, 1827, Storrs Papers, New York Historical Society. Wright said: "It is a part of my political creed always to act with my honest friends and to let the majority dictate that course of action." Wright to Flagg, December 20, 1827, Flagg Papers, New York Public Library. Stephen Van Rensselaer told the President that Wright was a "tool of Van Buren." Adams, *Memoirs,* VII, 397.

9. In 1837, on the Senate floor, Calhoun accused Wright of drawing up the bill, and the New Yorker admitted it. Garraty, *Silas Wright,* p. 61; Adams, *Memoirs,* VII, 397.

10. *Register of Debates,* 20th Congress, 1st Session, pp. 889–90.

11. *American State Papers, Finance,* V, 778 ff.

12. Wright to Flagg, January 16, 1828, Flagg Papers, New York Public Library.

13. Quoted in the Washington *National Journal,* February 19, 23, 1828.

14. February 19, 23, 1828.

15. According to Green, Van Buren wished to introduce McLane to a member of the committee. McLane wanted the committee to interview a manufacturer from Delaware. Green went on to state that "not one word of conversation passed between either Mr. Van Buren or Mr. M'Lane [and committee members] . . . relative to the provisions of the bill which the committee would report, or even relative to the objects it would embrace." *United States Telegraph,* February 26, 1828.

16. Marcy to Van Buren, January 29, 1828, Van Buren Papers, Library of Congress.

17. Wright to Flagg, December 20, 1827, Flagg Papers, New York Public Library; Porter to Clay, March 15, 1828, Clay Papers, Library of Congress; Ambrose Spencer to John W. Taylor, January 12, 1828, Taylor Papers, New York Historical Society.

18. On the surface these rates seem to be close to the Harrisburg proposals. A close study of the schedule is necessary for an understanding of the important differences. Taussig, *The Tariff History of the United States,* pp. 89–95, offers an explanation of this highly complex problem.

19. Possibly, too, the delicate feelings of Southerners helped stay their generous hand.

20. Wright to Flagg, April 7, 1828, Flagg Papers, New York Public Library. See also Hoffman to Flagg, February 2, 1828, *ibid.,* and Benton, *Thirty Years View,* p. 95.

21. Clay to Crittenden, February 14, 1828, in Mrs. Chapman Coleman, *The Life of John J. Crittenden,* I, 67. The same general sentiments can be found in Stephen Van Rensselaer to ?, March 21, 1828, Van Rensselaer Papers, New York Historical Society; John Miller to John W. Taylor, February 3, 1838, Taylor Papers, New York Historical Society; T. W. Griffin to Clay, February 15, 1828, Clay Papers, Library of Congress. It should be remembered that these men were hardly in a position to know what the Jacksonians planned to do.

22. Niles to John W. Taylor, February 14, 1828, Taylor Papers, New York Historical Society.

23. John Tyler to Dr. Henry Curtis, March 18, 1828, in Tyler, *Life and Time of the Tylers,* I, 385.

24. See John Tyler's remarks to Dr. H. Curtis when the bill reached the Senate. Tyler to Curtis, May 1, 1828, *ibid.,* I, 387.

25. *Argus,* February 1, 1828.

26. *Ibid.,* February 8, 12, 29, 1828.

27. Spencer to Taylor, April 5, 1828, Taylor Papers, New York Historical Society.

28. Flagg to Wright, March 13, 16, 1828, Flagg Papers, New York Public Library.

29. *Register of Debates,* 20th Congress, 1st Session, pp. 1836–70.

30. Van Buren to Flagg, March 31, 1828, Flagg Papers, Columbia University Library.

31. April 4, 8, 11, 22, 1828.

32. Wright to Flagg, April 7, 1828, Flagg Papers, New York Public Library.

33. Wright to Flagg, April 13, 1828, Flagg Papers, New York Public Library.

34. Webster to Joseph E. Sprague, April 13, 1828, in Webster, *Letters,* pp. 135–36.

35. Wright to Flagg, April 22, 1828, Flagg Papers, New York Public Library.

36. Hoffman to Flagg, April 27, 1828, Flagg Papers, New York Public Library; Adams, *Memoirs,* VII, 531; Calhoun to James E. Calhoun, May 4, 1828, in American Historical Association, *Annual Report,* 1899, II, 265.

37. John Tyler to Dr. H. Curtis, May 1, 1828, in Tyler, *Life and Times of the Tylers,* I, 387.

38. Van Buren to Wright, Wright to Van Buren, May, 1828, Van Buren Papers, Library of Congress.

39. Van Buren "Notes," dated May, 1828, Van Buren Papers, Library of Congress. He also collected a number of extracts from the writings of Washington, the elder Adams, Jefferson, and Madison which favored a tariff. He appeared to be gathering material to justify his entire position.

40. The remark had to do with Van Buren's efforts at conciliation regarding the spirits provision. The New York Senator claimed that "the manufacturer of rum would receive an encouragement from the duty of foreign spirits." Senator Henry S. Foote of Connecticut all but laughed in his face. See Foote's remarks on the Senate floor, May 8, 1828, *Register of Debates,* 20th Congress, 1st Session, p. 748.

41. Unfortunately, neither the debates on this bill nor a record of the individual voting by senators on the many amendments are

given in the *Register of Debates*. *Niles' Weekly Register* furnished most of the voting information used here.

42. Webster, however, had a few remaining doubts and went to Adams for advice. Adams, *Memoirs,* VII, 534.

43. Samuel Babcock to Bailey, May 7, 1828, J. B. Davis to Bailey, May 21, 1828, Bailey Papers, Massachusetts Historical Society; Thomas Cooper to Verplanck, May 15, 1828, Verplanck Papers, New York Historical Society.

44. This is not to imply that every "Eastern" senator voted for every amendment which would lower the rates on raw materials. This is expecting too much. A total of 17 amendments were suggested by the Senate committee, of which 10 were defeated.

45. Or, he could have induced his friend Levi Woodbury of New Hampshire to do the killing for him. Woodbury voted against the final tariff even though he voted for the various amendments to improve the schedules, including the woolens. His vote was opposite to Van Buren's on every important amendment, except the woolens.

46. Calhoun, *Works,* III, 50, 51.

47. Webster, *Works,* I, 165. Webster is very clear that without this amendment he would have voted against the final bill. See also Taussig, *Tariff History of the United States,* p. 101.

48. Tyler, *Life and Times of the Tylers,* III, 69 n.

49. Daniel Webster, Thomas Hart Benton, John Eaton, and Van Buren were among the majority.

50. *Register of Debates,* 20th Congress, 1st Session, p. 2576.

51. *Ibid.,* pp. 2700, 2708.

52. May 20, 1828. For the opposite view, see *Niles' Weekly Register,* May 17, June 28, July 26, 1828.

53. "I know," said Wright to Speaker Stevenson, ". . . that we are going to pass a tariff. . . ." James Gordon Bennett, Manuscript Diary, entry for June 12, 1831, New York Public Library.

54. Calhoun, *Works,* III, 48, 49.

55. Woodbury to Van Buren, July 1, 1828, Van Buren Papers, Library of Congress.

56. Van Buren's "Notes," dated August 4, 1840; Wright to J. S. Watkins, February 9, 1835, Van Buren Papers, Library of Congress; Marcy to Knower, May 6, 1832, Marcy Papers, Library of Congress; Thomas Hart Benton, *Mr. Benton's Letter to Major General Davis . . .,* pp. 9–10.

57. May 20, October 31, 1828.

58. March 3, 1829. Van Buren had been shrewd enough, however, to lay his instructions on the table during the tariff debate and "point to them as his power of attorney, and as containing the directions for his vote." The words within quotation marks are those of Daniel Webster made on the Senate floor, May 9, 1828, *Register of Debates,* 20th Congress, 1st Session, p. 750.

59. Cambreleng to Van Buren, March 1, 1829, Van Buren Papers, Library of Congress.

60. Edward Everett to Alexander H. Everett, December 2, 1828, Everett Papers, Massachusetts Historical Society.

61. J. De Graff to Flagg, December 27, 1828, Flagg Papers, New York Public Library; Wright to Van Buren, December 9, 1828, Van Buren Papers, Library of Congress.

Notes to XIII: REVOLUTION

1. Marcy to Van Buren, January 29, 1828, Van Buren Papers, Library of Congress.

2. *Argus,* July 15, 1828.

3. The *Argus* decried the "despicable" efforts of the "pander, Weed" to "appropriate the anti-masonic feeling" entirely to the political advantage of John Q. Adams. (April 8, July 15, 1828.) See also Weed, *Autobiography,* p. 304; Charles McCarthy, "The Antimasonic Party," in American Historical Association, *Annual Report for the Year 1902,* I, 378.

4. Van Buren, *Inquiry into the Origin and Course of Political Parties in the United States.*

5. Van Buren to Mr. Coleman, April 4, 1828, in Hamilton, *Reminiscences,* p. 77. See also Riker to Van Buren, April 14, 1828, Van Buren Papers, Library of Congress. Van Buren's speech in the Senate was delivered on February 12 and can be found in the *Argus* of May 2, 1828.

6. Weed, *Autobiography,* p. 253.

7. P. L. Tracy to John W. Taylor, July 10, 1828, Taylor Papers, New York Historical Society.

8. E. Griffin to Flagg, July 30, 1828, Flagg Papers, New York Public Library.

9. Thomas Ritchie to Van Buren, March 11, 1828, Van Buren

Papers, Library of Congress; *National Intelligencer,* February 23, 1828.

10. Edward Everett to Alexander H. Everett, October 1, 1828, Everett Papers, Massachusetts Historical Society; Calhoun to Van Buren, September, 1828, Van Buren, *Autobiography,* p. 516.

11. Verplanck to Van Buren, December 6, 1828, Van Buren Papers, Library of Congress.

12. Stanton, *Random Recollections,* p. 32. His movements were watched by the editor of the Albany *Daily Advertiser,* who immediately suspected evil designs. (August 5, 1828). See Croswell's answer, however, in the *Argus,* August 8, 1828.

13. Van Buren to Hamilton, August 25, 1828, in Hamilton, *Reminiscences,* pp. 78–79.

14. McCarthy, "The Antimasonic Party," in American Historical Association, *Annual Report for the Year 1902,* I, 379. Thurlow Weed went on to the Anti-Masonic convention in Utica and tried to solicit votes for the Adams ticket. The Anti-Masons demonstrated what they thought of his idea by resolving that they would disregard "the two great political parties" in New York. Since they refused to support "directly or indirectly" any person who was a Mason, no matter his services to the state or nation, they felt obliged to choose their own list of candidates. *Argus,* August 12, 1828.

15. The Anti-Masons first nominated Francis Granger, who had also been nominated by the administration party for lieutenant-governor. Under the mistaken notion that the Anti-Masons could still be wheedled into an alliance with the Adams men, Granger on August 28 refused the nomination for governor. McCarthy, "The Antimasonic Party," in American Historical Association, *Annual Report for the Year 1902,* I, 379. Hurriedly, then, the Anti-Masons called a second convention at LeRoy on September 7, and substituted Southwick for Granger.

16. Charles Butler to Flagg, September 5, 1828, Flagg Papers, New York Public Library.

17. E. T. Kelsay, "The Presidential Campaign of 1828," *The East Tennessee Historical Society Publication,* V (1933), 70.

18. William B. Lewis to Van Buren, August 8, 1828, Van Buren Papers, Library of Congress.

19. Notation by Van Buren to *ibid.;* Robert M. Johnson to Van Buren, September 25, 1828, Van Buren Papers, Library of Congress.

20. *National Intelligencer,* September 11, 13, 23, 25, October 4, 1828.

21. Van Buren to the editor of the Albany *Daily Advertiser,* October, 1828, Van Buren Papers.

22. R. M. Livingston to John W. Taylor, September 12, 1828, Taylor Papers, New York Historical Society; Francis Granger to Weed, September 28, 1828, October 26, 1828, Granger Papers, Library of Congress.

23. Van Buren did not list the names of these politicians himself. Van Buren to Hamilton, August 25, September 6, 16, 1828, in Hamilton, *Reminiscences,* pp. 78–79; Van Buren to Cambreleng, September 8, 18, 1828, William B. Lewis to Van Buren, September 27, 1828, Van Buren Papers, Library of Congress; Van Buren to P. I. Hoes, July 15, 1828, Miscellaneous Papers, Library of Congress; Jackson to R. K. Call, August 16, 1828, in *The Virginia Magazine of History and Biography,* XXIX (April, 1921), 191–92. Van Buren continued giving Jackson advice even after the election. Usually it was done through a third person. Van Buren to Hamilton, February 21, 1829, in Hamilton, *Reminiscences,* p. 94.

24. *Argus,* November 4, 1828.

25. Clay to Edward Everett, November 7, 1828, Everett Papers, Massachusetts Historical Society.

26. Edward Everett to Alexander H. Everett, October 1, 1828, Everett Papers, Massachusetts Historical Society.

27. Van Buren to Cambreleng, October 18, 29, November 7, 10, 1828, Van Buren to Butler, November 17, 1828, Van Buren to C. E. Dudley, August 24, 1828, Van Buren Papers, Library of Congress.

28. Crawford to Van Buren, October 21, 1828, Van Buren to Crawford, November 14, 1828, Van Buren Papers, Library of Congress.

29. Van Buren to Jackson, November 17, 1828, Van Buren Papers, Library of Congress,

30. Van Buren to Cambreleng, November 7, 1828, Van Buren Papers, Library of Congress.

31. Lewis to Hamilton, December 12, 1828, Van Buren Papers, Library of Congress.

32. Van Buren to Hamilton, February 21, 1829, in Hamilton, *Reminiscences,* p. 94.

33. Poore, *Perley's Reminiscences,* p. 91.

BIBLIOGRAPHY

MANUSCRIPT SOURCES

Buffalo Historical Society
    Peter B. Porter Papers
Columbia University Library
    DeWitt Clinton Papers
    Azariah C. Flagg Papers
    Charlemagne Towers, Manuscript Diary
Library of Congress
    Henry Clay Papers
    Francis Granger Papers
    Andrew Jackson Papers
    William L. Marcy Papers
    Martin Van Buren Papers
    Daniel Webster Papers
Massachusetts Historical Society
    John Bailey Papers
    George Bancroft Papers
    Jacob Brown Papers
    Edward Everett Papers
    Norcross Collection
    Theodore Sedgwick Papers
    Washburn Collection
New York Historical Society
    John Bailey Papers
    Henry Clay Papers
    DeWitt Clinton, Manuscript Diary
    Albert Gallatin Papers
    Jabez D. Hammond Papers
    Rufus King Papers
    Henry Meigs Papers

Henry R. Storrs Papers
John W. Taylor Papers
Martin Van Buren Papers
Stephen Van Rensselaer Papers
Gulian C. Verplanck Papers
New York Public Library
James Barbour Papers
James Gordon Bennett, Manuscript Diary
Benjamin F. Butler Papers
Percy Childs Papers
DeWitt Clinton Papers
Azariah C. Flagg Papers
Samuel Gouverneur Papers
James Monroe Papers
John W. Taylor Papers
Martin Van Buren Papers
Silas Wright Papers
New York State Library
Harmanus Bleecker Papers
Martin Van Buren Papers

PRINTED PRIMARY SOURCES

Complete files for the newspapers examined for various dates during the period under discussion are not always available. The scattered surviving copies were used whenever they could be found; sometimes a single issue of a local newspaper is all that remains.

The following newspapers are cited in the Notes: Albany Advertiser, Albany Argus, Albany Daily Advertiser, Albany Register, Charleston Southern Patriot, Columbia Telescope, National Advocate, National Intelligencer, New York American, New York Evening Post, New York Statesman, New York Tribune, Niles' Weekly Register, Raleigh Register, Richmond Constitutional Whig, Richmond Enquirer, Rochester Anti-Masonic Enquirer, United States Telegraph, Washington City Weekly Gazette, Washington National Journal.

Adams, John Quincy. Memoirs of John Quincy Adams. Edited by Charles Francis Adams. 12 vols. Philadelphia 1874–77.
American State Papers: Documents, Legislative and Executive, of

the Congress of the United States (Finance). Vol. V. Washington, D.C., 1859.

Annals of Congress. Second Session of Seventeenth Congress through Second Session of Eighteenth Congress. Washington, D.C., 1821–25.

Beardsley, Levi. Reminiscences. New York, 1852.

Benton, Thomas Hart. Mr. Benton's Letter to Maj. Gen. Davis, of the State of Mississippi. . . . Washington, D.C., 1835.

—— Thirty Years' View. 2 vols. New York, 1865.

Biddle, Nicholas. The Correspondence of Nicholas Biddle. Edited by Reginald C. McGrane. Boston and New York, 1919.

Bigelow, John, ed. "De Witt Clinton as a Politician," *Harper's New Monthly Magazine,* L (1874–75), 409–17, 563–71.

Blair, Francis P. General Jackson and James Buchanan; Letter from Francis P. Blair to the Public. 1856.

Bonney, Mrs. Catharina V. R. A Legacy of Historical Gleanings. 2 vols. Albany, 1875.

Breck, Samuel. Recollections of Samuel Breck . . . . Edited by H. E. Scudder. Philadelphia, 1877.

Brockway, Beman. Fifty Years in Journalism. . . . Watertown, N.Y., 1891.

Brown, Everett, S., ed. The Missouri Compromises and Presidential Politics, 1820–1825. . . . St. Louis, 1926.

Butler, William Allen. A Retrospect of Forty Years. Edited by Harriet A. Butler. New York, 1911.

Calhoun, John C. Correspondence of John C. Calhoun. Edited by Franklin Jameson. Vol. II of American Historical Association. *Annual Report for the Year 1899.* Washington, D.C., 1900.

—— "John C. Calhoun and the Presidential Election of 1824; Some Unpublished Calhoun Letters," T. R. Hay, ed., *American Historical Review,* XL (1934–35), 82–96, 287–300.

—— The Works of John C. Calhoun. Edited by Richard K. Crallé. 6 vols. New York, 1854–57.

Carter, Nathaniel H., and William L. Stone. Reports of the Proceedings and Debates of the Convention of 1821. Albany, 1821.

Clay, Henry. "Letter of Henry Clay to B. W. Crowninshield, March 18, 1827," *The Quarterly Journal of Economics,* Vol. II (1888).

—— The Private Correspondence of Henry Clay. Edited by Calvin Colton. Cincinnati, 1856.

Columbia County Historical Society. "Mary Livingston Memorandums," *The Bulletin,* No. 55 (January, 1942), 4–14.

Crockett, David. Autobiography of David Crockett. Philadelphia, 1865.

Davis, Matthew L. Memoirs of Aaron Burr. 2 vols. New York, 1869.

Dix, John A. "Dix Letters, 1812–1848," *Massachusetts Historical Society Proceedings,* L (January, 1917), 133–68.

—— Memoirs of John A. Dix. Compiled by Morgan Dix. 2 vols. New York, 1883.

Edwards, Ninian. "The Edwards Papers." Edited by E. B. Washburn. *Chicago Historical Society Collections,* III (1884).

Flagg, Azariah C. A Few Historical Facts Respecting the . . . Business of the State of New York. . . . 1868.

Foote, Henry S. Casket of Reminiscences. Washington, D.C., 1874.

Gallatin, Albert. The Writings of Albert Gallatin. Edited by Henry Adams. 3 vols. Philadelphia, 1879.

Gallatin, James. A Great Peace Maker; The Diary of James Gallatin. New York, 1914.

Hamilton, James A. Reminiscences of James A. Hamilton. New York, 1869.

Hone, Philip. The Diary of Philip Hone, 1828–1851. Edited by Allan Nevins. New York, 1936.

Jackson, Andrew. Correspondence of Andrew Jackson. Edited by J. S. Bassett. 6 vols. Washington, D.C., 1926–33.

Jay, John. The Correspondence and Public Papers of John Jay. Edited by Henry P. Johnston. 4 vols. New York and London, 1893.

Jefferson, Thomas. The Works of Thomas Jefferson. Edited by P. L. Ford. 12 vols. New York, 1904–5.

—— The Writings of Thomas Jefferson. Edited by Albert E. Bergh. 20 vols. Washington, D.C., 1907.

Journal of the Assembly and Senate of the State of New York, 1812–1828. Albany, 1812–28.

King, Rufus. The Life and Correspondence of Rufus King. Edited by Charles R. King. 6 vols. New York, 1898.

Lincoln, Charles Z., ed. Messages from the Governors. 9 vols. Albany, 1909.

Madison, James. Letters and Other Writings of James Madison. 42 vols. Philadelphia, 1867.

Mackenzie, William L. The Life and Times of Martin Van Buren. . . . Boston, 1846.

—— The Lives and Opinions of Benjamin Franklin Butler and Jesse Hoyt. Boston, 1845.

Mangum, Willie Person. The Papers of Willie Person Mangum. Edited by Henry T. Shanks. Vol. 1 (1807–32). Raleigh, N.C., 1950.

Monroe, James. "Monroe on the Adams-Clay 'Bargain,'" *American Historical Review,* XLII (January, 1937), 273–76.

Munsell, Joel. The Annals of Albany. 10 vols. Albany, 1859.

Newcome, A. R., ed. "Correspondence of John C. Calhoun, George McDuffie and Charles Fisher Relative to the Presidential Campaign of 1824," *The North Carolina Historical Review,* VII (October, 1930), 477–505.

Pinckney, James D. Reminiscences of Catskill. Catskill, 1868.

Poore, Ben Perley. Perley's Reminiscences of Sixty Years in the National Metropolis. 2 vols. Philadelphia, 1886.

Proceedings and Addresses on the Occasion of the Death of B. F. Butler of New York. New York, 1859.

Register of Debates in Congress. First Session of Nineteenth Congress through First Session of Twentieth Congress. Washington, D.C., 1826–28.

Richardson, J. D. Compilation of the Messages and Papers of the Presidents. 20 vols. Washington, D.C., 1908.

Ritchie, Thomas. "Unpublished Letters of Thomas Ritchie," *John P. Branch Historical Papers,* III (June, 1911), 199–254.

Sargent, Nathan. Public Men and Events. 2 vols. Philadelphia, 1875.

Scott, Winfield. Memoirs of Lieut.-General Scott. 2 vols. New York, 1864.

Seward, Frederick W., ed. Autobiography of William H. Seward. New York, 1877.

Smith, Mrs. Samuel Harrison. The First Forty Years of Washington Society. Edited by Gaillard Hunt. New York, 1906.

Stanton, Henry B. Random Recollections. New York, 1887.

Stuart, James. Three Years in North America. 2 vols. Edinburgh, 1833.

Swift, Joseph Gardner. The Memoirs of General Joseph Gardner Swift. Worcester, Mass., 1890.

Taney, Roger Brooke. Memoir of Roger Brooke Taney. Baltimore, 1872.

Van Buren, Martin. The Autobiography of Martin Van Buren. Edited by John C. Fitzpatrick. Vol. II of American Historical Association, *Annual Report for the Year 1918*. Washington, D.C., 1920.

—— Inquiry into the Origin and Course of Political Parties in the United States. Edited by Abraham and Smith Thompson Van Buren. New York, 1867.

Webster, Daniel. The Letters of Daniel Webster. Edited by C. H. Van Tyne. New York, 1902.

—— The Private Correspondence of Daniel Webster. Edited by Fletcher Webster. 2 vols. Boston, 1857.

—— The Works of Daniel Webster. Boston, 1853.

Weed, Thurlow. Autobiography of Thurlow Weed. Edited by Harriet A. Weed. Boston, 1883.

Wise, Henry A. Seven Decades of the Union. Philadelphia, 1881.

SECONDARY SOURCES

Abernathy, T. P. "Andrew Jackson and the Rise of Southwestern Democracy," *American Historical Review*, XXXIII (October, 1927), 64–77.

—— From Frontier to Plantation in Tennessee. Chapel Hill, N.C., 1932.

Adams, Henry. John Randolph. Philadelphia, 1898.

—— Life of Albert Gallatin. Philadelphia, 1879.

Alexander, D. S. "John W. Taylor," *Quarterly Journal of the New York State Historical Association*, I (January, 1920), 14–37.

—— A Political History of the State of New York. New York, 1906–23.

Alexander, Holmes. The American Talleyrand. New York and London, 1935.

Ambler, Charles Henry. Thomas Ritchie; a Study in Virginia Politics. Richmond, Va., 1913.

Anderson, Hattie M. "The Jackson Men in Missouri in 1828," *Missouri Historical Review*, XXXIV (April, 1940), 301–34.

Baker, Elizabeth F. Henry Wheaton, 1785–1848. Philadelphia, 1937.

Bassett, John S. The Life of Andrew Jackson. New York, 1931.

Bassett, John S. "Major Lewis on the Nomination of Andrew Jackson," *Proceedings of the American Antiquarian Society,* XXXIII (April, 1923), 12–33.

Bemis, Samuel Flagg, ed. The American Secretaries of State and Their Diplomacy. 10 vols. New York, 1927–29.

—— John Quincy Adams and the Foundations of American Foreign Policy. New York, 1949.

—— John Quincy Adams and the Union. New York, 1956.

Biographical Directory of the American Congress, 1774–1927. Compiled by Ansel Wold. Washington, D.C., 1928.

Biographical Sketch of Martin Van Buren.

Bobbé, Dorothie. De Witt Clinton. New York, 1933.

Booth, Edward T. Country Life in America as Lived by Ten Presidents of the United States. New York, 1947.

Bradbury, Mrs. Anna R. History of the City of Hudson. Hudson, N.Y., 1908.

Brown, Everett S. "The Presidential Election of 1824–25," *Political Science Quarterly,* XL (September, 1925), 384–403.

Bruce, William Cabell. John Randolph of Roanoke, 1773–1833. 2 vols. New York, 1922.

Bryan, Wilhelmus B. A History of the National Capital. 2 vols. New York, 1914–16.

Butler, William Allen. Martin Van Buren. New York, 1862.

Carroll, Eber M. "Politics during the Administration of John Quincy Adams," *South Atlantic Quarterly,* XXIII (1924), 141–54.

Chambers, William N. Old Bullion Benton, Senator from the New West. Boston, 1956.

Channing, Edward. History of the United States. 6 vols. New York, 1905–25.

Clark, Bennett C. John Quincy Adams, "Old Man Eloquent." Boston, 1932.

Coit, Margaret L. John C. Calhoun. Boston, 1950.

Coleman, Mrs. Chapman. The Life of John J. Crittenden. 2 vols. Philadelphia, 1873.

Cresson, W. P. James Monroe. Chapel Hill, N.C., 1946.

Crockett, David. The Life of Martin Van Buren. Philadelphia, 1835.

Current, Richard N. Daniel Webster and the Rise of National Conservatism. Boston, 1955.

Curtis, George T. Life of Daniel Webster. 2 vols. New York, 1870.

Dangerfield, George. The Era of Good Feelings. New York, 1952.

Dawson, Moses. Sketches of the Life of Martin Van Buren. Cincinnati, 1840.

Donovan, Herbert D. A. The Barnburners; a Study of the Internal Movements in the Political History of New York State . . . 1830–1852. New York, 1925.

Dow, Charles M. "Daniel D. Tompkins," *Quarterly Journal of New York State Historical Association,* I (January, 1920), 7–13.

Eaton, Clement. Henry Clay and the Art of American Politics. Boston, 1957.

Ellet, Mrs. E. F. The Court Circles of the Republic. Hartford, Conn., 1869.

Ellis, David M. Landlords and Farmers in the Hudson-Mohawk Region, 1790–1850. Ithaca, N.Y., 1946.

Ellis, Franklin. History of Columbia County, New York. Philadelphia, 1879.

Emmons, William. Biography of Martin Van Buren. Washington, D.C., 1835.

Erikson, Erik M. "Official Newspaper Organs and the Campaign of 1828," *The Tennessee Historical Magazine,* VIII (January, 1925), 231–47.

Fish, Carl R. The Civil Service and the Patronage. Cambridge, Mass., 1920.

Flick, Alexander C., ed. History of the State of New York. 10 vols. New York, 1919.

Fox, Dixon Ryan. The Decline of Aristocracy in the Politics of New York. New York, 1919.

—— "The Negro Vote in Old New York," *Political Science Quarterly,* XXXII (1917), 252–75.

Fuess, Claude M. Daniel Webster. 2 vols. Boston, 1930.

Garraty, John Arthur. Silas Wright. New York, 1949.

Gillet, R. H. The Life and Times of Silas Wright. 2 vols. Albany, 1874.

Hailperin, Herman. "Pro-Jackson Sentiment in Pennsylvania, 1820–1828," *Pennsylvania Magazine of History and Biography,* L (July, 1926), 193–240.

Hale, Edward E. "Anecdotes of Martin Van Buren," *Outlook,* LXX (April 5, 1902), 849–52.

—— William H. Seward. Philadelphia, 1910.

Hamilton, Milton W. The Country Printer, New York State, 1785–1830. New York, 1936.

Hammond, Jabez D. The History of Political Parties in the State of New York. 2 vols. Cooperstown, N.Y., 1845.

—— Life and Times of Silas Wright. Syracuse, 1848.

Hay, Thomas R. "John C. Calhoun and the Presidential Election of 1824," *The North Carolina Historical Review,* XII (April, 1935), 20–44.

Holland, William M. The Life and Political Opinions of Martin Van Buren. Hartford, 1836.

Holloway, Laura C. The Ladies of the White House. Philadelphia, 1884.

Horton, John T. James Kent, a Study in Conservatism, 1763–1847. New York, 1939.

Hosack, David. Memoir of De Witt Clinton. New York, 1829.

Howe, M. A. De Wolfe. Life and Letters of George Bancroft. 2 vols. New York, 1908.

Howell, George R., and Jonathan Tanney. History of the County of Albany. New York, 1886.

Ireland, John R. History of the Life, Administration and Times of Martin Van Buren. Chicago, 1887.

James, Marquis. The Life of Andrew Jackson. Indianapolis and New York, 1938.

Jenkins, John S. History of Political Parties in the State of New York. Auburn, N.Y., 1849.

—— The Life of Silas Wright. Auburn, N.Y., 1849.

—— Lives of the Governors of the State of New York. Auburn, N.Y., 1851.

July, Robert W. The Essential New Yorker, Gulian Crommelin Verplanck. Durham, 1951.

Kehl, J. A. Ill Feeling in the Era of Good Feeling; Western Pennsylvania Political Battles, 1815–1825. Pittsburgh, 1956.

Kelsay, Isabel T. "The Presidential Campaign of 1828," The East Tennessee Historical Society Publication, Vol V (1933), 69–80.

Kennedy, John P. Memoirs of the Life of William Wirt. 2 vols. Philadelphia, 1849.

Kent, Frank R. The Democratic Party, a History. New York, 1928.

Kirk, Russell. Randolph of Roanoke; a Study in Conservative Thought. Chicago, 1951.

Klein, Philip S. Pennsylvania Politics, 1817–1832: A Game Without Rules. Philadelphia, 1940.

Krout, John A., and Dixon R. Fox. The Completion of Independence, 1790–1830. New York, 1946.

Leading Citizens of Columbia County, New York. Boston, 1894.

Life and Speeches of Henry Clay. 2 vols. New York, 1943.

Longacre, James B., and James Herring. The National Portrait Gallery of Distinguished Americans. 4 vols. Philadelphia and New York, 1839.

Lynch, Denis T. An Epoch and a Man, Martin Van Buren and His Times. New York, 1929.

McBain, Howard L. De Witt Clinton and the Origin of the Spoils System in New York. New York, 1907.

McCarthy, Charles. "The Antimasonic Party: A Study of Political Antimasonry in the United States, 1827–1840," Vol. I of American Historical Association, Annual Report for the Year 1902, pp. 365–574.

McGuire, James K., ed. The Democratic Party of the State of New York. 3 vols. New York, 1947.

McMaster, John B. A History of the People of the United States. 7 vols. New York, 1901.

Malone, Dumas. Jefferson and the Rights of Man. Boston, 1951.

—— Jefferson the Virginian. Boston, 1947.

—— The Public Life of Thomas Cooper, 1783–1839. New Haven, Conn., 1926.

Martineau, Harriet. Autobiography. Boston, 1877.

—— Retrospect of Western Travel. 2 vols. London and New York, 1838.

Mayo, Bernard. Henry Clay. Boston, Mass., 1937.

Meigs, William M. The Life of John Caldwell Calhoun. 2 vols. New York, 1917.

Meyers, Marvin. The Jacksonian Persuasion: Politics and Belief. Stanford, Calif., 1957.

Miley, Cora. "A Forgotten President, The Enigmatical 'Little Magician,' Martin Van Buren," Americana, XXIII (1929), 169–81.

Miller, Peyton, F. A Group of Great Lawyers of Columbia County, New York. 1904.

"Mr. Van Buren," The United States Magazine and Democratic Review, XV (July, 1844), 3–9.

Moore, Glover. The Missouri Controversy, 1819–1821. Lexington, Ky., 1953.

Moore, John Bassett. "A Great Secretary of State, William L. Marcy," *Political Science Quarterly*, XXX (September, 1915), 377–96.

Morison, Samuel E. "The First National Nominating Convention," *American Historical Review*, XVII (July, 1912), 744–63.

—— The Life and Letters of Harrison Gray Otis, Federalist, 1765–1848. 2 vols. New York and Boston, 1913.

Murdock, J. S. "The First National Nominating Convention," *American Historical Review*, I (July, 1896), 680–83.

Myers, Gustavus. The History of Tammany Hall. New York, 1901.

Orth, Samuel P. Five American Politicians. Cleveland, 1906.

Ostrogorski, M. Democracy and the Organization of Political Parties. 2 vols. New York, 1902.

—— "The Rise and Fall of the Nominating Caucus," *American Historical Review*, V (1899–1900), 253–83.

"Pages from an Autograph Collection," *University of California Chronicles*, XXVII (1925), 331–45.

Parton, James. The Life and Times of Aaron Burr. 2 vols. Boston and New York, 1857.

—— Life of Andrew Jackson. 3 vols. New York, 1860.

Peckham, Harriet C. History of Cornelis Maessen Van Buren . . . and His Descendants. New York, 1914.

Powell, James H. Richard Rush. Philadelphia, 1942.

Rammelkamp, C. H. "The Campaign of 1824 in New York," in American Historical Association, Annual Report for the Year 1904, pp. 177–201.

Raymond, William. Biographical Sketches of the Distinguished Men of Columbia County. Albany, 1851.

"Recollections of an Old Stager," *Harpers*, XVLII, 753 ff.

Remini, Robert V. "The Albany Regency," *New York History*, (October, 1958), 341–55.

Reznick, Samuel. "The Depression of 1819–1820, a Social History," *American Historical Review*, XXXIX (October, 1933), 28–47.

Robinson, Charles M. "The Life of Judge Augustus Porter," *Publications of the Buffalo Historical Society*, VII (1904), 229–75.

Roseboom, Eugene H. A History of Presidential Elections. New York, 1957.

Schlesinger, Arthur M., Jr. The Age of Jackson. Boston and New York, 1946.

Schurz, Carl. Life of Henry Clay. 2 vols. Boston and New York, 1887.

Seaton, Josephine. William Winston Seaton of the "National Intelligencer." Boston, 1871.

Sellers, Charles G. James K. Polk, Jacksonian, 1795–1843. Princeton, 1957.

Shepard, Edward M. Martin Van Buren. Boston and New York, 1899.

Shipp, J. E. D. Giant Days, or the Life and Times of W. H. Crawford. Americus, Ga., 1903.

Simms, Henry. Life of John Taylor. Richmond, Va., 1932.

Sioussat, St. George L. "Some Phases of Tennessee Politics in the Jackson Period," *American Historical Review*, XIV (October, 1908), 51–67.

Smith, Culver R. "Propaganda Technique in the Jackson Campaign of 1828," *East Tennessee Historical Society Publications*, VI (1934), 44–66.

Smith, George W. "The Career of Michael Hoffman," *Herkimer County Historical Society*, No. 1 (1896), 5–26.

Stanwood, Edward. American Tariff Controversies in the Nineteenth Century. 2 vols. Boston and New York, 1903.

—— A History of the Presidency from 1788 to 1897. Boston and New York, 1898.

Stenberg, Richard R. "Jackson, Buchanan and the 'Corrupt Bargain' Calumny," *Pennsylvania Magazine of History and Biography*, LVIII (January, 1934), 61–85.

Stevens, Harry R. The Early Jackson Party in Ohio. Durham, N.C., 1957.

Stoddard, Francis H. The Life and Letters of Charles Butler. New York, 1903.

Stoddard, William O. The Lives of the Presidents: Andrew Jackson and Martin Van Buren. New York, 1887.

Styron, Arthur. The Cast-Iron Man John C. Calhoun and American Democracy. New York and Toronto, 1935.

Sydnor, Charles S. "The One Party Period of American History," *American Historical Review*, LI (April, 1946), 439–51.

Syrett, Harold C. Andrew Jackson; His Contribution to the American Tradition. Indianapolis and New York, 1953.

Taussig, F. W. The Tariff History of the United States. New York, 1914.

Turner, Frederick J. Rise of the New West. New York and London, 1935.

Tyler, Lyon G. The Letters and Times of the Tylers. 3 vols. Richmond, Va., 1884, 1896.

Van Deusen, Glyndon G. The Life of Henry Clay. Boston, 1939.

—— Thurlow Weed, Wizard of the Lobby. Boston, 1947.

Walters, Raymond, Jr. Albert Gallatin: Jeffersonian Financier and Diplomat. New York, 1957.

—— "James Gallatin's Diary: A Fraud?" *American Historical Review*, LXII (July, 1957), 878–85.

Ward, John W. Andrew Jackson. New York, 1955.

Wayland, Francis F. Andrew Stevenson. Philadelphia, 1949.

Weston, Florence. The Presidential Election of 1828. Washington, D.C., 1938.

Whitton, Mary O. First First Ladies, 1789–1865. New York, 1948.

Wiltse, Charles M. John C. Calhoun, Nationalist, 1782–1828. Indianapolis and New York, 1944.

—— John C. Calhoun, Nullifier, 1828–1839. Indianapolis and New York, 1949.

Wise, W. Harvey, Jr., and John W. Cronin. A Bibliography of Andrew Jackson and Martin Van Buren. Washington, D. C., 1935.

INDEX